# Parodies of Ownership

DIGITALCULTUREBOOKS

is an imprint of the University of Michigan Press and
the Scholarly Publishing Office of the University of
Michigan Library dedicated to publishing innovative
and accessible work exploring new media and its impact
on society, culture, and scholarly communication.

# Parodies of Ownership

## Hip-Hop Aesthetics and Intellectual Property Law

Richard L. Schur

The University of Michigan Press AND
The University of Michigan Library
ANN ARBOR

Published in the United States of America by
The University of Michigan Press and
The University of Michigan Library
Manufactured in the United States of America
⊚ Printed on acid-free paper

2012   2011   2010   2009      4   3   2   1

*A CIP catalog record for this book is available from the British Library.*

Library of Congress Cataloging-in-Publication Data

Schur, Richard L.
    Parodies of ownership : hip-hop aesthetics and intellectual
property law / Richard L. Schur.
       p.    cm.
    Includes bibliographical references and index.
    ISBN-13: 978-0-472-07060-2 (cloth : alk. paper)
    ISBN-10: 0-472-07060-6 (cloth : alk. paper)
    ISBN-13: 978-0-472-05060-4 (pbk. : alk. paper)
    ISBN-10: 0-472-05060-5 (pbk. : alk. paper)
       1. African Americans—Legal status, laws, etc.   2. Intellectual
property—United States.   3. Hip-hop—Influence.   4. African
Americans in popular culture.   I. Title.
    KF4757.S38    2009
    346.7304'82—dc22                                    2009004565

Portions of chapters 3 and 7 were previously published as part of "Stomping the Blues No
More? Hip Hop Aesthetics and Contemporary African American literature," in Lovalerie
King and Linda Selzer's edited collection, *New Essays on the African American Novel: From
Hurston and Ellison to Morrison and Whitehead* (Palgrave 2008). Those sections have been
reprinted here by permission.

ISBN-13 978-0-472-02449-0 (electronic)

# Preface

Through her camera, Martha Cooper captured much of the energy of the emerging hip-hop scene during the late 1970s and early 1980s. Cooper, a white photographer for the *New York Post*, gained entrance into graffiti culture and was provided an opportunity to document the birth of hip-hop.[1] Her photographs render the burgeoning aesthetic of early hip-hop culture, its socioeconomic context, and the youthful exuberance of the participants. Because photography is a visual medium, these pictures tend to privilege graffiti and break-dancing over deejays and emcees. Cooper's *Hip Hop Files* shows graffiti artists sketching ideas on notepads, kids painting in dimly lit train yards, and trains covered with designs that require multiple cars.[2] She also took photographs of the Rock Steady Crew, one of the earliest and most important break-dancing groups.[3] Her work depicts them training, practicing, and ultimately performing. These shots also provide evidence of how New York City was suffering from neglect and decay even as these early hip-hop pioneers were laying the foundation for a new cultural aesthetic.

Cooper documents, among other things, how property, cultural ownership, and materialism, in various forms, have shaped hip-hop culture. Cooper's photography portrays graffiti artists acquiring paint and canvases by whatever means possible and documents the disintegration of the Bronx and other boroughs. It also depicts how young people sought to reclaim a form of ownership over their crumbling communities. In retrospect, these photographs highlight battles over public space, private property, and intellectual property. Although the City of New York criminalized the participants, graffiti art, break-dancing, and deejays, at their best, sought to beautify a decaying urban landscape and create public spaces for post–Civil Rights era youth to enjoy the freedoms for which the Civil Rights Movement fought so gallantly.

These early elements of hip-hop culture quickly entered both mainstream and elite cultures. Break-dancing, due to MTV's emergence and the immense popularity of Michael Jackson, found adherents across the country and in many suburban communities. Graffiti art also soon merged into the New York art scene as graffiti writers, including Lee Quinones and Fab Five Freddy, became the subject of gallery shows during the early 1980s. Jean-Michel Basquiat, who gained as much or more celebrity in the art world than in the world of hip-hop, transformed graffiti into an "elite art" and soon became associated with Andy Warhol and other New York artists. Prefiguring intellectual property law's conflict with hip-hop, his work from the early 1980s frequently included ironic usages of copyright and trademark symbols. Richard Marshall argues that "the © is Basquiat's stamp of approval, authority, ownership, and originality." He further observes that "by symbolically copyrighting his SAMO sayings, Basquiat was not just identifying them as his own, but sarcastically commenting on the obsession with legitimacy, ownership, and authorship, even of his often cryptic, subversive, and anti-ownership phrases."[4] Long before sampling became the subject of copyright disputes, hip-hop aesthetes, like Basquiat, examined who "owned" American culture and how the distribution of property and putatively color-blind property law doctrines operated to produce racial inequalities.

Hip-hop would soon expand beyond New York and the United States. Although it has relatively quickly become a key element of youth culture worldwide and a form of mass or corporate culture, its initial concerns with ownership, property, and materialism remain integral elements of hip-hop. Hip-hop culture continues to provide a running dialogue, albeit sometimes confusing, contradictory, and highly metaphorical, about the material conditions of African American life and the relationship of Black America to American society and culture. The term *hip-hop aesthetics* denotes how these issues shape the content and form of contemporary African American cultural texts. My examination of hip-hop aesthetics seeks to explain the relationships among post–Civil Rights era art, literature, and music and view them as interrelated phenomena. By privileging artistic and literary texts in my account, I hope to transcend the debates about hip-hop lyrics, especially their violence and sexism, and focus on the underlying aesthetic strategies that shape their production.

Another purpose of this book is to try to make some sense of the confused debate about property, property rights, and materialism in the post–Civil Rights era. Law, economics, cultural studies, and the arts all lay claim to these words, and no one book could synthesize all these usages. Scholars have most frequently viewed this conflict as pitting hip-hop music, especially with its reliance on sampling, against copyright law's understanding of fair use. In part because this is well-worn territory, and because I thought this narrow focus has unintentionally omitted some key elements of the story, I have broadened the conflict to examine a wider range of visual and textual production and to provide an occasion to speculate in a more philosophical tone (as opposed to a doctrinal one) about the purposes and effects of intellectual property law. As I hope this book makes clear throughout, intellectual property law is not the sole or primary influence shaping contemporary African American cultural production. Rather, it has become one of the key contemporary battlegrounds for a wide range of social, cultural, economic, and political questions.

In its effort to synthesize the vibrant conversations around intellectual property[5] and hip-hop aesthetics,[6] this book, engaging in a thought experiment of sorts, asks what insights could be gleaned if we viewed hip-hop aesthetics and African American cultural history, more generally, through the lens of intellectual property law (with occasional slippages into property law) and if we imagined what intellectual property law might look like if it tried to use copyright and trademark regulations to create a more just circulation of racialized texts. Obviously, these questions are artificial ones, because neither legal nor cultural texts can be so neatly isolated. The "real world" is infinitely more complex. That being fully admitted, this thought experiment helps sheds light on how the mind-sets or worldviews promoted by hip-hop and intellectual property law conflict at a conceptual or theoretical level and further the contemporary racial divide.

To examine this interface between hip-hop aesthetics and intellectual property law, I rely heavily on critical race theory and Latino/a critical theory.[7] These models have helped me imagine how a color-blind area of law, intellectual property law, might be transformed into a discursive space where race-conscious remedies might be developed and a more just popular culture nurtured. In a nutshell, the overall structure of this book follows what I would term a critical race theory methodology, which seeks to examine the historical, popular, and cultural origins of today's debate about intellectual property and then proceeds to offer a number of case studies in which legal doctrine is applied to specific texts. The conclusion then tries to suggest how each discipline or field might be affected by this conflict between hip-hop aesthetics and intellectual property law. Because this project attempts to synthesize the work of so many scholars from numerous fields, I regret that it has been impossible to recognize every scholarly contribution to this book without destroying the flow of the text and the central argument developed herein.

The book begins in chapter 1 by examining the historical debate within the African American community about the role of property and materialism in shaping a social justice agenda. The second chapter shifts to an examination of African American popular culture and its relation to the development of critical race theory. I consider how Henry Louis Gates's influential description of vernacular and artistic practices within the African American community relies on assumptions that run directly counter to intellectual property law's assumptions about creativity. The third chapter draws on Anna Deavere Smith's *Twilight—Los Angeles, 1992* to map out the characteristics of hip-hop aesthetics and provide an overview of contemporary aesthetic strategies, highlighting how those strategies have resulted in legal conflict or led to the threat of legal conflict. Chapter 4 applies the hip-hop aesthetic to Toni Morrison's *Beloved* and Adrian Piper's *Vanilla Nightmare* series. Neither Morrison nor Piper is part of the hip-hop generation, but this chapter tries to show how the structure and themes of their work, especially their focus on the meaning of ownership, constitute a bridge between Civil Rights generation strategies for social justice and hip-hop era approaches. Chapter 5 examines copyright and trademark law's approach to fair use by engaging in a close reading of Colson Whitehead's *John Henry Days* and Michael Ray Charles's *Forever Free* series. The penultimate chapter considers the possibility of social transformation and what intellectual property law terms "transformative use" by exploring Alice Randall's *The Wind Done Gone* and the artwork of Fred Wilson. The book concludes by suggesting possible directions for future scholarship in African American literature, African American art history, intellectual property law, critical race theory, and hip-hop studies.

By examining hip-hop as an aesthetic structure that underlies a range of genres, this book can provide a fuller critique of contemporary social and cultural relations. *Parodies of Ownership* ultimately concludes that intellectual property law doctrine has contained and neutralized the critical impulse of hip-hop aesthetics even if contemporary African American writing and art have flourished. Despite attempting to transform how intellectual property law distributes ownership rights for ideas, expressions, and texts,

courts have been unwilling to modify copyright law even when practitioners of hip-hop aesthetics, such as Alice Randall, win their cases. The widespread popularity of hip-hop aesthetics has challenged but not transformed
intellectual property law.

Because this book regularly shifts among four academic disciplines (literature, art, law, and music) that do not always share premises or methods, I
must acknowledge a few of my working assumptions in writing this book:

1. While this study describes how hip-hop has influenced contemporary African American literary and artistic production, it is clear that hip-
hop is not solely an African American phenomenon. At its origins, hip-hop
blended multiple ethnic traditions in its aesthetic and continues to do so
today, especially as its popularity in Europe, Africa, and Asia attests. However, I have limited my study to hip-hop's effect on African American art
and literature in order to keep the project a manageable one and to maintain a fairly unified focus throughout.

2. While much contemporary African American cultural production fits
within the hip-hop paradigm, it would be a mistake to apply the model to
all people with a certain skin tone. Rather, this books identifies the central
elements of hip-hop, translates them to a number of aesthetic realms, and
demonstrates how a range of creative endeavors within African American
culture share a common methodology or approach.[8] Not all books by
African American writers will fit within this paradigm, nor will every piece
of art by African American artists. For example, this book does not examine "street lit," despite its recent popularity and its focus on hip-hop-re-
lated content, because these books tend not to display the aesthetic strategies discussed herein.

3. Hip-hop's journey through the legal system has been well-docu-
mented and analyzed, especially as it relates to the "fair-use" doctrine, by
numerous hip-hop and intellectual property law scholars. While this book
examines the fair-use doctrine and applies it to contemporary African
American cultural production, it spends most of its critical energy examining the abstract or philosophical meaning of intellectual property, rather
than engaging in doctrinal analysis. The doctrinal analysis of fair use's application to hip-hop has largely been accomplished, and the most pressing
issues in intellectual property law scholarship, from a lawyer's point of
view, have moved onto new terrain. Rather, this book is concerned with a
different set of questions. Who "owns" the American cultural imagination
and possesses the ability to rework and reconstruct it? What kinds of own-

ership rights can be asserted through art, music, literature, and law, especially by historically marginalized people? Do textual producers draw on
particular aesthetic or cultural traditions when they assert their ownership
claims, no matter whether they are making copyright, trademark, or even
patent claims? Although this book frequently relies on dominant legal
analysis as a point of comparison, I am even more interested in explaining
the cultural and philosophical significance of the gap between intellectual
property law and hip-hop aesthetics. I have chosen "intellectual property
law" as the key theoretical focus, despite the book's emphasis on copyright,
because it is a more general term and offers a more appropriate analog for
understanding what Rayvon Fouché terms "black vernacular technological
creativity," forming the basis for the hip-hop aesthetic during the post–
Civil Rights era.[9]

4. I rely on the term *property* to denote a range of meanings: self-ownership; a claim of ownership; a tangible good; the laws regulating the ownership of tangible goods, land, or texts; and property rhetoric/talk. Within
the context of African American historical experience and cultural criticism, one definition frequently blurs into the others, and literary, musical,
and visual references to any one aspect of property frequently constitute
metaphors for the other definitions of property. This slippage, I would argue, is intentional within African American cultural criticism because it is
designed to destabilize or challenge legal discourse. It also serves to question the existing distribution of property and property rights. To respect
this tradition, I have adopted this metaphorical usage of *property*.

5. As a heuristic device, I argue that contemporary African American
criticism reflects a shift from civil rights to property rights. For many
lawyers, this is a distinction without a difference because property rights
are civil rights too. I nonetheless use this language because property rights,
by and large, rely on the logic of alienability, where one's interest can be
bartered or traded away. Civil rights approaches, by contrast, tend to assume that one's rights to due process and equal protection cannot be alienated or given up as a part of negotiation or contract. (Again, I realize that
lawyers more familiar with the nuances of property and civil rights law
might disagree with this broad characterization.) Because of hip-hop's materialism and its emphasis on commodified forms of identity, I believe that
examining the shift from a rhetoric of inalienability (civil rights) to one of
alienability (property rights) and its legal ramifications is absolutely essential for any understanding of contemporary African American cultural production and its critique of dominant legal discourse.

6. Although I do see differences between the Civil Rights and the hip-hop generations, I also see many linkages.[10] If their parents generally saw the Civil Rights Movement as a romantic struggle to overcome racial injustice, then hip-hop children tend to view the earlier generation's accomplishments and their effects more ambiguously and ironically. My assumption, as a cultural historian, is not that these attitudes are incommensurate and unrelated. Rather, the purpose of this book is to trace out how and why the hip-hop generation has turned from romantic optimism to a more ironic attitude. The recent election of Barack Obama suggests that these two generations do share values and goals and that the cynicism and irony of the post–Civil Rights era may be transforming into a new cultural narrative or sensibility.

# Acknowledgments

Without the wisdom, encouragement, and guidance of family, friends, and colleagues, this book would not exist. The journey that culminated with this book began because Zan Skolnick, my father-in-law, nudged me to look into Toni Morrison's testimony in the copyright case about Alice Randall's *The Wind Done Gone*. That initial research received a warm welcome from Norm Yetman, then an editor of *American Studies*, and an audience at a Mid-American American Studies Association (MAASA) conference in St. Louis. Ted Vaggalis served as a regular sounding board for my ideas and was kind enough to read a rough draft of the entire manuscript. His comments and suggestions vastly improved the final version. Ken Egan, Charlie Ess, and Cheryl Ragar encouraged and helped mentor me through the process of publishing a book. Jaqueline Tygart, art librarian extraordinaire, assisted me in tracking down images and catalogs. Diane Ziegler and Marie Tracy provided amazing administrative support during the last few years.

I am deeply grateful that Michael Ray Charles, Huey Copeland, and David Sanjek granted my requests for phone interviews. Those conversations helped propel the project forward. Richard Delgado was a superb resource, and I appreciate his enthusiasm for the book at a time when I doubted that I would ever complete it. Julie Cohen offered numerous suggestions for improving the sections on intellectual property. Students in my African American literature and African American cultural studies classes helped hone and improve many of the ideas contained in this book. I am blessed by being a part of a supportive department. Jeanie Allen, Hueping Chin, Charlie Ess, Michael Hill, Erin Kenny, Sean Terry, and Ted Vaggalis are simply wonderful colleagues and make going to work each day a pleasure. Tony Clark, Lisa Esposito, Teresa Hornsby, David Katzman, Lovalerie King, Cheryl Lester, Elizabeth Paddock, Chris Panza, Greg Renoff, Ann Schofield, Sherrie Tucker, and Saundra Weddle all regularly asked about the book's progress and offered moral support. I would also like to express my appreciation of everyone associated with the University of Michigan Press, especially the blind reviewers whose comments guided my revisions.

I must acknowledge the tremendous imagination of the writers, musicians, and artists discussed herein. Their work, along with that of many other contemporary African American cultural workers, was an inspiration and provided a wealth of material to analyze and discuss. I hope that this book does justice to their artistry and encourages others to delve deeper into their work. Although I only know them through their writing, Rosemary Coombe, Henry Louis Gates, Nelson George, Norman Kelley, Lawrence Lessig, Kembrew McLeod, Mark Anthony Neal, Tricia Rose, Joseph Schloss, and Siva Vaidhyanathan provided the intellectual inspiration for this book. I would like to thank them for writing books that inspired me.

Last but not least, family and friends encouraged me throughout the journey of writing this book. Victor Schur, Eileen Schur, Blossom Skolnick, and Zan Skolnick are the best parents and in-laws a person could ask for. Roberta Schur, Elyse Tish, Gary Skolnick, Harriet Krauthamer, Ellen Mednick, Scott Tandy, Diane Smason, and Josh Flanders have been wonderfully supportive. I also want to thank my children, Ruth, Ari, and Max, for indulging my absentmindedness when I was lost in thought about this project. Most of all, I would like to thank Linda Skolnick. She supported this project from the beginning, agonized with me over it, and lent her considerable intellect to the challenges it presented.

# Contents

# From Chattel to Intellectual Property: Legal Foundations of African American Cultural Critique

Copyright and intellectual property are the real estate of the future.

      —Dexter Scott King, *Growing Up King*

Many critics charge that the King family has neglected King's social and moral legacy in favor of exploiting for themselves his commercial appeal.

      —Michael Eric Dyson, *I May Not Get There with You*

The U.S. Postal Service has issued over 150 stamps of African Americans. From Frederick Douglass and Harriet Tubman to Malcolm X and Charlie Parker, the images of African American leaders, musicians, athletes, scientists, and business leaders have been captured on stamps of all sizes and denominations. The watershed year for this representational emphasis is 1980. Between 1940 and 1980, about twenty African Americans appeared on postage stamps. In the last quarter-century, nearly seven times that number of African Americans have appeared on postage stamps and postcards. Despite the continued existence of racial hierarchy and white supremacist thought in American life, what does this sudden explosion of images from African American history mean? How does this shift in

American popular visual culture demand a rereading of the very tradition of African American cultural criticism these stamps seek to represent? How does the "materialization" of this tradition of dissent alter the very meaning of the original messages for contemporary readers? Does this commodification of such figures reveal absences, gaps, or new ways of reading and understanding these canonized figures?

The hip-hop and Post-Soul generations (who came of age after the March on Washington, but before the rise of commercialized hip-hop) encountered the great leaders of African American history not only within their homes and churches but within American popular culture as well. Unlike earlier generations, who learned about the accomplishments of Douglass, Jacobs, Cooper, Washington, and Du Bois primarily within the confines of the African American community, more recent generations have encountered the canonized versions of King and Malcolm X, alongside the African American community's memories. If their parents and grandparents knew their words, the hip-hop generation is just as likely to recognize the images of Martin and Malcolm as their ideas. On the one hand, this increased visibility demonstrates a shift in American culture because most people consider it "normal" to recognize African American heroes. On the other hand, more images within American visual culture do not necessarily translate into a broader-based commitment to end racism or white supremacy. Ironically, the civic recognition of King and others has persuaded many whites that racism is a thing of the past. The increased visibility of African American leaders may also cause the hip-hop generation to grow cynical about Civil Rights Movement heroes because the apparent widespread acceptance of their efforts has not helped to realize their visions of freedom and equality for African Americans.

From the hip-hop generation's viewpoint, the translation of the Civil Rights Movement into stamps or other commodities creates an ambiguity about the movement itself. Coupled with the general ironic attitude toward politicians, athletes, and Hollywood stars, this has led to widespread cynicism about social activists and activism. For example, the main character of *Barbershop* (Eddie, played by Cedric the Entertainer) calls Martin Luther King a "ho" because of his adulterous behavior and states that "Rosa Parks ain't do nothin' but sit her black ass down." These comments (and the ones critical of Jesse Jackson as well) reflect disenchantment with the Civil Rights Movement, its tactics, and its vision because the movement and its main figures have become unquestionable, especially as white leaders from across the political spectrum genuflect at the past while increasingly ignoring the continued legacy of racial hierarchy in American culture.[1]

This chapter provides an intentionally revisionist account of African American cultural criticism. My goal here is to trace the origins of the hip-hop generation's approach to property law and why materialism and propertizing one's identity, at least on the surface, appear to be more appealing than social activism for many young African Americans. Building on the work of many hip-hop commentators who have examined, criticized, and defended hip-hop's materialism, I seek to place hip-hop's attitude toward property in a historical context. My purpose is not to rehearse the arguments made so ably by Derrick Alridge, Regina Austin, Yvonne Bynoe, Jeff Chang, Nelson George, Robin Kelley, James Peterson, Ted Swedenburg, S. Craig Watkins, and Kristine Wright on this topic. Rather, I hope to find a broader historical explanation for this "return" to property rights and contextualize it as part of the ebb and flow of African American cultural criticism. Todd Boyd has begun this project by articulating the dawning self-consciousness among the hip-hop generation.[2] Regina Blackburn has also initiated the project of revising African American cultural history through the lens offered by hip-hop.[3] This chapter, in essence, is equal parts archaeology, genealogy, and hermeneutics. Using the material practices and frequent materialism of hip-hop as a primary analytic, I reread the classic texts of African American studies to help them speak to the challenges of the post–Civil Rights era.

Stephen Best has recently argued that slave law in the nineteenth century laid the foundation for the contemporary *propertization* of life via intellectual property law.[4] In this chapter, I seek to extend his account and show how African American culture has increasingly placed property law at the center of cultural criticism. Rather than providing a definitive reading of any one text or period, I am trying to stitch together remnants of historical memory and develop a narrative to explain recent shifts in African American cultural production. This new/old narrative breaks up African American intellectual history into three periods based on the main question the period posed for property law. The first period (1780–1880) asked *who could own property*. While there was a range of writings, sermons, and speeches during this period, I am specifically interested in how some of the most famous slave narratives addressed this question about the subject in property law.[5] The second period (1880–1964) begins with the enactment of Jim Crow laws and caused African Americans to struggle with the question of *where could African Americans own property* and the spatial logic of property law. These questions about the geography of race can be found in the debates between Du Bois and Washington and between Malcolm X and Martin Luther King. The last period (1964 to the present) represents the beginnings of a new era in which the question becomes *who owns the imaginary domain out of which African Americans form cultural identity*. In this section, I explore the lawsuit between Rosa Parks and Outkast. The post–Civil Rights era has been marked by multiculturalism and identity politics. The legal battle over Parks's name suggests how the ownership over the symbols and metaphors of American and African American life has become a central issue in African American cultural criticism.[6] My rereading of African American history through the lens of property implies both continuity and change between generations or historical periods.[7] While admittedly painting with a broad historical brush, my goal here is to provide a historical context for hip-hop aesthetics and its attitude about property.

## Slave Narratives

Slave narratives depict the monstrous cruelty of slavery, enabling formerly enslaved African Americans to write themselves into American culture and providing a forum for demonstrating how slavery tainted the entire country with immorality. According to Robert Stepto, "The strident, moral voice of the former slave recounting, exposing, appealing, apostrophizing, and above all *remembering* is the single most impressive feature of a slave narrative."[8] These highly crafted narratives allowed certain talented writers, like Frederick Douglass, to assume a high level of authorial control in spite of the many generic restrictions and engage in social, cultural, and political criticism.[9] Hazel Carby notes that "in the slave narratives written by black women the authors placed in the foreground their active roles as historical agents."[10] Carby's study also demonstrates that African American women used the slave narrative both to assert control over racial and gender stereotypes and to create, via writing, a more authentic self. Henry Louis Gates argues that because slave narratives frequently were honed and perfected on the speaking podium prior to being written down, the texts incorporate both authorial intent and audience response.[11] Gates contends that from the beginning, slave narratives constituted revisionist accounts of African American history. Hip-hop's rereading of slave narratives thus merely serves as the latest iteration of revisionist criticism.

Hip-hop's rereading of slavery and slave life is perhaps no more shocking than Booker T. Washington, who downplayed the hardships of slavery to promote the value of labor, but it nonetheless clashes with more established views and fosters tensions between generations of African Americans.[12] Near the conclusion of Jake Lamar's *The Last Integrationist* (1996), Emma Person, one of the main characters, states quite bluntly that "what the slave wants is not freedom, but a slave of his own."[13] Through Emma Person, Lamar argues that freedom is not the main goal of the slave—property ownership is. If Lamar alone had articulated such a position about slavery, it might be idiosyncratic to highlight it here. However, Edward P. Jones won the 2004 Pulitzer Prize for fiction for his novel *The Known World* (2003), where he presents a complex portrait of antebellum life that includes a former slave becoming a slave owner himself. In Jones's fictional account, Henry Townsend, a freed slave and plantation owner, quickly adapts and adopts the attitudes toward property held by whites of the period. In the visual arts, the MacArthur Foundation presented Kara Walker with a prestigious "genius" grant for her black cut-paper silhouettes that resurrect forgotten images of African Americans from the South. Walker has been criticized for producing work that so closely resembles forms and images designed originally to demean and oppress African Americans. Because Walker's silhouettes tell complex stories, Thelma Golden once commented to Walker, "I imagine that there must be 500 pages of some sort of parody of a slave narrative lurking in your studio."[14]

Do these fairly well-received instances of contemporary artists and writers rewriting slave life suggest how hip-hop is revising our understanding of slavery? Annette Dixon writes: "Adopting the antiquated medium of the silhouette, Walker turns it into a power tool with which she evokes the system of slavery, exploring themes of exploitation, accommodation, and complicity in the institution of slavery on the part of both the powerful and the oppressed."[15] Novels about slavery written in the transition period between the Civil Rights era and the full-blown emergence of hip-hop aesthetics in the late 1980s, such as Ernest J. Gaines's *The Autobiography of Miss Jane Pittman* (1971), Gayl Jones's *Corregidora* (1975), and Sherley Ann Williams's *Dessa Rose* (1986), retain a much more reverent attitude toward those who were enslaved and clearly criticize every aspect of racism from that era. More recent images and novels present a much more ambiguous image of slave life and the goals and hopes of enslaved African Americans. By analyzing a few select passages from three of the more important slave narratives, I will bring attention to several moments in these texts that critics have tended to overlook but that are likely to gain in importance as a result of the hip-hop challenge to African American cultural criticism.

Most scholars identify Olaudah Equiano's text as one of the earliest slave narratives. A hip-hop rereading of the text might, for instance, focus on the narrative's conclusion, after Equiano is free and is attempting to find success in a postliberation (at least for him) setting. The narrative's ultimate anecdote relates his efforts to serve the English government and aid a group of Africans the British wished to return to Africa. Initially, Equiano refused to join the mission but was ultimately convinced to participate. The misappropriation of funds by government officials, however, caused the ship to lack the basic requirements needed to complete the journey. A number of the Africans perished as a consequence of this misuse of public property. As a result of the improprieties, the government relieved Equiano of his position. Equiano then uses his narrative to protect his integrity and incorporates in his text a number of letters that demonstrate that his virtue was ultimately vindicated by later investigations.

A hip-hop reader is likely to focus on this passage because it confronts the dilemma of hip-hop culture: how does one maintain one's integrity (i.e., keep it real) in a material world? This concluding story from his narrative allows Equiano to remind his readers one last time that slavery constitutes barbarity and a form of theft. Equiano demands that English law take seriously its own property laws. Slavery circumvents property law properly understood and undermines the budding capitalist ethic. Equiano's argument is structurally similar to hip-hop's critique of contemporary property law because both reiterate the value of protecting property interests but question what can and cannot be owned. Even though the narrative as a whole is much more concerned with developing a critique of slavery and stating the case for abolition, its attention to property relations allows the book to speak in a different register to contemporary audiences, especially as it makes clear that the evil of slavery is that it is not a small step from the misappropriation of black bodies to the misappropriation of government property.[16]

Similarly, Harriet Jacobs's *Incidents in the Life of a Slave Girl* concludes by reinforcing the importance of reconstructed property law for African Americans. Although one might assume that a woman, such as Jacobs, who had been an object of property would demand a complete abolition of the propertization of life, Jacobs endorses ownership as long as the subject of property law (i.e., *who* can own things) is expanded to include African Americans. Under antebellum law, slave owners stole a slave's labor. To this, Jacobs responds, "When a man has his wages stolen from him, year after year, and the laws sanction and enforce the theft, how can he be expected to have more regard to honesty than the man who robs him?"[17] She argues that property law will be just only if the right to own property (i.e., the power to exclude others from enjoying or reaping the benefits of an object) is guaranteed to those at the bottom of society as it is those at the top. A society that limits the rights of ownership to a specific class of men will necessarily be an unstable one because it will be, in effect, condoning theft. Jacobs's slave narrative concludes with the claim that "the dream of my life is not yet realized. I do not sit with my children in a home of my own. I still long for a hearthstone of my own, however humble. I wish it for my children's sake far more than for my own."[18] The last scene suggests that freedom and property ownership are intertwined and that the realization of property ownership will help her achieve her ultimate dream. Jacobs's last wish, however, links property ownership with virtue because it is primarily for the sake of her children that she wishes to become a property owner. Within this context, freedom from slavery is not freedom enough. The final liberation occurs, at least textually, when the freed slave becomes an owner herself and can transmit her wealth to her children.

If Jacobs and Equiano attack slavery while explicitly arguing for the importance of property ownership, Frederick Douglass appears to assume the necessity of property rights for achieving freedom and equality.[19] In his speech "What to the Slave Is the Fourth of July?" Douglass announces his support for John Locke's approach to property in his *Second Treatise* and its inclusion within the Declaration of Independence and the Constitution.[20] In *My Life and Bondage*, Douglass discusses the controversy that arose when abolitionists purchased his freedom while he was visiting England. In defending the abolitionists, he argues that this action should be viewed "in light of a ransom, or as money extorted by a robber," and that such an action did not violate "the laws of morality." In addition to absolving his liberators from any moral guilt, Douglass reminds abolitionists that the problem with slavery is not the possession of a right of property, but of "a right of property *in man*."[21] Because James Wright immediately manumitted Douglass, the laws of morality were satisfied by his actions, and property law was rehabilitated.

While these three moments cannot represent the entirety of the slave narrative tradition, they do point to a contemporary reading of African American history that emphasizes ethical forms of ownership. This reading of the tradition diverges significantly from Marxist or radical analyses in which the elimination of property rights should theoretically lead to a greater equality among all Americans. In the post–Civil Rights era, critical race theorists (and hip-hop artists as well) have pretty much accepted capitalism as a necessary ground for any social change. For example, Cheryl Harris argues in her 1993 article, "Whiteness as Property," that whiteness has functioned as a property interest for most white Americans and that affirmative action has been and continues to be necessary to remedy the effects of this ongoing racial legacy. She concludes that "in protecting the property interest in whiteness, property is assumed to be no more than the right to prohibit infringement on settled expectations, ignoring countervailing equitable claims that are predicated on the right to inclusion. It is long past time to put the property interest in whiteness to rest."[22] It is crucial to note that Harris seeks to redefine property by eliminating racialized properties, which her revisionist legal history traces back to the antebellum period, not to dismantle the property concept altogether.[23] While the slave narratives can be (and have been) read in a number of ways, recent debates about multiculturalism, property rights, and reparations help define the meaning of the slave narratives for the hip-hop generation. Perhaps the hardship most shared by the slaves and today's hip-hop generation is a general exclusion from the market economy. Hip-hop aesthetics reenacts the slave narratives' desire to become the subjects of property law.

## The Great Debate: Washington and Du Bois

My attempt to offer a new periodization for African American cultural criticism jumps from the great slave narratives (from the mid-nineteenth century) to the turn-of-the-twentieth-century debate between Booker T. Washington and W. E. B. Du Bois. The transition from the slave narratives of Equiano, Jacobs, and Douglass to Washington and Du Bois's nonfiction clarifies the categorical differences between the two periods' approaches to property law. Once the crisis of defining objects and subjects of property law (or who can own what within property law) gets resolved, at least temporarily, through the Civil War, the battle within legal discourse turns increasingly to the geography of race and the spatial dimensions of property law. Although few historians have described it as such, the debate between Washington and Du Bois concerns geographic distinctions within property law, as Jim Crow segregation primarily attempted to create spatial distinctions to replace the status distinctions that had been outlawed with the

Emancipation Proclamation. The question shifted from *wh*
*where* do the boundaries of property law extend.

Booker T. Washington's Atlanta Exposition speech iɪ
grounds for this new debate about property law. The speec
that of two ships meeting. One of the ships is suffering fro... .....
When the distressed ship asks for water, the response is, "Cast down your
bucket where you are."[24] Washington, unlike many others of this period,
urges African Americans to remain in the South and "put brains and skill
into the common occupations of life."[25] He advocates using whatever materials people can find and whatever skills they have toward earning money
and building wealth.[26] Washington specifically refuses to dismantle Jim
Crow laws first. Rather, he argues that material prosperity will lead the way
to other forms of equality.

"In all things that are purely social," Washington says, "we can be as
separate as the fingers, yet one as the hand in all things essential to mutual
progress."[27] His famous symbol of the hand provides a ready metaphor to
describe the fight for equality and prioritizes the struggles that African
Americans will need to overcome. The first hurdle is economic for Washington. For African Americans to succeed economically, Washington advocates an initial acceptance of Jim Crow and the geography of race in the
South. African American material prosperity will "bring our beloved South
a new heaven and new earth."[28] Much like the writers of the slave narratives, Washington reinforces the importance of property rights. He demands neither the immediate abolition of property rights nor the dismantling of Jim Crow. Rather, his autobiography condemns theft early and
often in order to demonstrate how the logic of self-improvement hinges on
property rights.[29] Washington is careful to align the goals of the African
American community with those of the white community. What Washington, in effect, requests is that the South respect the very racial lines it has
drawn and allow African Americans to acquire property within those
boundaries. Washington thus answers the question of *where* can or should
African Americans own property by saying, wherever whites allow African
Americans to do so, as long they consistently respect those boundaries. At
least one hip-hop studies scholar has argued that the rhetorical construct of
the "hip-hop mogul," and its performance by Russell Simmons, Sean
Combs, and others, embraces Washington's approach to racial uplift.[30]

For Du Bois, Washington's answer is unacceptable. Du Bois argues that
the Atlanta Exposition speech "represents in Negro thought the old attitude of adjustment and submission" and that the "program practically ac-

cepts the alleged inferiority of the Negro races."[31] While criticizing the economic tenor of Washington's thought, Du Bois appears to exit the language of property and adopt *politics*, *civil rights*, and *education* as key words in his analysis of Jim Crow. It is my contention, though, that Du Bois does not fully abandon economics or property law in his critique of American culture. Rather, his analysis of the relationship between geography and property relies on psychological metaphors to emphasize that ownership is not how a person relates to an object, but how communities determine the relations between objects and subjects. What Washington attempts to stabilize in his Atlanta Exposition speech (the boundary lines where African American property claims will be respected), Du Bois remaps entirely. Du Bois argues that any strategy for African American liberation must first create the conditions where social and self-respect can be won and then rework the rules about property ownership based on this new psychological geography.

In the opening chapter of *The Souls of Black Folks*, Du Bois articulates his famous notion of double consciousness. In an oft-quoted passage, Du Bois writes:

> It is a peculiar sensation, this double-consciousness, this sense of always looking at one's self through the eyes of the other, of measuring one's soul by the tape of a world that looks on in amused contempt and pity. One ever feels his twoness,—an American, a Negro; two souls, two thoughts, two unreconciled strivings; two warring ideals in one dark body, whose dogged strength alone keeps it from being torn asunder.[32]

Many argue that this passage constitutes an attempt to represent the struggles faced by African Americans. Earnest Allen has recently challenged this view. Allen notes that despite the popularity of this concept, especially in the post–Civil Rights era, he doubts Du Bois found it a successful description of the psychic condition of African Americans because he quickly abandoned the phrase after introducing it.[33] Allen presents a compelling case for rethinking the now standard interpretation that focuses on self-esteem or self-realization. Certainly, the recently rediscovered and rereleased collection of photos Du Bois prepared for the 1900 Paris World Fair displays no signs of "unreconciled strivings" or "warring ideals." The images reflect dignified middle-class African Americans striving to improve themselves and the race.[34]

Viewing this famous quotation through hip-hop aesthetics' engagement with intellectual property law suggests Du Bois deployed psychological terminology to describe the spatial problem at the heart of property law and thus to respond to Washington's embrace of economics. Du Bois has taken the racialized or segregated geography that Washington accepts and tries to move it within the body in order to show its danger. He develops three arguments against Washington. First, Du Bois, relying on psychology, argues that segregated spaces ultimately lead to segregated minds and that segregated minds cause madness, not empowerment. Du Bois concludes that Washington's bargain with the South is a failure because it would allow African Americans to own only a part of themselves. Limiting African American ownership claims to restricted areas within the black community, for Du Bois, is not really ownership at all: "He [Washington] is striving nobly to make Negro artisans business men and property-owners; but it is utterly impossible, under modern competitive methods, for workingmen and property-owners to defend their rights and exist without the right of suffrage."[35] In this passage, Du Bois makes clear that his disagreement with Washington is over not the importance of property rights, but how African Americans can best attain them.

The geography of difference and ownership is inscribed in a second way in Du Bois's account of double consciousness. Du Bois posits a scene where identity is constructed through a series of views.[36] Although many rely on this account to explain how identity is constructed and how the visual shapes cultural formation, reading Du Bois's description of double consciousness through property law theory suggests a different meaning. An object (in this case, a person) does not have identity a priori. Rather, identity is a product of human effort that gets mixed with a seemingly natural object (in this case, the body). In other words, Du Bois relies on a theory of racial consciousness where the properties of identity always already require a network or constellation of views or perceptions.

By insisting that the social matters for acts of self-ownership, Du Bois undermines Washington's reliance on an uncritical rhetoric of self-improvement. Washington implicitly endorses the capitalist ethic. Central to this ethic is John Locke's theory of property. Locke writes:

Every man has a *property* in his own *person*: this no body has any right to but himself. The *labour* of his body, and the *work* of his hands, we may say are properly his. Whatsoever then he removes out of the state that nature hath provided, and left it in, he hath mixed his *labour* with, and joined to it something that is his own, and thereby make it his *property.*[37]

In his account of how property is created, John Locke argues that a human being owns himself, without regard to social rule or custom, and owns whatever his labor touches. Washington, however, quickly retreats from an orthodox Lockean position because he cannot talk of natural property rights without running afoul of segregation laws because within a segregated society, a person is prohibited from owning whatever his labor mixes with unless it falls within the limited geography permitted by Jim Crow laws. Through his speech, Washington implicitly accepts the Southern attempts to define African Americans regardless of how individuals define themselves. Du Bois's description of double consciousness allows him to unmask the failed foundation of "segregated ownership" as a philosophy. Ownership claims within the limited spaces left to African Americans constitute incomplete acts of ownership because a racialized legal discourse could just as easily ignore or repudiate them. According to Du Bois, the central problem of African American history has not been the failure to demand self-ownership, but the failure of whites and legal discourse to recognize those demands.

Du Bois's third and final critique of Washington's approach to property also involves the *where* question, but holds that the most important properties are cultural—not material. As is well-known, Du Bois and Washington differed greatly on the kind of education that African Americans needed. Du Bois advocated for higher education, and Washington favored vocational training. A way of understanding this debate is to consider it an effect of how they answered the question about *where* African Americans should own property. Du Bois believed that cultural properties would lift up the race, while Washington preferred a focus on the accumulation of material objects.

Following Du Bois's lead, many African Americans sought to create social and cultural institutions that challenged segregation. For example, the early twentieth century saw a boom in African American fraternal lodges. Frequently, African Americans tried to model their organizations after successful white organizations, such as the Elks or the Masons. Borrowing regalia and symbols, they frequently gave their organizations names like the Black Elks and the Black Masons in an effort to show solidarity with white lodges. Despite the appearance of segregation, participants viewed themselves as integrating into American culture by joining these civically minded organizations. Anticipating more contemporary debates and controversies, the white lodges frequently resorted to law, sometimes even intellectual property law, to prohibit their black counterparts.[38] Interestingly, the courts relied on theories of "territorial jurisdiction," with its connection to Jim Crow segregation, to determine when and where black organizations could appropriate the regalia and symbols of white lodges.[39] Some scholars have argued that these lawsuits helped develop the legal tactics that would be deployed later, during the Civil Rights Movement.[40] These disputes illustrate how African Americans sought to claim ownership over segregated spaces and objects in American culture.

In addition to its effects on political and social life, segregation created tremendous barriers for African American musicians. Ironically, the modern music industry developed concurrently with Jim Crow segregation during the late nineteenth and early twentieth centuries, and Jim Crow thus contributed to its overall structure. K. J. Greene argues that three factors made it difficult for jazz and blues musician, especially African Americans, to succeed: "(1) inequalities of bargaining power, (2) the clash between the structural elements of copyright law and the oral predicate of Black culture, and (3) broad and pervasive social discrimination which both devalued Black contributions to the arts and created greater vulnerability to exploitation and appropriation of creative works."[41] In many ways, intellectual property rights issues, which are the subject of this book, had not ripened because artists had to overcome other barriers first. Russell Sanjek and David Sanjek note that segregated unions also affected the ability of many African American musicians to earn a living, play music live, and participate in recording sessions.[42] Even industry practices regarding recording contracts differed based on the musician's race. Frank Kofsky describes how Billie Holiday and Charlie Parker worked under particularly ungenerous contracts.[43] The first major copyright clearinghouse (ASCAP) had rules that made it difficult for many blues and folk musicians to join. Without the creation of BMI in the 1940s, artists such as Huddie Ledbetter, Arthur "Big Boy" Crudup, and Fats Domino may not have been able to receive royalties from their work.[44] Because the question of segregation dominated this historical moment, African American criticism about the definition and distribution of ownership rights over cultural texts has only recently become a central concern. Even though intellectual property law has become a focal point in the ongoing quest of racial justice, hip-hop artists still face numerous political, economic, social, and contractual hurdles.[45]

The rise of Jim Crow and the entrenchment of segregation presented the problem of *where* African Americans should own property. Washington went along with the racialized geography in order to help African Americans build material wealth and an economic base. Du Bois looked to psychology, sociology, and culture as more fertile and ultimately more significant areas for making claims of ownership. While the debate between these two giants of African American thought has long been foundational to African American studies, a hip-hop rereading of their disagreement helps us understand how property concerns shaped the debate's terrain. As will become apparent in later chapters, hip-hop culture has not embraced *either* Washington or Du Bois, but both of them. Of course, this produces tension and can appear paradoxical or contradictory, but it also reflects the hybrid nature of hip-hop, where samples of seemingly contradictory beats, rhythms, or melodies can be brought into a certain harmony through hip-hop artistry.

## Martin Luther King and Malcolm X

Despite the nearly fifty years between the Washington–Du Bois and the King-X debates, the question about *where* African Americans should own property remained an open one even after *Brown v. Board of Education* ruled that "separate but equal" was unconstitutional. Lorraine Hansberry's *A Raisin in the Sun* (1959) portrays the debate within a fictional black family, the Youngers. Through the play's dialogue, Hansberry considers which kinds of property claims will best serve the family after they receive an insurance check following the father/husband's death. On a basic level, the play asks whether it is better to own a liquor store in segregated Chicago or purchase a home in an integrated neighborhood. The Youngers ultimately opt to demand integration.[46] While Hansberry's play explores other issues and conflicts besides property law, it nonetheless provides a ready bridge to connect debates between Washington and Du Bois with those between King and Malcolm X. Although not typically considered primarily critics of property law, Martin Luther King and Malcolm X returned to the Washington–Du Bois debate about property (although some would say it never completely left African American culture). In more conventional histories of the period, King comes to represent integration, and Malcolm X becomes a spokesperson of Black Nationalism. For King, integration means the ability to own property alongside or next to white people and would allow African Americans to buy homes where they wanted, open businesses, and participate fully in society. Black Nationalism, on the other hand, argues that African Americans must develop their own businesses, social structures, and cultural institutions in order to gain true equality. In contrast to integration, true liberation will occur when African Americans develop their own resources without relying on or mixing with white people and their institutions. For Malcolm X, integration would prove a failure because it would force African Americans to give up or sell their birthright (Black culture) as the price of social recognition.

James Hal Cone, quite astutely, points out that any mapping of Martin Luther King and Malcolm X into an ideological binary is simple and incomplete: "We should never pit them against each other. Anyone, therefore, who claims to be for one and not the other does not understand their significance to the black community, for America, or for the world. We need both of them and we need them *together.* Malcolm keeps Martin from being turned into a harmless American hero. Martin keeps Malcolm from being an ostracized black hero."[47] Cone argues that over the course of their lives, their respective philosophies moved closer together. For my purposes here of exploring a hip-hop rereading of King and X, however, it is interesting to examine how their words invoke a series of property claims. Both sought to answer the question of *where* should African Americans own property.

In two of his most important texts, King relies on property talk to lay a foundation for his appeal for equality. Neither moment has become part of the national myth, like King's dream that his children "will not be judged by the color of their skin, but the content of their character" or his claim that he is "an extremist for love." However, his appeals to property law suggest that it forms an emotional and theoretical basis for his call for integration. Hip-hop generation readers of King's "Letter from Birmingham Jail" find King's lament about how "you suddenly find your tongue twisted and your speech stammering as you seek to explain to your six-year-old daughter why she can't go to the public amusement park" particularly powerful.[48] This image helps white readers "feel" the emotional pain caused by segregated property rules. A hip-hop revision emphasizes the consumerist or materialist mentality that underlies this powerful historical moment. Even though King eventually questioned capitalism as an engine for equality, in this justly famous letter he updates Du Bois's argument about segregated spaces to include how a segregated marketplace leads to fundamental unfairness and inequality. Probably because of the class divisions within the

African American community, King initially emphasized the "ordinary" middle-class longings of African Americans in order to build a bridge with whites and demonstrate the plausibility and inevitability of integration in a market economy. The vocabulary of property and loss marked within this anecdote suggests that property- or materially based critiques were not completely foreign to the Civil Rights generation. In fact, even King, the Student Nonviolent Coordinating Committee (SNCC), and the Southern Christian Leadership Conference (SCLC) relied on such metaphors to mobilize middle-class African Americans and to persuade whites that all people wanted the same (material) things.

In his "I Have a Dream" speech, King lays the theoretical groundwork for his dream by noting that the ideals of the Declaration of Independence and the Constitution have not been realized. The metaphor that he chooses to represent this failure is that of a returned "promissory note" that "has come back marked 'insufficient funds.' "[49] According to legal discourse, a promissory note is a property interest. Akin to cash or stock, a promissory note allows its owner to protect his interests and confers rights and remedies on the owner if a problem arises. Within the speech, King relies on social contract theory to explain the origins of American democracy and to appeal to conventional notions about how society works. King reiterates the founding contract, which brought the United States into being, in order to write African Americans back into that contract. He also suggests that the basic rules of exchange and contract require white America to respond in good faith and live up to their promises. According to King, "we've come to cash this check, a check that will give us upon demand the riches of freedom and the security of justice."[50] This promissory note, this property interest, becomes the driving force in "purchasing" liberty and justice. Within the logic of the speech, King's dream must be purchased through the transfer of property. The unspoken, but all too dearly paid consideration for this transaction, was the labor of slaves and the burdens imposed by segregation.

Obviously, Malcolm X would not have relied on such a metaphor because he argued that whites could not be persuaded into giving African Americans rights and that this framework perpetuates the central lie of American culture (i.e., that the American Revolution, the Declaration of Independence, and the Constitution offered freedom to all). Nor would Malcolm X have quite endorsed efforts to gain the right to eat with or play with white people because integration was not his solution to race in America. Malcolm X answered the question of *where* African Americans should own property quite differently and thus deployed property rights to other ends. Malcolm X argued that revolutions are "based on land" and that "a revolutionary wants land so he can set up his own nation, an independent nation. These Negroes [Martin Luther King and other more moderate or integrationist approaches] aren't asking for any nation—they're trying to crawl back on the plantation."[51] Malcolm X argued that *where* African Americans should own property was the crucial question. For him, this question was not simply one of physical geography, but of how culture and social institutions define and transform a space into a place. In "Message to the Grass Roots," Malcolm argues that integration cannot be a sufficient response to the *where* question because that will only address the effects, not the causes of white supremacy in America. Later in the same speech, Malcolm states that "this modern house Negro loves his master. He wants to live near him. He'll pay three times as much as the house is worth just to live near his master."[52] Malcolm X belittles integration because it fails to redefine ownership. In many ways, he blends Booker T. Washington's economics and Du Bois's sociology to transcend existing property rules and create a more just social structure.

Malcolm X does not just criticize King and other reformers without offering his reformulated definition of property and true ownership:

> The economic philosophy of Black Nationalism is pure and simple. It only means that we should control the economy of our community. Why should white people be running all the stores in our community? Why should white people be running the banks of our community? Why should the economy of our community be in the hands of the white man? Why? If a black man can't move his store into a white community, you tell me why a white man should move his store into a black community.[53]

For Malcolm X, a revised property law must go beyond looking at who owns individual tracts of land. Rather, Malcolm X looks at patterns of ownership and seeks to build networks of property relations. Black Nationalism, according to Malcolm X, transcends Booker T. Washington's approach to property law because it refuses to ignore overall economic structures and the tremendous inequalities they produce. Self-reliance or self-help without concerted effort and a desire to take control of the community cannot empower the entire community. It only enriches certain chosen individuals. Unlike Martin Luther King, Malcolm X does not believe that increased property exchanges, which lead to more integrated neighborhoods, will improve the situation of the African American community. Integration only further isolates African Americans from one another. The goal of Black Nationalism is to draw new cultural boundaries, not accept existing ones, as integration does. Because African Americans would establish these new spatial divisions, they would be empowered. Black Nationalism thus stresses the geography of ownership, perhaps even more so than other theoretical orientations, because it subordinates individual property rights in favor of communal needs. In this instance, the answer to the question of *where* African Americans should own property is not so much a particular physical space, but a metaphysical or cultural one.

The only meeting between Martin Luther King and Malcolm X occurred during the congressional hearings about the Civil Rights Act of 1964. This act transformed American culture by granting formal equality to African Americans in public facilities and marked the beginning of the end of this debate. Within the context of my argument that African American cultural criticism has frequently focused on property law, it is important to review with some care this watershed moment for the Civil Rights Movement and the hip-hop generation. The legislation states, "All persons shall be entitled to the full and equal enjoyment of the goods, services, facilities, and privileges, advantages, and accommodations of any place of public accommodation." The bill continues by identifying the physical spaces covered by these rights:

(1) any inn, hotel, motel, or other establishment . . . ;

(2) any restaurant, cafeteria, lunchroom, lunch counter, soda fountain, or other facility principally engaged in selling food for consumption on the premises, including, but not limited to, any such facility located on the premises of any retail establishment; or any gasoline station;

(3) any motion picture house, theater, concert hall, sports arena, stadium or other place of exhibition or entertainment.[54]

While Congress would wait until the Civil Rights Act of 1965 to address inequalities in voting, and the Civil Rights Act of 1968 to specifically address home ownership and apartment rentals, this first major legislative victory focused squarely on opening up public spaces, especially sites of interaction and entertainment, to integration. The underlying logic of this and other Civil Rights acts implicitly endorses a property-centered analysis of African American cultural criticism. This legislation transforms equality into a consumer transaction.

This victory (clearly more integrationist than Black Nationalist) set the wheels in motion for a new property paradigm to take hold in African American cultural criticism. Physical integration, for better or worse, would become the new national paradigm for improving race relations and the quality of life for African Americans. Although advocates for "color-blind" jurisprudence would see this as the logical end for civil rights activism and African American cultural critique, raced cultural criticism continues.[55] Instead of focusing on delineating the physical boundaries that limit black life, the question, mirroring a much wider debate in American culture, centers on *who owns the imaginary domain out of which African Americans form cultural identity.* This battle not only pits African Americans against whites but has also created a rift between the Civil Rights and the hip-hop generations.

## Rosa Parks and Outkast

Despite the wonderful idealism of Civil Rights leaders, their legacy has become the subject of property disputes. After the deaths of King and Malcolm X, heated battles ensued over who owns the rights to their work and who should have the right to purchase and display their intellectual property. The King estate has sought to control his legacy by threatening and initiating lawsuits against Boston University, the television program *60 Minutes*, and even the federal government for planning to use King's likeness in a memorial without paying for the rights.[56] The King family has asserted its *intellectual property* rights in his papers and his image in order to protect his legacy. While we might question from whom or what they are protecting him, it is quite clear that copyright law allows King's heirs to control access to and authorize who may copy his papers. These rights have allowed the King family to claim ownership over a central figure of African American culture and American history. The life and thoughts of Martin Luther King have become *propertized* and transformed into a resource to be developed, managed, marketed and sold. Obviously, this situation is troubling, or at least an impediment, to students of American culture and anyone who wishes to claim and extend King's legacy.

But King is not alone in becoming the subject of intellectual property disputes after his death. Lost to history, the papers of Malcolm X suddenly appeared in an eBay auction in February 2002. A few weeks later, eBay pulled the auction because the auctioneers, who had presented the materials, could not adequately determine the legitimate title for the materials. Academics argued that these items needed to remain together within an archive or library that could appropriately manage them.[57] The Shabazz family and scholars feared that intellectual property law would allow important historical, cultural, and literary data about Malcolm X to slip behind a "veil" of private ownership and possibly be lost to scholarly inquiry.[58] One scholar even suggested that these documents constitute the inalienable inheritance of all African Americans.[59] Ultimately, the Schomburg Center for Research in Black Culture purchased the documents and is preparing them for further study and public display.

The controversies surrounding the cultural legacies of Martin Luther King and Malcolm X reveal the increasing importance of intellectual property law for regulating how contemporary African Americans remember these icons, pay homage to them, and build upon their ideas. The academics who commented on the Malcolm X papers saw a need to protect some private ownership rights for the Shabazz family and to allow some form of cultural ownership rights for all African Americans. These cases suggest the difficulties inherent in drawing a line between the public domain, what is "our" common heritage from which we may borrow, and the needs of individuals to hold their own documents, ideas, and stories in private ownership.

The lawsuit between Rosa Parks and Outkast demonstrates just how much the debate about property within African American culture has changed and become much more complicated because it involves tensions not only between blacks and whites but between generations of African Americans as well.[60] Mark Anthony Neal argues that the Outkast "song can be seen as a tribute to her [Parks] and the movement that her actions helped incubate. I see the use of Rosa Parks in this context as one of the components of Post-Soul strategies that willingly 'bastardize' black history and culture to create alternative meanings, a process that was largely introduced to the Post-Soul generation via the blaxploitation films of the 1970s."[61] Todd Boyd argues that Parks's actions reveal how the Civil Rights generation misunderstands hip-hop.[62] Building on the astute analyses of Neal and Boyd, I would add that both Outkast and Parks willingly propertize, or transform their ideas and values into potential property interests. Who won the dispute is of less interest to me than how their economic motives for commencing the lawsuit undermine their ability to articulate any kind of claim that does not appear motivated by materialism or greed. The Civil Rights ethic of working together to create a more just world has appeared to slip away. Besides Rosa Parks, Bobby Seale claimed that a film company falsely represented him in its movie about the Black Panthers, and Faith Ringgold filed suit against Black Entertainment Television (BET) for using a reproduction of her art as part of the scenery in an episode of *Roc*.[63] Neither won their case, but both activists, who had previously made claims about the collective cultural experiences of African Americans, articulated their claims under the rubric of private property.

In 1998, Outkast released the album *Aquemini*, which features the song "Rosa Parks." The song does not really reference Rosa Parks or her famous refusal to stand in 1955, which led to the Memphis bus boycott, but it does contain the line: "Ah ha, hush that fuss / Everybody move to the back of the bus." Parks sued Outkast because she claimed that the use of her name (1) constitutes false advertising, suggesting that Parks either approved of the music or endorsed the compact disc; and (2) intrudes on her right of publicity. Based on documents submitted in the lawsuit, it is clear that Parks did not want her name associated with a hip-hop album because she had recently licensed an album of gospel recordings, *Verity Records Presents: A Tribute to Mrs. Rosa Parks*. This lawsuit suggests that Parks and, by implication, the Civil Rights generation have shifted focus from civil rights to property rights. Parks displays some of the same motivations and values for which the Civil Rights generation criticizes the hip-hop generation. The lawsuits filed by Civil Rights era leaders and their heirs, from Martin Luther King to Malcolm X to Bobby Seale to Faith Ringgold to Rosa Parks, seem to reflect more continuity with the hip-hop generation's concerns than most would like to admit. Nelson George identifies a key moment in this transition to a new approach to property: "Public Enemy made politics seem cool. In the process, they also made politics a commodity."[64] The reparations movement offers another example of the influence of property rhetoric on African American cultural criticism. Proponents of reparations hope to use the money from any settlement to remedy poverty, unemployment, and illiteracy and/or create museums, libraries, and educational curricula.

In district court, Outkast successfully defended itself as the court ruled that the bus reference establishes a strong connection between the song and its title and that the group's First Amendment rights allow them to use Parks as a symbol within their song. That court dismissed the lawsuit after

Outkast submitted a motion for summary judgment.[65] Parks appealed this decision to the U.S. Court of Appeals for the Sixth Circuit, which overturned the lower court's decision. The Court of Appeals questioned the connection between the title and the song and determined (through its own reading of the lyrics) that little binds the song to the title and that therefore it was possible for a jury to conclude that the song merely uses Parks's name to get free publicity. Therefore, it denied Outkast's motion for summary judgment and returned the case to the district court for a trial.

Both juridical attempts to determine "whether there is any artistic relationship between the title and the underlying work" deserve close scrutiny because they reveal the new tensions within African American culture as it confronts contemporary intellectual property doctrine.[66] Before exploring these analyses, it should be noted that Rosa Parks and Outkast brought different interpretative lenses to the text. Parks argued that her name had nothing to do with the song's meaning and that Outkast simply wanted to get free publicity. She took a fairly literal reading of the song and determined that because there was no mention of the Civil Rights Movement, Montgomery, or the 1955 bus boycott, the song had no connection to her. Parks relied on Civil Rights era understandings of racial narratives in which racial uplift serves as the primary storyline in her interpretation of the song. Because there is no clear view expressed in the song about politics or culture, the lens Parks brings to "Rosa Parks" cannot make any connection between the song and its title.

In the court documents, Outkast did not really explain how Parks's name is connected to the song or why they had chosen to use it. The district court judge argued that the lyrics about moving to the back of the bus connect Outkast's boasting about their excellence to Rosa Parks's famous refusal to give up her seat. Within the aesthetic of hip-hop, referencing people, places, and trademarked objects constitutes a primary method of establishing location and identity. Unlike other forms of poetry or writing, hip-hop does not always aim to build a coherent narrative, but to construct a flow or rhythm out of "used" phrases or images. (Hip-hop can be described as an aural analog to the scrap quilts of Gee's Bend, Romare Bearden's collages, or David Hammons's sculptures made out of discarded objects.)[67] In other words, the aesthetic of hip-hop requires the use of names, locations, and objects to establish one's context, one's identity, and one's hip-hop virtuosity. Robin Kelley writes that "what counts more than the story is the 'storytelling'—an emcee's verbal facility on the mic, creative and often hilarious use of puns, metaphors, and similes."[68] For Outkast, Rosa Parks was simply another possible referent to add to their repertoire of imagery and wordplay.

The Sixth Circuit, however, needed to resolve which interpretation would define the meaning of "Rosa Parks" for its decision. Speaking for the three-judge panel, Judge John Holschuh attempted to discern the "plain meaning" of the song. Based on a blend of judicial common sense and *YZ's Unofficial Rap Dictionary*, the court concluded that "there is a genuine issue of material fact whether the use of Rosa Parks' name . . . is artistically related to the content of the song."[69] The court, however, did not believe that this question could be easily answered, and it remanded the case to the district court for a hearing on this issue. By returning the case to the district court, the Sixth Circuit Court allowed the opportunity for both sides to call witnesses and experts to explain whether or not Parks's name has any connection to the song. Ultimately the case settled and legal discourse was not forced to choose which interpretative lens, that of the Civil Rights generation or the hip-hop generation, would be adopted in this case. For at least awhile longer, the question of *who owns the imaginary domain out of which African Americans form cultural identity* remains unanswered.

The dispute between Parks and Outkast shows the continued importance of property law to African American culture because the shift from slavery to segregation to intellectual property both (1) demonstrates property's continued central role in African American thought and (2) sets the stage for the emergence of critical race theory as a major force in shaping how African American culture criticizes law and legal discourse. By focusing on hip-hop aesthetics throughout the remainder of this book, I will deploy hip-hop culture as a practical example of critical race theory's attempt to "race" legal discourse through a philosophical rewriting of law's foundation. The Sixth Circuit's decision in *Parks v. Laface Records* demonstrates that law, especially intellectual property law, must increasingly make interpretative judgments about cultural matters to apply legal doctrine. Without attending to the origins of cultural practices, it is impossible to apply intellectual property doctrines fully or fairly.

## CHAPTER 2

# Critical Race Theory, Signifyin', and Cultural Ownership

By the 1980s, Civil Rights–era strategies and reasoning no longer could respond effectively to evolving forms of racism. The impediments to equality and freedom had been altered from the physical violence of Bull Connor to the representational violence of the Reagan era. The post–Civil Rights era transformed the grammar and syntax of racism, racialization, and white supremacy. The success of the 1963 March on Washington and the "I Have a Dream" speech altered how Americans argued for a status quo where many African Americans (though not all) lived with de facto second-class citizenship. If political leaders previously relied on consciously racist language to keep African Americans "in their place," the 1970s and 1980s saw a resurgence of property rights and state's rights rhetoric that evaded overt references to race while tapping into racialized fears.

In legal discourse, *Arlington Heights* (1977) exemplifies the limits of Civil Rights strategies that rely on legal decision makers to remedy racial inequality. A housing developer wanted to change the zoning classification of a parcel of land so he could build apartment buildings for low-income families in a mostly white suburb of Chicago. At the zoning board hearings, some people objected to the possibility of poor African Americans moving from the city to the suburbs, but most focused on the potential change to "settled" zoning laws and the town's strategy to create buffer zones between commercial and residential districts. The town refused to change the zoning rules, and the developer filed suit. Because the record did not establish a clear and overt racial bias, the court found no discriminatory purpose in denying the zoning change. The town fought the construction of a low-income development probably due to racialized fears. Because it relied on the "color-blind" rhetoric of property rights, the court could not "see" the presence of race.[1]

Radical legal scholars became concerned about the increasingly limited efficacy of legal discourse in remedying social problems. Weaving together strands of Marxist and postmodern thought, a movement of like-minded scholars created critical legal studies (CLS) to identify the contradictions of liberal legal thought that had created an impasse in the effort for meaningful social reform. Mark Kelman identified three main contradictions that CLS found in liberal legal ideology: (1) the contradiction between a commitment to "mechanical rules" and law's claim to review all cases on their own merits; (2) the contradiction between liberal thought's valuation of individual desires as the basis for social life and its appeal to universal reason and objective knowledge when it engages in legal reasoning; and (3) the implicit tension between trying to validate and respect personal choice and acknowledging how social forces shape individual lives.[2] Roberto Unger, one of the earliest proponents of what became CLS, concluded that "without a guiding vision, legal reasoning seems condemned to a game of easy analogies."[3] As a result, CLS focused on the crisis of legitimation in which legal discourse, because it contains a range of attitudes and perspectives, can be used to legitimate contradictory conclusions about a legal problem. As a postmodern legal movement, CLS focused on the language's rhetorical slippage and the failure of reason to explain human behavior and legal decisions.[4]

From legitimation, CLS turned to its attention to power, especially as described by Michel Foucault in *Discipline & Punish* (1995) and *The History of Sexuality, Volume 1* (1990). Illustrative of these concerns, Peter Goodrich argued that law is concerned with "the transmission of power from person to person and from place to place by invisible means." Goodrich argues further that "power is unseen, it can be imagined through the surfaces upon which it is inscribed."[5] To locate this unseen flow of power, scholars increasingly looked toward popular culture for the traces of law's power. In the language of Foucault, these endeavors sought to map out the microphysics of power. Rather than being means to develop strategies to end discrimination and oppression, textual indeterminacy and the sketching of cultural power soon became ends in and of themselves. CLS came to represent nihilism because it became identified with "trashing" law and liberalism due to its efforts to uncover the cultural biases of legal discourse but appeared to offer little hope about law's utility for promoting cultural or social change.[6]

Initially, legal scholars of color supported the CLS movement, but they slowly grew disenchanted with the direction in which it was headed.[7] Kimberlé Crenshaw invited a number of scholars of color, including Richard Delgado, Neil Gotanda, Mari Matsuda, Stephanie Phillips, and Kendall Thomas, to attend the first "Critical Race Theory" (or CRT) workshop in 1989. Crenshaw convened the meeting to discuss how lawyers could continue the work of dismantling racial hierarchy in the context of CLS's growth in the legal academy.[8] At the meeting, the participants organized their discussions around two common interests. First, they shared an understanding that white supremacy inhered in dominant and formally equal institutions as an endemic feature rather than as a deviation. They argued that lofty legal ideals, while in theory neutral and fair, have relied on unstated and unconscious racial assumptions. Thus, they expressed a certain amount of shared skepticism of legal principles such as the rule of law, objectivity, and equal protection as necessarily neutral. Second, they shared a commitment to altering racial hierarchy in the United States.[9] While not all attendees shared a common perspective on how to accomplish their goals, all desired to use law to transform American culture. Other factors also shaped the birth of CRT. Its adherents were also concerned about the increase in urban violence, the "War on Drugs" and the incarceration of black men, chronic unemployment and underemployment, and white flight to the suburbs. The same factors that produced a shift in legal discourse also laid the foundation for the birth of hip-hop culture.[10]

Frustrated with postmodern legal theory, Derrick Bell, then a professor of law at Harvard, began writing short stories to illustrate the limits of traditional formal legal analysis, how it failed to connect with the lived experiences of African Americans. Bell's stories, which were collected in his *And We Are Not Saved* (1987), demonstrated that law produced and regulated racial identity and that racialized discourses constituted a necessary foundation for the efficient operation of legal reasoning.[11] Unlike their postmodern counterparts, Bell and other critical race theorists insisted that human beings have created the category of race to realize particular social and economic ends and that the social construction of race affects individual lives.[12] Patricia Williams, another founding member of CRT, wrote a book that blended legal critique, autobiography, and cultural commentary in order to demonstrate how cultural narratives influence the content of rights discourse.[13] The work of Williams, Bell, and Richard Delgado, author of *The Rodrigo Chronicles* (1995), challenged not only the boundaries of law but also the proper writing style for legal scholarship. By penning short stories (Bell), neo-Platonic dialogues (Delgado), and legal autobiographies (Williams), these authors sampled various literary styles, layered different voices from within the African American community in their writing, emphasized the orality of African American culture and the practices of everyday life, and included moments of humor and irony in their writing. Much as hip-hop has been criticized as a dangerous nihilistic enterprise, CRT has been accused of attacking reason and engaging in a wholesale cultural war.[14]

Some CRT proponents, such as Richard Delgado, argue that the new grammar of race requires a shift in tactics away from formal civil rights or constitutional law to other areas such as tort law. Delgado urges courts to articulate "an independent tort for racial slurs" that "would protect the interests of personality and equal citizenship that are part of our highest political traditions and moral values, thereby affirming the right of all citizens to lead their lives free from attacks on their dignity and psychological integrity."[15] In his seminal article "Words That Wound," Delgado announces both a return to a fundamental premise of the Civil Rights Movement (that the movement was an effort to demand that dominant culture recognize the humanity and subjectivity of marginalized people) and a shift in orientation. He goes beyond focusing on *where* African Americans could or should own property to explore how the next stage in the civil rights struggle requires a remapping of knowledge that can acknowledge realms or dimensions "unseen" by the majority. For Delgado and other critical race theorists, post–Civil Rights era discrimination is not labeled publicly or obviously, like the signage of the segregated South. Thus, it appears to be invisible for legal discourse. By recognizing a tort for racial epithets, Delgado, in effect, argues that cultural discrimination may not leave visible scars, but it nonetheless affects the psyche. In the vocabulary of Carl Gutièrrez-Jones, we need to develop a new rhetoric of injury that is capacious enough to capture those aspects of racism, such as hate speech, that the Civil Rights Movement could not address and that thus remain invisible to dominant culture.[16]

## Henry Louis Gates and Signifyin'

Mark Anthony Neal observes that Henry Louis Gates "has positioned himself as one of the most prominent gatekeepers of black intellectual property" in large part because his book *The Signifying Monkey* set the terms of the debate about African American literature during the culture wars of the 1980s and 1990s. Even more astutely, Neal observes that Gates, in his role as one of the "deans" of African American letters, has come to understand that "black intellectual thought and criticism are wed with the demands of the mainstream marketplace."[17] *The Signifying Monkey* sought to uncover or make visible the connections between black vernacular speech and the African American literary tradition.[18] Gates is most clearly responding to the theoretical turn in literary studies during the 1970s and 1980s that emphasized importing French theories, especially Derrida, to counter the New Critics' formalistic analysis of American literature, which attempted to stabilize the meaning and value of literary texts. *The Signifying Monkey* thus attempts to provide African and African American origins for debates about textual indeterminacy and the coherence of cultural traditions. Gates seeks to show how trickster figures from African and African Caribbean culture are transformed on the journey to America, not to establish rules or laws of historical development but to demonstrate the connection between African and African American cultural forms in the present day.

For Gates, the central theoretical principle that unifies and explains the African American literary tradition is signifyin'. Adopted and adapted from scholarly literature in anthropology and linguistics, signifyin', Gates concludes, "is a metaphor for textual revision."[19] It can appear in everyday parlance as "*talking shit, woofing, spouting, muckty muck, boogerbang, beating your gums, talking smart, putting down, putting on, playing, sounding, telling lies, shag-lag, marking, shucking, jiving, jitterbugging, bugging, mounting, charging, cracking, harping, rapping, bookooing, low-rating, hoorawing, sweet-talking, smart-talking,* and no doubt a few others that I [Gates] have omitted."[20] In each of these versions, signifyin' "depends on the success of the signifier at invoking absent meaning ambiguously 'present' in a carefully wrought statement" that playfully mines the indeterminacy of language to say one thing but mean another.[21] Frequently, signifyin' relies heavily on citing and rewriting well-known symbols, metaphors, or objects.

Because some have limited signifyin' to the dozens, it has been wrongly reduced to a game of verbal aggression. However, Gates makes clear that signifyin' cannot be reduced to the dozens because the practice, rightly understood, is simultaneously humorous and deadly serious, conveying meaning as much with style as with substance.[22] It signals a "triumph of wit and reason" based on verbal acuity.[23] According to Robin Kelley, signifyin' is "an effort to master the absurd metaphor, an art form intended to entertain rather than to damage."[24] Claudia Mitchell-Kernan clearly differentiates the insulting or verbally aggressive components of the dozens from its signifyin' aspects. She argues that signifyin' "incorporates essentially a folk notion that dictionary entries for words are not always sufficient for interpreting meanings or messages, or that meaning goes beyond such interpretations."[25] While insults or verbal aggression can accompany signifyin', they are not necessarily linked. To place signifyin' at the center of African American literature is not to emphasize hostility or linguistic violence. Rather, such a focus emphasizes wordplay, textual revision, and metaphor.

Although he rarely directly states this, Gates seeks to infuse literary studies with an African American subjectivity. Signifyin' stands in for a historically and culturally specific way of creating and understanding textual production, which Gates traces back to the late eighteenth century with the trope of the talking book. If postmodern literary theorists (the literary analog of CLS) sought to reframe literary analysis from the self-sufficient text assumed by the New Critics, Gates seeks to demonstrate that racial subjectivities shape how scholars read texts. Similar to critical race theorists, Gates wants to decenter the dominant cultural attitudes and narratives that have structured literary interpretation and limited the horizons of literary discourse. Following nearly identical paths, CRT and Gates both write over postmodern concerns about textual indeterminacy and the ubiquity of contradiction within acts of judgment to emphasize how the very discourses of law and literature themselves have been raced or racialized. Neither Gates nor CRT sees the gains of Civil Rights activists as being sufficient to transform social relations. Another step, one that recognizes how race unconsciously infects perception and judgments based on those perceptions, is needed.

A central element of Gates's theory is that African American originality departs significantly from dominant notions of creativity. Gates succinctly notes that "the originality of so much of the black tradition emphasizes refiguration, or repetition and difference, or troping, underscoring the foregrounding of the chain of signifiers, rather than the mimetic representation of a novel content."[26] In essence, Gates argues that the creativity of black vernacular speech emphasizes language use over language meaning. It matters not whether a speaker/writer first coined a phrase, idea, or expression; what matters is the art by which it is used to convey a new meaning and make a new connection. Thus, the pleasure of a signifyin' text is how well it opens up the meaning of a seemingly well-defined and settled word or image.

A recent but excellent example of signifyin' occurs in Aaron Mc-Gruder's comic strip, *The Boondocks*. In one strip, Huey Freeman, a young radical African American boy, overhears several loud sounds outside his window as he reads the newspaper. When he goes outside, he sees Cindy, a white girl, with a football and Riley, Huey's "thuggish" brother, lying on the ground asking, "But how was I supposed to know she . . ." Throwing the newspaper at him, Huey interrupts and replies, "Read Dummy!"[27] In the strip, McGruder has refigured Charles Schultz's classic *Peanuts* situation where Lucy pulls the football away when Charlie Brown is attempting to kick it. At its most basic level, the strip signifies on Riley for not reading the newspaper, as "Read Dummy" is the slogan of Huey's radical newspaper, which Riley has never had time to read. If Riley did read Huey's or any other newspaper, he would know that in *Peanuts* cartoons, the girl always pulls the ball away from the boy. By framing this as an interracial encounter, McGruder reminds his readers that when African Americans trust whites, they tend to get fooled and wind up on their rear ends. It also suggests that black men should be careful in their encounters with white women, thus racializing the frequent instances of sexual tension that appear in comic strips. Lastly, it reinforces the unconscious norm of whiteness that underlies *Peanuts*, despite the occasional appearance of Franklin, and comic strips more generally.[28] Gates identifies this kind of textual revision, which emphasizes textual indeterminacy, as distinctive to African American art and culture.

To illustrate how vernacular influences literary culture in *The Signifying Monkey*, Gates occasionally turns to the jazz music of Count Basie, Louis Armstrong, Duke Ellington, Jelly Roll Morton, and Charlie Parker, or the musical criticism of Ralph Ellison, Langston Hughes, and Zora Neale Hurston. Gates identifies John Coltrane's version of "My Favorite Things" as an exemplary instance of formal parody: it begins with the melody of the classic Julie Andrews version before veering off into a completely different direction.[29] Jazz has long constituted the soundtrack for African American culture, and Gates follows the standard scholarly approach of placing music at the center of African American cultural productions, with other arts, such as writing and painting, occupying a derivative or secondary status. Although Gates is first and foremost a literary scholar, he nonetheless recapitulates this historical ordering of African American culture.

## Signifyin' and Hip-Hop

A hip-hop rereading of signifyin' may appear to follow this pattern. For example, Aaron McGruder's *Boondocks* updates John Coltrane's rewriting of "My Favorite Things" by providing hip-hop-based lyrics for the song.[30] If Coltrane signified on Julie Andrews and suggested that jazz was the new "Sound of Music," then *The Boondocks* writes over Coltrane's revision and announces that hip-hop is the new "Sound of Music." McGruder thus signifies on critics who use jazz as the quintessential African American art form, especially during the age of hip-hop. This parody also shows the limits of Gates's jazz-influenced construction of signifyin', which includes both pastiche and parody as central features of African American cultural production. Pastiche, which Gates describes as unmotivated revision, focuses on the form of a text and how literary history names itself. Parody, or motivated revision, infuses words—taken from another text—and provides them with a new context and subverts their apparent meaning.[31] Because Gates relies on jazz as his musical basis and on literature written before 1982, his attempt to map out the contours of African American cultural production does not quite seem to align with the hip-hop aesthetic that was emerging as he wrote his groundbreaking work. Greg Tate goes so far as to argue that Gates's approach to signifyin' has cut Gates off from contemporary African American cultural styles and themes, including hip-hop.[32] This book's examination of recent art and literature suggests that hip-hop aesthetics has emphasized parody over pastiche in its use of signifyin' primarily because the increased circulation of racialized texts and new technology has made sampling or cutting and pasting popular images, sounds, or texts easier than ever before. The "calling out of one's name" also appears to have more commercial appeal than the "naming" of a tradition, and it certainly provides grist for the advertising and publicity mills that rule mass culture.[33]

During the culture wars, scholars and activists sought to revise the norms, values, and direction of American culture in accord with multicultural paradigms. Conscious or motivated efforts to revise canons, institutions, and culture exploded. Hip-hop music and the hip-hop aesthetics it spawned emphasized parodic forms because they echoed and reinforced ongoing dialogues about diversifying public life. Pastiche or unmotivated revisions that borrowed material without substantial modification appeared "old school," accommodationist, or simply not radical enough to face the challenges of the post–Civil Rights era. I want to emphasize that pastiche as form of signifyin' did not disappear after the 1980s, as the endless samples from George Clinton and James Brown attest, but it becomes a residual or minority form within African American culture. Hip-hop aesthetics prefers parody or irony because it mocks dominant culture and expresses the disappointment and despair attendant to the breaking apart of the Civil Rights coalition.[34] It also enables African American cultural workers to foreground the irony of African American life in a formally color-blind society, but one in which race still shapes so much for so many. Parody, not pastiche, as motivated revision provides a form that matches the cultural ethos.[35]

To explore the differences between hip-hop and earlier iterations of signifyin', I will briefly contrast Frederick Douglass's parody of the nineteenth-century hymn "Heavenly Union" with A Tribe Called Quest's "Can I Kick it?" Scholars frequently overlook that Douglass's first *Narrative* concludes with a note of parody. Douglass, whom Gates identifies as "a master Signifier," culminates his attempt to write himself into freedom by crafting new lyrics to a common church hymn.[36] In the "original," a nameless narrator describes how his/her soul is saved and he/she attains a "heavenly union" with Jesus. In Douglass's much longer version, he "borrows" lines and the rhythmic pattern from the hymn but transforms its meaning and criticizes the hypocrisy of American churches, which supported slavery. In the standard version, the opening stanza proclaims that God "gave" the singer a heavenly union, whereas Douglass's parody states that churches merely "sing" of it. The bloody "fire and brimstone" imagery of the original, describing hell and sin, is reworked to depict the brutality of African American slavery. If churchgoers sang of their aspirations to unite with Jesus, Douglass emphasizes how the nation, or the "union" of states, constitutes a parody of real heavenly union because it has failed to realize its lofty political and Christian ideals.[37] Douglass clearly mocks Christian apologists for slavery and reworks one of their own texts to demonstrate their hypocrisy. This is signifyin' par excellence.

In many ways, A Tribe Called Quest follows the signifyin' ways of Douglass in its 1990 song "Can I Kick It?" which parodies and deconstructs Lou Reed's "Walk on the Wild Side." The song samples from and criticizes Reed's ode to sexual adventurism. In his song, Reed has "bitten," or stolen, African American R&B rhythms from the 1970s and exoticized black urban spaces through his sexualized lyrics. A Tribe Called Quest's parody, however, operates primarily through its samples, rather than the lyrics themselves. The samples rework Reed's song, deconstructing its references to drug use, interracial sexuality, and societal rebellion. When he asks, "Can I Kick It?" Q-Tip of A Tribe Called Quest calls out Lou Reed for both identifying the location of his "walk on the wild side" as New York City and including African American girls within that walk.[38] Q-Tip questions Reed's ability to walk his streets or "hang" with A Tribe Called Quest. Although the lyrics do parody Lou Reed's, the group signifies on Reed primarily through the rhythm tracks and the melody. By reclaiming a stolen or bitten rhythm line, A Tribe Called Quest is engaged in a turf war with rock and roll. This battle is not about a physical space, but appropriated elements of intellectual property. Later in the song, Q-Tip asks David Dinkins, "Would you please be my mayor?" This references the election of the first black mayor of New York City and extends the parody and the claim of cultural ownership over New York City. A Tribe Called Quest calls out not only Lou Reed and rock and roll but the white political establishment that has attempted to dominate black urban spaces. "Can I Kick It?" simultaneously constitutes a parody of white popular culture and a demand for political and cultural freedom. The form of the music, although it shares some characteristics with Douglass's parody, also suggests a new use of signifyin' in the post–Civil Rights era.

Signifyin' functions like a trademark or copyright symbol. A successful instance of signifyin' constitutes an act of rhetorical ownership over an object, a text, or even an individual. For example, Douglass's parody demonstrated his moral superiority over Christian apologists through his verbal acuity, and A Tribe Called Quest asserts claims of cultural ownership over rock and roll and New York City. In both cases, African American cultural workers write over well-known texts. Signifyin', especially in the case of hip-hop, adds an "ironic spin" on the original, frequently "contradicting the original meaning."[39] The practice of signifyin' also refuses to acknowledge the seemingly settled distribution of property rights, which legal discourse purports to confer, and writes over them.[40] Although Gates does not call attention to this explicitly, he describes how signifyin' offers a method and a form to claim cultural and personal ownership over an object, sound, image, text, or trademarked logo. As a clandestine or alternative property-ownership system, signifyin' allows participants within African American culture to write over an unjust distribution of intellectual and cultural resources. This competing legal structure "allocates" rights over intangible objects within African American culture without following the requirements identified in copyright or trademark law. For popular and vernacular culture, law, as written in the statute books, is simply irrelevant.

Keith Aoki asserts that, especially during the formative years of blues and jazz, the lack of official copyright protection fostered creativity and innovation among African American musicians.[41]

Signifyin', as described by Gates, constitutes a second-level legal order. This legal order does not possess the *judicial* authority to adjudicate claims, levy fines, or order parties to desist from certain conduct, but it does possess *cultural* authority in conferring status, power, and authority within African American culture. Such recognition frequently can translate into market success within the white community.[42] Eduardo Penalver and Sonia Katyal have argued, in the case of property law, that property outlaws or dissidents have been the catalysts for legal change.[43] Applying their analysis to the expansion of intellectual property law, Katyal argues that we have entered into a period of marked "semiotic disobedience," in which "social activism exposes the need for alternative political economies for information.[44] In many ways, I am arguing that Gates's description and canonization of signifyin' constitutes a strategy of semiotic disobedience.[45] This strategy may ultimately transform the definition and distribution of intellectual property rights.

## Signifyin' and Copyright Infringement

Gates's theory of signifyin' does not explicitly purport to undermine the foundations of American jurisprudence, but it does, however, uncover a paradox or contradiction at the heart of liberal legal theory: the self-evident nature and meaning of cultural properties. Gates, along with a bevy of hip-hop artists and critical race theorists, arrives at similar criticisms about the role of subjectivity in shaping what an object or text means. Speakers, writers, artists, and viewers bring a set of narrative assumptions about the world when they interpret the meaning of a text. These narrative assumptions frequently are connected to their identity and their experiences. Texts, in and of themselves, may be indeterminate and open to endless deconstruction—an argument made by Derrida, his followers, and legions of postmodern thinkers. Hip-hop aesthetics, as articulated through Gates, and the rise of hip-hop respond to Derrida's call by demonstrating how cultural specificity works to create interpretative networks or lenses that simultaneously specify a determinate meaning and keep texts open for reinterpretation.[46] This paradoxical property of signifyin' produces an impasse—or *aporia*, in Derrida's vocabulary—for legal discourse. Intellectual property law has increasingly protected copyright holders from any trespass, including those that might constitute fair use. Such borrowings, however, are fundamental to African American vernacular practices, especially as prescribed by Gates's theory of signifyin'.[47] The very boundaries that intellectual property law seeks to establish to protect intellectual properties directly conflict with how African American vernacular culture and hip-hop aesthetics operate. Thus, hip-hop aesthetics, when read through Gates's theory of signifyin', constitutes an outlaw practice because it values long-standing cultural practices over the recent expansion of intellectual property doctrines.[48]

The initial question that drove my scholarship (and resulted in this book) is whether hip-hop's use of sampling constitutes copyright infringement.[49] In what follows, I hope to demonstrate that while hip-hop aesthetics fails to conform to legal fictions about cultural and property law boundaries, the result is not a pervasive, infringing cultural aesthetic. Rather, intellectual property law has failed to untangle abstract legal fictions about creativity from how ordinary people within a shared cultural system convey meaning through the reordering of signs, symbols, metaphors, and icons.[50] Copyright law reserves to bona fide intellectual property owners, not necessarily the artist who produced a work, the right to reproduce a work, create a derivative text of it, distribute it, perform it, or display it publicly.[51] Copyright infringement is engaging in any of the aforementioned acts without the appropriate permission or license. What if these very acts of potential infringement follow established patterns of and attitudes about creativity and constitute a conscious attack on the limited (and racialized) assumptions of legal discourse? Should relatively recent changes in intellectual property law require a shift in longstanding practices of African American signifyin'? Do African American cultural workers need a license to signify now, even though signifyin' was "free" in the past?[52] As the domain of intellectual property increases, does culture become a source of oppression, rather than a potentially liberatory force?[53] Does the growing epistemological violence of copyright law constitute a contemporary analog for establishing racial supremacy, as lynching and other racist practices did in an earlier era?

An examination of Robert Colescott's *Les Demoiselles d'Alabama vestidas* and *Demoiselles d'Alabama desnudas* illustrates all of the issues surrounding the question of whether signifyin' constitutes an act of copyright or trademark infringement. Colescott's work functions as a bridge between earlier African American artists and contemporary ones, who more fully develop hip-hop aesthetics.[54] In a pair of 1985 paintings, Colescott signifies upon Picasso's *Les Demoiselles d'Avignon* by re-visioning the scene and accentuating the racialized nature of art history, which looks to Europe for models and paradigms. The contents of the paintings serve as mirror images. In his *Les Demoiselles*, Picasso depicts five naked (all ostensibly white) women, three with faces that stress their resemblance to their "real" faces and two with African-inspired masks or facades. The forms, borrowing on African-inspired aesthetics, incorporate Cubism and emphasize the women's angularity.

Colescott's pair of *Les Demoiselles* paintings talk back to Picasso and art historians by rewriting Picasso's famous scene both to accentuate the unspoken racial gaze of art criticism and to focus on Picasso's own borrowings of African cultural practices and forms. The 1985 works invert the races of the women depicted in the original and emphasize the fullness of the women's forms, rather than relying on a sparse angularity. Colescott translates Picasso's image into black vernacular by transforming the three ostensibly white women into African Americans and changing the women with African-inspired masks for faces into white women. This color or race adjustment underscores how liberally Picasso borrowed from African sources to create a "radical" vision of art and works to reclaim cultural ownership of modernist techniques "stolen" from African culture. Colescott also provides a more curvaceous depiction of the women to demonstrate the differences between African American and dominant conceptions of beauty. For Picasso and by implication Western art, thin or angular white women have become the very definition of feminine beauty. Colescott's fuller women project an entirely different perspective on feminine beauty, one that resonates with dominant attitudes within the African American community.

While repainting Picasso's *Les Demoiselles d'Avignon* in itself would constitute signifyin', Colescott multiplies the effect of his critique by replacing a singular image with a pair of paintings. One revision would be insufficient to respond to Picasso's image and his Cubist aesthetic. The difference in content between the two images focuses on the extent to which the painting "reveals" the truth of the women. By portraying clothed and nude women, Colescott parodies Picasso's reliance on African-inspired forms and images to reveal human nature. If anything, Colescott's paired critique emphasizes the play of absence and presence inaugurated by visual culture. Thus, Picasso's attempt to reveal the women of Avignon through the lens of primitivism merely recapitulates the masking of reality that he attempts to uncover, even if the women appear to allow the artist view them in a natural state. The primitive or natural scene Picasso sought to capture constitutes nothing but a mask for Colescott, a mask whose existence he can highlight only by offering a pair of revisions. In addition to unmasking the fictitious foundations of art history that place Picasso within the pantheon of revered painters, Colescott also undermines the very ideal of romantic authorship, which has driven scholarship in both art history and legal theory. If Modernist primitivism itself had no choice but to rely on a "borrowed" cultural foundation to depict humankind's natural core, then Colescott interrogates the foundations of both property and art because both discourses recognize Picasso as the owner and originator of certain conventions from African art. Colescott's revision of Picasso certainly invites the question of cultural ownership because he interrogates how art history has identified Picasso as a genius, placed him at the center of twentieth-century art, and granted him ownership rights over certain African-influenced forms. What does Picasso or his estate own in regard to *Les Demoiselles*? What parts of it, if any, are available for the long-standing practice of signifyin' within African American and African communities? What principles will courts rely on to determine and distribute ownership interests when a form of African American cultural dialogue depends on extensive citation as critical practice?[55]

By emphasizing signifyin' as the narrative center of his vernacular theory of African American literature and culture, Henry Louis Gates has apparently authorized and perhaps even encouraged others to continue engaging in signifyin' practices. Who wins when cultural practices, described and endorsed by a major academic, potentially conflict with developments in legal theory? Do property or cultural rights triumph in this conflict? Many Civil Rights activists relied on rights discourse to argue for social change and civic recognition.[56] The Civil Rights generation's progeny, however, have seen the limitations of that strategy and have deployed black vernacular practices to reframe freedom and equality in the language of property rights. Signifyin', as it appears in contemporary African American art, music, and literature, constitutes a necessary complement to the political and social claims made by integrationists and the Black Power movement. The question is whether this challenge to property law will ultimately be recognized by legal discourse; cause a reconfiguration of intellectual property doctrine; and transform social, political, and economic relations. Can Gates's turn to vernacular culture recenter literary discourse and redistribute property rights?

## Sampling, Signifyin', and Copyright Law

By the late 1980s, hip-hop music's use of sampling had become the subject of numerous controversies. The first major case to consider hip-hop's use of samples was *Grand Upright Music v. Warner Brothers* (1991).[57] It involved Biz Markie's use of three words from a Gilbert O'Sullivan recording. The copyright owners of the song, Grand Upright Music, brought suit for copyright infringement against Biz Markie and his record company, Warner Brothers, for illegally copying the original recording in their song "Alone Again." The legal question the U.S. District Court for the Southern District of New York had to answer was whether the inclusion of a sample constituted a copyright infringement. Warner Brothers and Biz Markie argued that because sampling had become a common practice within hip-hop culture, the court should not consider it an infringing action. The court did not find Biz Markie's defense satisfactory. Judge Duffy began his opinion by quoting the Ten Commandments: "Thou shalt not steal." He continued: "The defendants . . . would have this court believe stealing is rampant in the music business and, for that reason, their conduct here should be excused."[58] In these opening comments, Judge Duffy reveals his assumption that property matters more than aesthetic or cultural considerations within his legal approach and his hostility toward hip-hop's use of sampling.

The court pointed to letters sent by Biz Markie and Warner Brothers attorneys to the copyright owners of the sampled material, requesting permission to sample. Judge Duffy argued that these letters demonstrate copyright infringement.[59] In my reading of these letters, it is clear that Warner Brothers sought to protect itself from how copyright law might be applied to the "new" aesthetic offered by hip-hop. A similar argument about legal uncertainty was made by the court on behalf of 2 Live Crew in *Campbell v. Acuff-Rose* (1994). This uncertainty arises from the application of intellectual property law not simply to new practices, but to a musical form that was linked to raced and classed bodies.[60] In the 1980s and 1990s, CRT explored how legal discourse operated in a racialized manner without ever mentioning race.[61] In addition to his heavy-handed biblical opening, Judge Duffy included a curious footnote in his opinion: "The argument suggested by the defendants that they should be excused because others in the 'rap music' business are also engaged in illegal activity is totally specious. The mere statement of the argument is its own refutation."[62] Duffy refuses to explore the artistry of hip-hop, its connection to jazz- and blues-inspired creativity, or its legal and cultural criticisms. By stating without reason or argument that hip-hop clearly constitutes an illegal activity, Duffy relies on unspoken cultural narratives that both criminalize young black men and locate artistic genius and historical memory within white America. For Duffy, signifyin' is nothing more than stealing. Even though Gates and others had attempted to describe African American vernacular culture since the late 1960s, Judge Duffy felt empowered to regulate African American culture without any apparent knowledge of its operation. Although hip-hop does not necessarily denote race or social class, it has erroneously become synonymous with African American culture and has become a raced practice. As CRT has long noted, Judge Duffy or any other judge cannot accuse a person of being "criminal" because of their race. However, a color-blind liberal legal theory has permitted racialized music, clothing, or linguistic usage patterns as proxies for criminality.[63] Although this judicial opinion is relatively brief, it makes clear that the music itself is criminal because "we all know" that its performers are really just thieves.

Following *Grand Upright Music*, copyright owners asked courts to determine how much and what kind of sampling constitutes copyright infringement. In *Jarvis v. A&M Music* (1993), a court found that sampling even short nonverbal sounds could constitute copyright infringement.[64] Some courts have found that "fragmented literal similarity," or distorting the original, is not actionable,[65] nor is borrowing a note.[66] More recently, the Sixth Circuit held that any copying, no matter how small, could constitute a copyright infringement.[67] This ruling, however, appears to conflict with an earlier Seventh Circuit decision that allows for complementary copying but not substitutional copying.[68] In other words, this court wanted to consider whether the "copied" item would directly affect the sales of the original one. Although it is generally clear that producers must clear samples, the kind of sampling that triggers this requirement is ambiguous.

The U.S. Supreme Court, in *Campbell v. Acuff-Rose* (1994), explored parody and how it fits within copyright and fair-use jurisprudence. This case involved 2 Live Crew's use of lyrics and music from Roy Orbison's "Oh, Pretty Woman" in its song "Pretty Woman." Tracing the origins of parody to ancient Greece, the court found that this hip-hop parody constituted a fair use of a copyrighted text.[69] Applying the four-part balancing test for fair use, the court determined that hip-hop parodies were unlikely to serve as "market substitutes" for the original.[70] Even though 2 Live Crew sold many copies of its song, the Supreme Court found it sufficiently critical of Orbison's to warrant a "fair-use" defense against copyright infringement.[71] Although it took several cases, lawyers began to see that characterizing hip-hop aesthetics as parody (not signifyin') allowed them to deploy fair use to defend some claims of copyright infringement.

What remains unspoken or unseen within the courts' stated reasoning is the role race plays in legal thinking. Except for a footnote defining rap as "black American pop music," the decision omits all discussion of race.[72] The races of Luther Campbell and Roy Orbison are also omitted. The case report, as written, exemplifies liberal legal theory's commitment to color-blind jurisprudence. The court only invoked the culture of ancient Greece to demonstrate the "timelessness" and potentially "civilized" origins of parody. Did race, however, shape how the court applied fair-use doctrine to hip-hop? While no direct evidence exists to answer this question, the decision in *Rogers v. Koons* suggests that racial considerations do matter when applying the rules of fair use.[73] In that case, Art Rogers, a photographer, sued Jeffrey Koons because he had transformed one of his photographs of a couple holding several puppies into a parodic or satirical sculpture mocking the original photograph's sentimentality. The court had to determine whether Koons's self-described parody constituted fair use. Unlike in *Campbell*, the court in *Rogers* found that Koons had, in fact, infringed on Rogers's copyright because he had borrowed too much from the photograph, and the resulting sculpture was merely satirical of sentimentality in general, rather than specifically commenting on or criticizing Rogers's picture. Koons had attempted to defend his actions under the rubric of appropriation art, but the court found this to be merely an indication that marketability, not artistry, had determined Koons's choice of subject matter.

Comparing *Campbell* and *Rogers*, one notable difference between the two cases is race. In *Campbell*, the court did not state, but clearly knew, that Orbison was white and Campbell was African American. By contrast, in *Rogers*, both were deemed white. Race matters when applying the "fair-use" doctrine because Campbell could claim an implicit racial critique of Orbison. Koons had no such claim against Rogers. Campbell could also rely on the academic authority of Henry Louis Gates because Gates had testified on 2 Live Crew's behalf in its obscenity trial.[74] As part of his defense of 2 Live Crew, Gates argued that the group's use of obscene language followed patterns of African American vernacular culture, also known as signifyin'. Although signifyin', as an African American vernacular practice, failed to be mentioned in *Campbell*, its omission probably might have allowed 2 Live Crew to emerge victorious in its case. Signifyin' necessarily involves borrowing, appropriation, and inversion, but those critical practices, even if part of an artistic tradition, frequently appear as copyright infringement within intellectual property law. The Supreme Court's omission of signifyin' and thus of the specificity of African American cultural production simultaneously ignores race in "good" color-blind fashion and allows race to retain its unspoken and unconscious force in liberal legal theory.

Gates's articulation of signifyin' clearly differentiates African American cultural texts. African American cultural workers' reliance on mimicry and appropriation as aesthetic principles produces a conflict between cultural theory and intellectual property law.[75] Hip-hop's expansion of signifyin' in an age of increasing copyright protections only deepens the crisis. Ironically, hip-hop's popularity has caused African American writers and visual artists to develop hip-hop aesthetics further and create a potentially unbridgeable rift between African American culture and intellectual property law. The unspoken legal context of Gates's theory of signifyin' presents both a potential legal liability for African American artists and an opportunity to realize critical race theory's mission to produce a color-conscious jurisprudence.

## CHAPTER 3

# Defining Hip-Hop Aesthetics

Scholars have long relied on musical styles to describe, define, and symbolize African American cultural production. Gospel, blues, jazz, soul, and now hip-hop have come to represent how both dominant culture and academics view and analyze African American life. The primacy of music within African American cultural criticism can be traced back at least to Frederick Douglass's discussion of sorrow songs, developed by W. E. B. Du Bois in *The Souls of Black Folk*. In the late 1960s, Leroi Jones, now Amiri Baraka, characterized African Americans as a "Blues People."[1] Novels such as *The Color Purple* (1982) and *Corregidora* (1975) have relied on blues singers as central characters.[2] Richard Powell has viewed African American art through a "Blues Aesthetic."[3] Sterling Brown and Langston Hughes frequently created blues-influenced poems and short stories. Jazz improvisation has frequently inspired literary style, and jazz innovators have been frequent subjects of literature. Ralph Ellison, John Edger Wideman, Toni Morrison, Michael Harper, and others have turned jazz into literature. Scholars have applied jazz categories and metaphors to understand the art of Archibald Motley, Aaron Douglas, Jacob Lawrence, Romare Bearden, and many others.

While music certainly has proven fertile ground for cultural analysis and criticism, rarely have the relationships among music, literature, and visual art been symmetrical ones. Musicians, composers, and music critics have rarely turned to literature or visual art for inspiration or artistic paradigms. The traditional explanation for this hierarchical or core-periphery structure within African American cultural criticism has been that music is the most immediate repository of African American vernacular culture. In other words, the orality of African American culture can be most easily translated into music—not art or literature. The transcription of Black English, for example, has proven extremely problematic within literature, even as Black English has been common within musical lyrics. Gates's theory of signifyin' counters these trends, attempting to remove music in this account of how African American orality gets translated into literature. Even though Gates includes lyrical analysis in his book, he turns folk songs, blues lyrics, and urban toasts into literary documents. The sound and humor of black life get muted in order to place parody, satire, and metaphor as the identifying or core features of African American vernacular culture. This ambitious structure, however, merely inverts the asymmetry between cultural forms rather than explaining how art, music, and literature constitute complementary practices.

By downplaying the blues, the sorrow song, and jazz improvisation, Gates's theory of vernacular culture in effect depoliticizes African American literature and dampens the critical vision (both explicit and implicit) contained within many texts. Although African American cultural criticism has long focused on property, the structure of Gates's argument accentuates how the African American literary tradition is based upon writers reading and writing over one another. African American literature needed this organizing principle, according to Gates, to solidify its status in English departments during the culture wars of the 1980s. This highly technical argument, however, furthered the split between literary discourse and social activism. Even though signifyin' involves both redefining and redistributing ownership interests over cultural and imaginative texts, Gates fails to make explicit connections to the burgeoning "property rights" movement of the 1980s. In contrast, hip-hop boldly announces its materialism to mock the moralizing impulse of idealistic Civil Rights leaders. Hip-hop, not Gates, succeeded in an aesthetic form in which a critique of property law could be articulated through African American vernacular culture.

The purpose of this chapter is to establish the basic elements of hip-hop aesthetics and show how this form shapes its cultural message.[4] Hip-hop aesthetics possesses four central characteristics: (1) sampling, (2) layering, (3) rhythmic flow and asymmetry, and (4) parody or irony.[5] In identifying these characteristics, it is my intention to create a sufficiently broad definition of hip-hop aesthetics to explore the interaction among contemporary visual artists, musicians, and writers. Hip-hop aesthetics frequently relies on compositional and lyrical signifyin', but not exclusively so. The goal of deejays, b-boys, graffiti artists, and emcees is to entertain, amuse, and create—not merely to signify. Any discussion of hip-hop aesthetics that omits how much fun it is makes an error similar to a discussion that confuses blues music with feeling "blue."[6] One key aspect of hip-hop is the vicarious experience of making ownership and authenticity claims in a postmodern world where self and communal ownership are constantly in flux. Hip-hop finds pleasure in ownership rights at the very moment they may seem either irrelevant or insufficient for realizing America's promises of freedom and equality. Analogous to Albert Murray's reading of the blues, hip-hop aesthetics is not necessarily postmodern, but the tonic for the crises postmodernism has brought: the rupture between an object and the word, image, or sound that represents the object. Hip-hop initiated neither the deconstruction of black musical history nor the destruction of our nation's urban centers. Rather, hip-hop chases away the "blues" of postmodern America and attempts to stitch together the ruptures of postindustrial America so ordinary folks can once again claim ownership over their cultural traditions, which the culture industries have commodified and transformed into their own private property.

The work of Anna Deavere Smith, which blends sound, image, movement, and wordplay, provides a wonderful illustration of how hip-hop aesthetics operates. I have chosen Smith's work to illustrate hip-hop aesthetics for a number of reasons. First, her work allows me to discuss hip-hop aesthetics without potentially exposing her to legal liability. Smith appropriates or samples from comments elicited during her interviews with people, and she probably obtained releases and/or permission to use their words. Even if Smith did not do this, copyright protection requires that words be fixed in a tangible medium before copyright attaches. Because her interviewees *spoke* to her, they would not have any ownership rights over their comments. As a result, Smith is well-protected from potential lawsuits even though her methodology bears a striking resemblance to that of Biz Markie, Public Enemy, De La Soul, N.W.A., and the Beastie Boys, all of whom have been subject to lawsuits because of the texts they chose to sample. One of the challenges of researching and writing about hip-hop aesthetics is that a poorly chosen topic could open up the subject of the research to a lawsuit! Another factor in my choice of Smith as my exemplar is that she is the first hip-hop aesthete to win major recognition for her artistry. The MacArthur Foundation recognized her work in 1996 with a "genius" grant. Finally, her work includes all the foundational aspects of hip-hop culture. To offer such an interdisciplinary model of hip-hop aesthetics will undoubtedly make the familiar strange for some readers because most studies of "hip-hop" focus almost exclusively on music and musicians. Hip-hop culture, however, demands a more thorough account of its diverse effects, especially as it captures the ethos of the post–Civil Rights era.

A significant challenge faces anyone who attempts to define hip-hop aesthetics: it is continually in flux. Myriad forms and genres of hip-hop have come and gone. Battles between boroughs, coasts, record companies, and generations have marked hip-hop's history. Technical innovations and legal decisions have also contributed to the quick pace of change within hip-hop. Music videos, trends in film, and demographic shifts have also impacted the aesthetic. This book selects 1991 as the approximate average or mean for identifying the characteristics of hip-hop aesthetics for three reasons. First, *Grand Upright Music* changed the legal environment for sample-based hip-hop music production and caused a split in how art, music, and literature apply the elements of hip-hop. Second, acts like Public Enemy had by this point become crossover artists, merging with rock, shifting the audience for commercialized hip-hop.[7] Third, this year serves as an approximate midpoint between the earliest days of hip-hop and today's very different scene.[8] For my purposes, it constitutes the "average" or "norm" of an ever-shifting cultural formation. The downside of this approach is that I am forced to generalize. The resulting generalizations asserted here cannot and will not explain every song, artwork, or writing by Americans of African descent, nor could any other generalization. Rather, the traits of hip-hop aesthetics help illuminate how hip-hop's approach to artistry (and pleasure) frequently incorporates a critique of legal and economic institutions.

During the 1980s, Anna Deavere Smith began working on a series of performances pieces entitled *On the Road: A Search for American Character.* To create these "scripts," Smith "interviews people and later performs them using their own words."[9] Her most well-known pieces from this series focus on exploring racial tensions surrounding explosive issues in various locales. For *Fires in the Mirror,* Smith interviewed a range of residents (African Americans, Jewish Americans, and Caribbean Americans) from Crown Heights following the killings of Gavin Cato and Yankel Rosenbaum and the violence that ensued. *Twilight—Los Angeles, 1992* examines local responses to the riot that followed the first Rodney King verdict.

Throughout these performances, Smith shifts her tone, posture, syntax, and appearance to signal changes in character. Smith's work constitutes a perfect instance where word, image, movement, and sound converge within a shared aesthetic framework. To distinguish the literary, musical, or visual from the rest would reduce the richness of her work. As one-person shows, these performances highlight Smith's virtuosity as an actress and her ability to synthesize a "polyphony of perspectives" within a coherent performance text.[10] Critics such as Debby Thompson and Tania Modleski have analyzed these texts through the lens of postmodernism and have concluded that Smith's approach to racial performance repeats or mimics racial identities to recognize their lethal hold on our imaginations and the possibilities for freeing our minds.[11] By illustrating hip-hop aesthetics through Smith's work, this chapter seeks to connect her creative process to developments throughout contemporary African American culture and demonstrate how such artistic strategies cannot be confined to distinct media, such as art, music, and literature, but form an aesthetic unity. This chapter concludes by considering how Smith's work, and thus hip-hop aesthetics more generally, deconstructs several central principles of intellectual property law.

## Sampling

> The Negro, the world over, is famous as a mimic. But this in no way damages his standing as an original. Mimicry is an art in itself.
>
> —Zora Neale Hurston,
> "Characteristics of Negro Expression"

My description of hip-hop aesthetics begins with sampling—not lyrical analysis or the beats. Much writing on hip-hop downplays its production to focus on the violence, misogyny, or cultural nationalism of its lyrics or to connect its polyrhythmic complexity to African origins. While these issues or elements require careful consideration, overemphasizing them causes critics and scholars to overlook the underlying aesthetic processes hip-hop embodies and its critique of political economy. Sampling, as a creative method or framework, bridges the acts of consumption and production. It requires cultural workers to rearrange the symbols, phrases, rhythms, and melodies circulating within American culture into something completely new. Sampling is part active listening and part production. Hip-hop is relentlessly engaged with the world of sounds, images, texts, and commodities through which African Americans and others experience contemporary life. Hip-hop did not originate with political or artistic manifestos, but at dance parties and in public parks. Deejays played records on turntables and then transformed these songs by emphasizing, looping, or repeating the parts audiences enjoyed (i.e., the breaks) and disregarding the rest. Sampling developed a refined aesthetic based on transforming recognizable elements into something new and fresh.[12]

Joseph Schloss describes hip-hop, in part, as a sonic collage.[13] In many ways, collage is an apt metaphor for hip-hop aesthetics because the newer generation of writers and visual artists has foregone extended studies of individual characters or situations. In its place, we often find a collection of loosely related characters, scenes, storylines, images, logos, and narratives. This strategy not only challenges the pacing or rhythm of contemporary African American texts but also constitutes a further elaboration of signifyin'. Sampling or collage, unlike the blues, is not primarily concerned with bending notes, wringing experiential angst out of a familiar song,[14] or writing over tradition,[15] but locating a "cohesive organizing principle" that fuses together the familiar elements in an aesthetically satisfying way.[16] To produce a text, the hip-hop aesthete must understand the sociohistorical context of the sampled material and comment ironically on it through layering and rhythmic flow.

To please and surprise their audiences, deejays such as Afrika Bambaataa, Afrika Islam, and Kool Herc DJ, sought out beats from all kinds of music, from soul to jazz to rock to calypso to reggae to Bugs Bunny soundtracks.[17] Grandmaster Flash explains that "to every record, there's a great part. This is what we used to call 'the get down part.' . . . And this particular part of the record . . . unjustifiably, was maybe five seconds or less. This kind of pissed me off. I was like, 'Damn, why'd they do that?' You know? So, in my mind, in the early seventies, I was picturing. 'Wow, it would really be nice if that passage of music could be extended to like five minutes.'"[18] For Flash, the technology of the 45 and the structure of the single, with its series of verses and repeating choruses, had caused both musicians and record producers to bury the sounds to which people wanted to dance.

According to Schloss, the break—what Flash names the "get down part"—does not exist until a deejay hears a rhythm or percussion track and identifies it as a sample for use in a related but completely different composition. DJ Jazzy Jeff claims, in an interview with Schloss, that many initial musicians and producers didn't understand the very music that they had recorded. It took hip-hop producers who created samples from their work to show them the importance of the sounds and rhythms they had created.[19] Schloss even suggests that hip-hop producers can transform compositions from other musical forms into hip-hop merely by listening to them with an ear practiced in identifying samples. Domino claims that merely by listening to a Beatles song, his ear can change its rock and roll sensibility into hip-hop.[20]

While record companies, copyright holders, and legal discourse tend to view sampling as theft, hip-hop producers understand the process as being much more like research and development.[21] Samples, within the logic of hip-hop, have an affinity with heretofore unknown elements or with land for which no one useful economic purpose has been found. According to John Locke, the architect of modern theories of property, property is created when a person does labor on an object and thus marks it as her own.[22] Hip-hop sampling embodies that moment when an artist mixes her work with a sound, text, logo, or image and redefines that object due to her own labor. Locke's theory of property argues that humans will never exhaust nature's bounty because our creativity will constantly find new uses for discarded or devalued items. Although few tend to connect hip-hop artistry and John Locke, the practice of sampling echoes his optimistic view about the creativity of the human mind. Locke, like the proponents of hip-hop culture, argued that government's central purpose was to protect property rights. Within hip-hop, piracy or biting another's style—not sampling—constitutes theft because it does not add anything to the original.[23] If a new perspective, beat, or take on something old is created, then it is sampling. Sampling thus constitutes a fairly unique and culturally specific way of defining originality, even if it relies on words, images, or sounds produced by another person.

Samples of conversation, clothing, and mannerisms form the basis of Anna Deavere Smith's performance pieces. Although Smith is rarely viewed as part of the New Black Aesthetic (NBA), or the Post-Soul generation, her method of textual production exemplifies precisely what is new about hip-hop aesthetics. Smith is a relentless "sampler." If deejays must pay their hip-hop dues by "digging in the crates" to find the right sounds,[24] then Smith has paid her dues by interviewing hundreds of people to find the "samples" for *Fires in the Mirror* and *Twilight—Los Angeles, 1992*. She makes no attempt at creating unique characters or plots de novo. Rather, she employs the personas and words of actual people to craft her own narrative or performance out of borrowed poses, tones, mannerisms, hair-styles, and statements. Much like Grandmaster Flash on the turntable, Anna Deavere Smith uses the interviews to locate the poetry within her in-terviewees.[25] It is precisely these poetic moments that Smith isolates from an hour-long interview and samples via a two-to-seven-minute mono-logue. Smith explains how she chooses to include a sample within her per-formance: "I try to find a section that I don't have to interrupt [the voice of the character with the questions she asked in the interviews]. The perfor-mance is much more difficult if I've created chaos in their frame of thought."[26]

Hip-hop producers, such as DJ Jazzy Jeff and Domino, argue that they transform original sounds by the mere act of listening with an ear trained in the hip-hop aesthetic. Without specifically drawing on hip-hop deejaying to illustrate her methodology, Smith outlines a very similar process for con-structing her performance pieces. In her introduction to *Fires in the Mirror,* Smith prefaces her discussion about her methods by referencing one of her grandfather's favorite phrases: "If you say a word often enough, it becomes your own."[27] Although her father disputes the exact phrasing, Smith is clearly concerned with the very problems that have haunted hip-hop musi-cians: is sampling an original act, and who owns a text based on samples? Again, Smith makes no explicit connection to hip-hop, but she tries to show that through her presenting herself "as an empty vessel, a repeater," the words spoken during her interviews have demonstrated their power and al-lowed her to learn about contemporary American culture.[28] This approach enables Smith to go beyond traditional acting methodologies that ask actors to look inside themselves to develop a character. Rather, sampling has con-vinced Smith "that the activity of reenactment [her term for sampling] could tell us as much, if not more, about another individual than the process of learning about the other by using the self as a frame of reference."[29] A bit later, Smith claims, "To develop a voice one must develop an ear."[30] These quotations taken together articulate the ethos behind sampling in post–Civil Rights era African American cultural production. Smith uses sampling to both focus an audience's attention on the best parts of a person's view or critique of American culture and demythologize any and all racial categories by demolishing stereotypes and monolithic conceptions of iden-tity. Smith claims that her use of sampling allows her to get beyond the worn stereotypes of mass culture and complicates simplistic portrayals of raced individuals, presenting their stories with humor and pathos.

## Layering

Whatever the Negro does of his own volition he embellishes.
—Zora Neale Hurston,
"Characteristics of Negro Expression"

In addition to relying on sampled sounds, hip-hop has also relied on extensive references to local landmarks, popular culture, celebrities, and high-priced commodities. Although these references are not recorded and reworked through the aid of technology, mixing, rapping, graffiti, and breaking have consistently invoked popular culture and translated it into their compositions. A typically humorous example of this is EPMD's "The Steve Martin," where the lyrics describe a dance where the goal is to imitate and mock Martin's dance moves as the lead character in the 1979 film *The Jerk*, about a white person raised by blacks who never quite fits despite his best efforts to act "black." By layering this Steve Martin reference (which is as much a visual reference as a musical one) over drum, horn, and bass tracks, along with scratching sounds, as Erick Sermon and Parrish Smith rap back and forth, the layering of sounds, images, and symbols opens a space for giving these items a new meaning, thus creating a way for hip-hop artists to make ownership claims over texts. Tricia Rose argues that "hip hop has always been articulated via commodities [i.e., already owned objects] and engaged in the revision of meanings attached to them."[31] Layering is one way to "deterritorialize" dominant images, sounds, and phrases and make fun of and out of them.

The power of Anna Deavere Smith's performances hinges on her ability to weave together an underlying narrative out of the multiple characters and issues she presents. Her plays are deceptively simple because they move so quickly among characters, settings, and viewpoints that the viewer rarely has time to reflect upon the sutured nature of the narrative. In the terminology of hip-hop aesthetics, *Fires in the Mirror* and *Twilight—Los Angeles, 1992* relentlessly layer sample upon sample to complicate any simplistic attempt at realism or representation through the development of one character, story, or theme. Rather, these works seek to examine the nature of perception itself. Smith's performances tie together a range of emotional responses, idiosyncratic views, and disparate images. There is nothing *necessary* about their connection to one another. What Smith produces is a bricolage that comes to represent the perceptions these events elicited, not the events themselves. By editing, shaping, and organizing these samples, she imposes a kaleidoscopic order upon the chaos of human experience. Within a kaleidoscope, objects produce random shapes that a mirror will form into complex patterns. Smith, in effect, orders the random views offered by local residents and fashions them into a singular object.

Smith's use of layering is not unprecedented within African American cultural history. On the contrary, this tradition is long-standing, even if the contemporary era has refocused the practice. In perhaps its earliest African American form, the strip quilt illustrates the layering within African American cultural production: "In this type of quilt the scraps of cloth are first sewn into strips, which are then assembled into various patterns."[32] While people from many ethnic and racial groups have engaged in scrap quilting, African American versions distinguish themselves through five characteristics: "(1) the dominance of strips; (2) bright, highly contrasting colors; (3) large design elements; (4) offset designs; and (5) multiple patterning."[33] Layering appears to have a long history within African American cultural production, predating the invention of electronic samplers. African American women layered fabrics into elaborate designs that conformed to African aesthetic standards, emphasizing asymmetric patterns. Quilting, as a paradigm, emphasizes both working-class and female perspectives because it moves away from the artist as solitary genius and places her or him within a social context where creations serve both pragmatic and artistic purposes.

Any analysis of Smith's performance pieces must attend to their layered structure and their methodological connection to strip quilting, especially as a gendered paradigm for cultural production. *Fires in the Mirror* and *Twilight—Los Angeles, 1992* do not provide linear or chronological accounts of the events they explore. Rather, they form a quilt, with multiple patterns but no clear narrative or geometric center. These strips of commentary, however, all contain brilliant hues of experience and emotion. Scrap quilting, although a traditional folk art, anticipates developments in postmodern and postcolonial theory. According to Tania Modleski, "Smith radically and viscerally contests ideals of authenticity, in effect 'deterritorializing' her characters and getting them to act on new common ground—the stage."[34] Modleski relies on postcolonial theory to argue that Smith's aesthetic breaks down traditional ideas about artistic genius and reality in order to demonstrate the constructed nature of cultural truths and products. The postcolonial provocateur, according to Modleski, must deconstruct as she creates because the hidden truth of cultural production, African American or not, is that the quilting circle presents a better paradigm for describing artistic processes and the social construction of reality than other models do. Layering, the selection and placement of samples, constitutes an essential element of African American cultural work, especially in the post–Civil Rights era.

To give a specific example of how layering works within Smith's method, I want to explore the section "Hair" from *Fires in the Mirror*. In this relatively brief section, Smith performs three characters who articulate the relationship between hair and identity and demonstrate what all human beings share—concern with appearance—and how racial discourses articulate that concern in culturally specific ways. The first portrait, of an anonymous teenage black girl, presents the claim or call to which the following sampled characters will respond. She starts by explaining how she learned she was black and then quickly adds the 1960s Black Power slogan, "Black is beautiful." Like fabric redeployed in a strip quilt, Smith takes this tired and now empty phrase and tries to build a new pattern around it. The girl then adds, "White is beautiful too," indicating that she is taking this conversation in a different direction than the original phrase might have suggested, especially within the context of a play about racial conflict.[35] The girl then describes how her black friends "bite" the styles—everything from hairstyles to gym shoes—of their Puerto Rican classmates.[36] In this monologue, the anonymous girl borrows the phrases of her parents, a previous generation, and her friends, presenting a layered text within a layered text.

Smith next provides a portrait of Al Sharpton discussing how he patterned his own hairstyle after James Brown's hair. Sharpton promised to do so because Brown took the fatherless Sharpton under his wing. Performing as Sharpton, Smith says: "It's a personal thing between me and James Brown. And just like in other communities people do their cultural thing with who they wanna look like, uh, there's nothing wrong with me doing that with James. It's. It's *us*. . . . So it's certainlih not a reaction to Whites. It's me and James's thing."[37] Smith interviewed Sharpton because he had organized protests after the Crown Heights riots, but she selected his comments about his hair to include within the play because they best fit the theme about identity she sought to develop. Last in this section, Smith explores how Lubavitcher women approach the relationship between hair and identity. Through Rivkah Siegal, Smith shows how Hasidic women shave their heads and wear wigs. Rivkah describes how she wears five different wigs and how her coworkers believe that she has cut or dyed her hair. This scene culminates with Rivkah stating: "I've gone through a lot with wearing wigs and not wearing wigs. It's been a big issue for me."[38]

Although these three portraits fill only ten pages within *Fires in the Mirror*, they suggest how carefully Smith chooses and layers each sample or "fabric strip." As part of the opening movements of the performance, the section on "hair" incorporates analysis of gender, race, religion, and marital status through a borrowing of the visual appearance, words, and syntactical patterns from two "ordinary" people and one famous person. While ostensibly exploring the origins and consequences of the Crown Heights riots, Smith stops to meditate on the cultural foundations of beauty within African American and Jewish communities. Brilliantly, she both exposes the historical connection between whiteness and beauty and suggests that *this* relationship may be breaking down even as institutional racism persists. When the anonymous girl introduces the hip-hop phrase "biting" into the conversation about beauty and style, it suggests Smith's awareness of hip-hop's reliance on sampling and her acknowledgment that the aesthetic standards of hip-hop rely on incorporating existing styles into one's own style, potentially transforming the borrowed style. Sharpton's defense of his trademark hairstyle homage to James Brown, itself reminiscent of hip-hop's sampling from Brown's oeuvre, illustrates the danger of appropriation, as some members of the black community claim Sharpton's hairstyle relies on white standards of beauty. Smith, however, tries to show that Sharpton's reuse of Brown's style is a thing of a beauty because it symbolizes his emotional connection to a father figure. Last, Rivkah Siegel's concern about her extensive reliance on wigs suggests that "borrowing" too much can lead to as many problems as it solves. By layering these three samples next to one another, Smith comments on her own aesthetic practices even as she humanizes both sides of the Crown Heights riots. This methodology also transforms the meaning of the original words from Smith's interviews and helps connect the interviewees in ways they had not originally conceived.[39] Layering thus allows Smith to juxtapose a wide range of concerns—many of which would remain socially invisible without her intervention—within a relatively concise space.[40]

## Flow and Asymmetry

> The presence of rhythm and lack of symmetry are paradoxical, but there they are. Both are present to a marked degree. There is always rhythm, but it is the rhythm of segments.
> —Zora Neale Hurston,
> "Characteristics of Negro Expression"

Perhaps the most recognizable element of hip-hop music is its rhythm or its driving beat. According to Tricia Rose, "rap music centers on the quality and the nature of rhythm and sound, the lowest, 'fattest beats' being the most significant and emotionally charged."[41] She argues further that hip-hop "involve[s] the repetition and reconfiguration of rhythmic elements in ways that illustrate a heightened attention to rhythmic patterns and movement between such patterns via breaks and points of musical rupture."[42] While the idea of the break, the moment where the drummers and bassists briefly improvise or solo, has long been a part of music, it took early hip-hop deejays to repeat this evanescent moment and transform into a song in its own right.[43] By identifying, sampling, and repeating funky bass and drum tracks, the driving rhythm of hip-hop was born. As Rose suggests, the "flow" or rhythm of hip-hop was essentially repetitious because only the best sections of music were repeated over and over again, frequently for humorous effect. De La Soul, for example, sampled a familiar section of a Steely Dan's "Peg" to ground their "Eye Know," and Boogie Down Productions relied on a sample of ACDC's "Back in Black" to articulate their claim that they have a "Dope Beat." As time passed and the technology developed, deejays selected only particular instruments within a track to sample and created layered and "fat" rhythms to drive their sonic collages.[44]

While hip-hop does not offer a uniform beat that all songs share, it does contain a fairly unique attitude toward repeated, rhythmic patterns. The idea that African American music is rhythmically oriented has been long assumed. Ronald Radano, however, has recently challenged this view and demonstrated that percussive rhythms have been associated with African American music only since the Civil War.[45] Rhythm is not a natural element of African American music, but one that has been nurtured and constructed over time. The rhythmic patterns that underlie hip-hop, in its many forms, are not simply retentions or "holdovers" from African musical culture, but the product of particular choices made by artists at distinct historical moments.

Part of hip-hop's innovation has not just been the repetition of the break, but the shifting of rhythmic, base, and percussion tracks in the middle of a song. Tricia Rose has called this rupture.[46] Hip-hop both presents a rhythm or flow and deconstructs it, by stopping or modifying the beat. It is not uncommon that a rhythm or bass line will fade away or be cut off abruptly, producing this rupture or asymmetrical effect. Audiences learn to take pleasure in the rhythm and the deejay's ability to break down one rhythm or vibe and replace it with a completely different one. Both rhythmic flow and asymmetry follow from hip-hop's extensive use of samples and layering. Unlike jazz or blues musicians, who tend to improvise from or bend notes and melodies from within one song, hip-hop musicians' attitude toward flow and rupture requires a much larger palette of sounds, from which one lays down a rhythm track.[47] In this account, sampling and layering enable the very rhythmic effects for which hip-hop is well-known. Ideas and aesthetic judgments about samples, repetition, and rhythmic flow "push along" not only hip-hop music but other forms of contemporary African American cultural production as well. Frequently, rupture appears as rhythmic asymmetry in visual and literary art.

Although most commentators and audience members initially notice the content of her work, or its subject matter, Smith's *On the Road* performance pieces also constitute experiments in dramatic time and timing. While many academics have emphasized how Smith performs identity within a postmodern framework, they have neglected the temporal aspects of these performances. In other words, even though the postmodern is frequently represented as the compression of space and time, scholars of performance and identity formation tend to emphasize the spatial logic underlying race over the temporal aspects when confronting *On the Road*.[48] Smith's intervention into the public dialogues about the Crown Heights riots and the Rodney King verdict both imitate and interrogate the temporality of contemporary cultural discourse. In the introduction to the book version of *Fires in the Mirror*, Smith comments, "American character is alive inside the syntactical breaks."[49] She adds that the piece "was not originally intended for the printed word. Our effort has been to try to document it in such a way that the act of speech is evident."[50] Smith clearly held some reservations about publishing a book from her performances because "words are not an end in themselves. They are a means to evoking the character of the person who spoke them. Every person that I include in the book, and who I perform, has a presence that is much more important than the information they give."[51] In these quotations, Smith signals her trepidation that the book versions of the performances will cause readers to overvalue the words and neglect the images and sounds that specify the meaning of these words. Her concern is that words alone lack the rhythmic or temporal elements that can provide the necessary clues for proper understanding. For Smith, the rhythms of speech can convey as much meaning as the words themselves. In preparing the written version, she took great pains to include all of the verbal miscues and accompanying gestures. Both books also contain photos from the performances, which convey how Smith's posture and appearance shaped the word's meanings as well.

The emphasis on rhythm is not confined to her portrayal of individual characters, but pervades the rhythmic flow and asymmetry that the performance and text create. The pace of *Fires in the Mirror* and *Twilight—Los Angeles, 1992* is relentless. The viewer/reader does not have more than a few minutes to acquaint herself with a particular persona and his or her rhythm. Part of what Smith performs through the vast array of personae is the hurried pace or rhythm of contemporary dialogues on race. The pace is more important than the words. In a more musical vein, Smith privileges conversational rhythm over the topics or melodies of the dialogue. Jazz music developed the break, what Albert Murray defines as "a temporary interruption of the established cadence . . . which usually requires a *fill*" or solo.[52] It was in the break between rhythmic patterns that jazz virtuosity could be displayed and performed. Smith's performance pieces create a cadence or flow, which in turn produces the expectations for rupture. The audience/reader of Smith's performance pieces comes to listen and watch for the breaks and contemplate their meaning, as much as the content provides. Murray argues that "on the break you are required to improvise, do your thing, to establish your identity, to write your signature on the epidermis of actuality."[53] Unlike the jazz musician who improvises on the break, Smith embraces hip-hop's approach of bending, deconstructing, and reconstructing a melody or rhythm by layering samples on top of samples.

The emphasis on rhythmic flow and asymmetry in her composition causes the audience to respond in a positive manner toward Smith's work. Comparing her work to a film documentary or a news report, Janelle Reinelt quite rightly notes that Smith's performance pieces convey an ambiguous critique of race relations. Reinelt also observes that Smith's "objectivity and fairness is noted in almost every review; she earns the right to speak for others because the performance creates the impression of fidelity and fairness to the interviewees."[54] Keeping in line with hip-hop aesthetics, Smith is trying to "keep it real." Her ability to weave her interviews into a flowing whole creates the semblance of truth despite the many fragment of truth contained therein. In these plays, offering authenticity, or the illusion of authenticity via flowing layered samples, becomes more important than stating a clear or coherent critique. In the introduction to *Twilight—Los Angeles*, Smith is very clear that she "is looking at the *processes* of the problems. Acting is a constant process of becoming something. It is not a result, it is not an answer. It is not a solution."[55] Although Smith never explicitly connects these processes with hip-hop, the dialogue she performs replicates the very conversations cultivated by hip-hop aesthetics.

Tricia Rose has described hip-hop as "black noise" or a "black cultural expression that prioritizes black voices from the margins of urban America. Rap music is a form of rhymed storytelling accompanied by highly rhythmic, electronically based music."[56] Although not music, Smith's performances also present marginalized voices and stories through flowing layered samples. It is not just the content, but the method and rhythm of presenting that content, which defines hip-hop aesthetics.

## Irony and Parody

> The Post-Soul imagination, if you will, has been fueled by three distinct critical desires, namely, the reconstitution of community, particularly one that is critically engaged with the cultural and political output of black communities; a rigorous form of self and communal critique; and the willingness to undermine or deconstruct the most negative symbols and stereotypes of black life via the use and distribution of those very same symbols and stereotypes.
>
> —Mark Anthony Neal, *Soul Babies*

Up to this point, my discussion of hip-hop aesthetics emphasizes structures or methods, not the themes or subject matter of contemporary African American cultural production. Analysts and critics of hip-hop music, contemporary visual arts, and recent literature tend to focus on the meaning, not the processes that created the texts. As a result, reading contemporary African American cultural criticism would cause many readers to conclude that the message dictated the artistic processes that created the resultant texts. By foregrounding sampling, layering, and rhythmic flows and ruptures, my goal has been to counter this scholarly trend and suggest that there is a mutually constitutive relationship between form and content. According to Albert Murray, the blues could be used to narrate tragedy, comedy, melodrama (or romance), and farce. The blues, at least according to Murray, could tell whatever story the artist wanted to tell.[57] While most hip-hop critics acknowledge how hip-hop's aesthetic structure shapes its message, it is still not uncommon to encounter scholarly and popular analyses of hip-hop's lyrics or messages that separate the two. After reviewing a broad array of contemporary African American music, art, and literature, it appears that hip-hop aesthetics provides an ironic form for those who deploy it. Sampling, layering, and rhythmic flow/asymmetry, as a unified aesthetic system, undermine strong political or cultural state-ments—either nationalist or integrationist—despite the efforts of some message rappers.

Traditional analyses of irony, such as Northrop Frye's, define the prac-tice as giving "form to the shifting ambiguities and complexities of unide-alized existence."[58] The most ironic moments are those where the position or view of the creator is most submerged, leaving the audience to interpret the many possible meanings and to wonder whether the irony is intended or incidental.[59] Hayden White has argued that irony can constitute a mode of historical narration: "Irony tends to dissolve all belief in the possibility of positive political actions . . . it tends to engender the belief in the 'mad-ness' of civilization itself and to inspire a Mandarin-like disdain for those seeking to grasp the nature of social reality."[60] Offering a more pragmatic account, Richard Rorty argues that much postmodern criticism embodies this ironic attitude and that the ironist questions the value of any and all terms, ideas, texts, images, or sounds because they offer mere representa-tions of reality, which in turn can be redescribed.[61] Rorty concludes, much like Hayden White, that irony is irredeemably private and will not serve as the basis for social justice movements.[62]

Postmodernists, on the other hand, tend to offer more positive ac-counts about the potential political effects of irony. Gilles Deleuze argues that it is the primary way to challenge law's inequities.[63] For Deleuze, irony creates the very concept of difference because it highlights contradictions, paradoxes, and language's complexity.[64] Translated to hip-hop aesthetics, irony—at least for Deleuze–creates the very racial, gender, and class differ-ences hip-hop frequently seeks to articulate.[65] Linda Hutcheon develops this point further to show how irony can make explicit the conflicting as-sumptions between interpretative communities.[66] Hutcheon's argument is premised on the idea that irony is only possible when multiple discursive communities exist and create contrasting interpretations of a given text.[67] In his study of African American satire, Darryl Dickson-Carr examines how degenerative irony has operated within African American literature.[68] Basing his analysis on Hutcheon's theoretical approach, Dickson-Carr ar-gues that irony in the post–Civil Rights era targets both the narratives that found Western culture and the contradictions and tensions within the African American community.[69]

Within the logic of hip-hop aesthetics, keeping it real is a claim about the need for artistic authenticity and being true to one's roots, not a desire for realism in art per se.[70] When a hip-hop artist insists on keeping it real, it does not mean that he or she is producing a verbatim or completely accurate image or description of existence. Rather, realness requires an unsentimental perspective on contemporary life that recognizes how the mere repetition of a text, sound, or image illustrates the ongoing production of discursive communities based on race, gender, and sexuality. As the epigraph to this section notes, Neal has identified cultural critique and deconstruction of stereotypes (both positive and negative ones) as central goals of contemporary African American cultural production. Central to articulating these criticisms, hip-hop aesthetics deploys irony to insist on the continuing importance of race in shaping discursive communities, social experiences, and legal doctrines.

Both the music of Dead Prez and the comedy of Dave Chappelle illustrate how irony operates by exploring existing social cleavages. Dead Prez is a hip-hop group whose name simultaneously references both money, because U.S. currency tends to celebrate past political leaders, and a revolutionary politics, which would lead to the metaphorical deaths of our current leaders.[71] Dead Prez is unusually political by hip-hop standards. Its conscious deployment of irony is designed to remind the hip-hop nation of its putative political commitments and assert that community's cultural, political, and racial difference from the mainstream.[72] The group's race-conscious politics have caused them tremendous difficulty in securing a recording contract. On the other hand, Dave Chappelle has found commercial and popular success with his ironic commentaries about the myth of a color-blind America. In one skit, Chappelle imagines how the country would respond to George W. Bush's public persona and his policies if he were black.[73] Through his ironic portrayal of President Bush, Chappelle demonstrates how race still shapes public opinion, the political order, and perhaps most importantly the country's sense of humor. Both Dead Prez and Chappelle examine the illusion of authenticity demanded by hip-hop. Dead Prez reveals the "false consciousness" of hip-hop stars who create radical street personas but willingly trade that persona for material success, which disconnects them from their community. Chappelle deconstructs racial stereotypes and taboo topics in a putatively color-blind society. Even as he questions the logic of authenticity, Chappelle relies on his racial identity to save his own racialized representations from being viewed as racist depictions.[74] Unlike Dead Prez, whose antiracist and anticapitalist politics are pretty clearly presented, Chappelle has politics that are harder to discern.

Perhaps no song more than N.W.A.'s "Fuck tha Police" better represents the irony implicit within hip-hop lyrics. The song questions legal authority and seems to advocate armed resistance against the police when necessary. Due to this song, a number of police departments made it difficult, if not impossible, for N.W.A. to perform.[75] They read the song's lyric literally and mistakenly believed that N.W.A. advocated the killing of law-enforcement officials.[76] What such a literal reading missed was the literary framing of the song. The song begins by claiming that the "NWA court" has begun and that Ice Cube must take an oath that his testimony will be truthful. The scene is clearly fictional and fantastic, as Dr. Dre plays the judge and the prosecuting attorneys include Mc Ren, Ice Cube, and Easy E. Moreover, by parodying the traditional courtroom oath, the song clearly understands itself as an imagined response to the struggles of urban life and a parody of the false racial truths typically offered in courtrooms during the height of the War on Drugs. The song concludes with the fictional court rendering the judgment that the police officer is a "redneck, whitebread, chickenshit muthafucka."[77] The officer immediately cries that he wants justice. Despite the harsh language and vivid imagery, the song is clearly fictional and ironic. Some whites heard the song as echoing their own fears about black lawlessness, but N.W.A. seems to criticize how race affects police actions and legal decisions. It is not the exhortation to anarchy some understood it to be, but a plea to inject hip-hop youth's perspective on law enforcement into public dialogues. If law enforcement ever experienced the other side of the police stick, as Ice Cube suggests, it too would cry injustice. Following Deleuze, N.W.A.'s irony merely accentuates the social cleavage that already existed.

My study of hip-hop, as a result, suggests that its approach to metaphor is primarily ironic because the standard meaning for a word or a phrase is rarely asserted or invoked. Tricia Rose argues that hip-hop relies on a "hidden transcript" with "cloaked speech and disguised cultural codes" that can "comment on and challenge aspects of current power inequalities."[78] Rapping provides emcees a way to articulate social criticisms that still are not quite "utterable" even if law guarantees formal equality. Hip-hop has thus become highly metaphorical, creating new words and terms and resignifying established symbols and icons. Sampling and layering have only added to the obfuscation within hip-hop, because lyrics, beats, rhythms, and even sound bites all produce and deconstruct messages simultaneously. If blues testified to the need to overcome existential angst and jazz attempted to forge identity and respect through improvisation, hip-hop finds joy in its technological and lyrical play but doubts that any transcendence or respect is forthcoming, especially from the world outside one's neighborhood.[79]

Some have found hip-hop nihilistic or self-indulgent. I would argue that its overall message, especially as articulated in art and literature, is primarily ironic. This irony, however, can have negative consequences because its very performance and potential inaccessibility have the potential to recapitulate the very stereotypes the form attempts to deconstruct. This emphasis on irony also undermines efforts to build a hip-hop-based coalition to challenge inequality and injustice.

From the outset, critics both admired the realism of Smith's performance pieces and worried about the potential for her work to reinforce worn stereotypes. By analyzing *Fires in the Mirror* and *Twilight—Los Angeles* through the lens of hip-hop aesthetics, it is possible to understand them as ironic revisions of contemporary American history. Through these performances, Smith asserts that the words themselves should be understood not as literal truths, but as symptoms of a bigger problem:

> I am interested in the difficulty people have in talking about race and talking about difference. This difficulty goes across race, class, and political lines. I am interested in the lack of words and mistrustful of the ease with which some people seem to pick up new words and mix them in with the old. The new words seem to get old quickly. This means to me that we do not have a language that serves us as a group.[80]

In the introduction to *Twilight—Los Angeles*, Smith restates her assumptions more economically: "Our race dialogue desperately needs this more complex language [one that can accommodate multifaceted identities]."[81] In these quotations from the introductions of both performance pieces, Smith tries to make clear her ironic use of metaphor and language. Romantic, tragic, or even comic modes of narration can submerge the "truth" of identity under stereotypical forms. Instead, Smith refuses to allow the Rodney King or Crown Heights riots to be understood through these tropes. Rather, the performance pieces rely on sampling, layering, and rhythmic flow/asymmetry to undermine the narrative renderings various interviewees use to convey their viewpoint about the events.

The last section of *Twilight—Los Angeles, 1992* ("Justice") illustrates how Smith deploys an ironic mode of narration to present an unidealized image of the riot's causes and effects. To conclude her chronicle, Smith presents a defense lawyer for one of the acquitted (Harlan Braun), a Korean who owned a liquor store in South Central (Mrs. Young-Soon Han), a Latina activist (Gladis Sibrian), and the organizer of a gang truce (Twilight Bey). Through these individuals, Smith articulates a multifaceted critique of how media accounts oversimplified the events in order to narrate the riots as romance, tragedy, or comedy. Unlike the standard versions of the riots, the picture Smith presents is much more ambiguous. Smith selects Harlan Braun to draw one possible conclusion about the riots: "'What is truth?' And it's a haunting question here too, isn't it? Is it the truth of Koon and Powell being guilty or is it the truth of the society that has to find them guilty to protect itself?"[82] Through Braun, Smith demonstrates the irony of those who sought to find a single truth in the riots. Braun questions the very nature of truth and thus reminds the audience that Smith has layered her samples to interrogate the "linear" conceptions of truth in which events result from one primary cause and yield one lesson. Second, Smith performs the words of Mrs. Young-Soon Han. Han describes how the riots changed her once-favorable view of the United States and caused her to question the very ideal of justice. She also wonders whether Korean Americans will be able to find common ground with African Americans and live together with them peaceably. By placing Han's voice after Braun's, Smith deconstructs the racial binary on which most commentators relied to understand the case and demonstrates the multiple issues and views that shaped people's perspectives of the event.

Third, Smith presents Gladis Sibrian, the director of the Farabundo Martí National Liberation Front. Sibrain discusses the powerlessness that people, especially African American and Latino/a youth, felt as a result of the riots. For Sibrian, the violence that ensued constituted anarchy because no one organized and channeled the emotions the court decision caused. The riots symbolize a failure because they reinforced feelings of powerlessness across racial and ethnic lines even as people took events into their own hands. Through Sibrian, Smith shows that no transcendence followed from this social explosion. The failure, however, did not result from a fatal flaw (as in tragedy), but is reflective of the irony implicit in the post–Civil Rights era. This section and the play culminate with Twilight Bey and his metaphor of twilight to describe the metaphysical uncertainty the performance piece presents. Although the putative theme of this section is justice, Smith leaves the audience with the image of twilight, the fleeting moments between day and night. This metaphor emphasizes the evanescence of the historical event and the perspectives on it, suggesting that justice itself may be an ephemeral condition.

Ironically, the former gangbanger gets the last word of the play, but those final thoughts do not possess a determinate meaning, nor did he construct them for the exact purpose to which they are here used. Rather, he comes to embody the failure of grand narratives through his name and his philosophy. Twilight Bey becomes a metaphor for liminality himself, thereby losing the very individuality Smith appears to offer her interviewees. The layers of samples, culled from her many interviews, suggest that all perspectives contain some truth, even if no one perspective possesses the entire truth. The rhythmic flow, which is so central to the virtuosity of Smith's performances, implies that the play of "time" holds the key to justice, not a discrete principle. Smith claims, in her introduction to *Fires in the Mirror*, that if one repeats a word enough times, it becomes one's own.[83] Yet this statement obscures the ironic form of ownership her performance methodology confers. The words she comes to own have been transformed through her own sampling, sorting, and pasting into a "new" composition. By sampling the words of her interviewees and then reconstructing them into a layered and flowing text, Smith interrogates who owns the performative spaces that the theater offers.[84] While the people portrayed do gain some access to the stage, it constitutes an ironic access because Smith's virtuosity as a performer and the stories of Crown Height and Los Angeles overpower their thoughts and personalities. Moreover, their words gain value within Smith's narrative precisely to the extent her performance reshapes their meaning.

## Hip-Hop Aesthetics and Intellectual Property Law

Anna Deavere Smith's performance pieces exemplify not only the characteristics of hip-hop aesthetics but how its assumptions conflict with intellectual property law. *Fires in the Mirror* and *Twilight—Los Angeles, 1992* both share the copyright warning, common to most books or plays:

> All rights, including but not limited to live stage performing rights (professional and amateur), motion picture, radio and television broadcasting, recording, recitation, lecturing, public reading, and the rights of translation into foreign languages are expressly reserved to the author and subject to royalty.

This copyright warning seems particularly ironic because Anna Deavere Smith did not actually write *any* of the words she performed. Rather, she selected these quotations/samples from her interviews, layered them in patterns, and then claimed ownership in the compiled or collaged text. Moreover, this legal claim seems to contradict the very assertion she makes about who owns the stage in her introductions. While I am not questioning her artistic ability or her creativity, there appears to be tension between the hip-hop methodology employed and the legal form that allows Smith to assert some level of control over her creation and disseminate her art. Smith's plays help reveal how intellectual property law enables texts created by hip-hop aesthetes to circulate within popular culture and threatens the vitality of hip-hop aesthetics as an ongoing cultural paradigm for textual production.

Intellectual property law creates properties out of written or visual texts (copyright); manufacturing processes and business inventions (patent); company names, logos, and slogans (trademark); and even celebrity personas (right of publicity). Copyright, patent, trademark, and the right of publicity are loosely connected legal constructions, to which different legal doctrines frequently apply. What they share, however, is the ability to create property out of intangible objects. As is frequently noted in the literature, especially by its strong proponents, intellectual property law (1) provides incentives for creators to create intangible property, (2) enables third parties to invest in other people's ideas and the expression of those ideas, (3) allows our intellectual resources to flow to their most valuable uses, and (4) fosters private ownership and thus permits decentralized decision making about creativity and scientific discovery.[85] According to the U.S. Code, intellectual property owners have the right to make copies of and distribute their work.[86] The U.S. Supreme Court has recently made it clear that courts must create a "sound balance between the respective values of supporting creative pursuits through copyright protection and promoting innovation [and creativity]" when interpreting and applying intellectual property law.[87]

While property rights are ostensibly color-blind and race neutral, Cheryl Harris astutely notes that they have always been linked to identity traits, such as gender, religion, race, ethnicity, national origin, and social class.[88] Unspoken assumptions about creators, authors, and scientists have limited the applicability of intellectual property doctrines because they tend to include romantic assumptions about authorship: creators of all kinds work alone, create new works of art or make discoveries through leaps of genius, and ignore historical or cultural contexts when they work.[89] Hip-hop aesthetics does not follow the romantic conception of genius that underlies intellectual property law.[90] As its practitioners and critics alike note, hip-hop aesthetics is concerned with "keepin' it real" and authenticity claims as much as it is concerned with monetary rewards—although its practitioners willingly take the money. Even if hip-hop music has frequently concerned itself with the legality of sampling, hip-hop artists nonetheless assert their ownership rights over their songs and their styles.[91]

Anna Deavere Smith's performance pieces suggest a similar conflict of values and assumptions. Smith must blur the line between verbatim reportage and solitary artistic genius as she develops her project in order to please both the requirements of the theater community and the legal requirements for intellectual property protection. Her attempt to perform her critique that theater omits the multiplicity of voices that comprise the United States creates a potential legal conundrum: if she samples too directly, then she opens herself up to a lawsuit. If she samples wisely, as she does from excerpts taken from private interviews, she comes to "own" the very words she claims have been missing from the public dialogue. Thus, she has "stolen" from the very people with whom she claims solidarity. A number of groups and hip-hop stars have encountered similar dilemmas, seeking to include phrases from Martin Luther King speeches or samples of George Clinton and James Brown as testaments to their groundbreaking artistry. In these instances, hip-hop musicians must either pay up or delete the homage they wanted to make.

As I have tried to argue throughout this chapter, sampling, layering, and rhythmic flow/asymmetry lead hip-hop aesthetics toward ironic forms of narration and ambiguous criticisms of American culture. Intellectual property law and legal discourse, however, have historically assumed that meaning is directly correlated to the words, sounds, or images of a given text. While irony revels in ambiguity and double meanings, intellectual property law operates as if words have a distinct meaning without reference to any particular audience or cultural context. One of the primary analytical tools upon which courts have relied in copyright law is the idea/expression dichotomy.[92] Thus, an author can own the expression or particularly wording of a concept, but not the concept itself, because legal discourse has determined that allowing authors to own particular articulations of an idea provides the necessary balance between innovation and property rights and between the creator and the public.

This scheme functions properly as long as particular expressions denote one distinct idea. Hip-hop aesthetics challenges this assumption of copyright law because its aesthetic theory presupposes ambiguity and double meanings and carefully constructs these texts to produce these ironies through sampling, layering, and rhythmic flows/asymmetries. Rather than assuming that a particular text constitutes a subset or articulation of a given idea, hip-hop aesthetics turns this relationship upside down and attempts to transform a single expression into a multiplicity of ideas. For example, when Jay-Z samples from the musical *Annie* in his song "Hard Knock Life," he transforms the meaning of a "hard knock life" even if copyright law required him to pay a royalty for merely copying the song. The idea/expression dichotomy breaks down when applied to hip-hop producers because their verbatim copying frequently shows how multiple ideas exist within a single expression. It is precisely this free play of ideas, which hip-hop promotes, that intellectual property law regulates and limits.

The goal of hip-hop aesthetics is thus to reconstruct a textual object so that what appears solidly romantic, tragic, or comic becomes an elusive, ambiguous, and ironic commentary on contemporary social relations. Emphasizing authenticity or "keepin' it real" is actually an ironic plea that serves as an antidote to the excesses of other narrative modes. Hip-hop does not dismiss tragedy, romance, and comedy because these narrative modes affect social relations even if they fail to represent cultural life adequately. Hip-hop aesthetes must engage tragedy, romance, and comedy to demonstrate how they saturate American culture and fill it with "white noise." Contra postmodernism, hip-hop does not lament the "emptiness" of mass culture but deconstructs its "weight" and influence. It makes fun out of that "cultural baggage" by transforming the meaning of a text even as it appears to use a verbatim copy of it. Hip-hop aesthetics reveals that ownership, especially of cultural texts, is ultimately more bound by cultural and racial contexts than existing intellectual property law doctrines suggest. Thus, Smith's claim in the copyright notice that she owns the expressions *Fires in the Mirror* and *Twilight—Los Angeles, 1992* appears more coherent because she emplotted them, through sampling, layering, and rhythmic flows/asymmetries, into an ironic collage for the theater.

Smith's performance pieces exemplify hip-hop aesthetic's criticism of intellectual property law. Smith makes clear that the key to her meaning lies in her performance, not in its composition or as an abstract text. For her, identifying her work as a performance attempts to protect it from being reduced to a mere text or expression. Smith resists any effort to transform the ambiguity of her work into a romantic, tragic, or comic tale that falsifies the messiness of the Crown Heights or Rodney King riots. Intellectual property law, however, cannot protect this kind of integrity because it does not acknowledge how particular expressions get plotted with distinct narrative modes. This gap within the assumptions of hip-hop aesthetics and intellectual property law reveals how legal discourse seeks to resolve such textual ambiguity by expanding (intellectual) property's rule. Given its historic role in creating racial, gender, and class inequality, it is ironic that contemporary society is asking property concepts to resolve a whole host of ongoing cultural conflicts in the post–Civil Rights era.

## CHAPTER 4

# Claiming Ownership in the Post–Civil Rights Era

The origins of hip-hop can be traced to the late 1960s in Jamaica, but the music began capturing national attention during the 1980s.[1] During hip-hop's early years, Ronald Reagan's election deepened existing cultural divides and furthered the "culture wars" that dominated the attention of African American activists, intellectuals, writers, musicians, artists, and politicians. These activists and intellectuals sought to complete the social transformation begun during the 1950s and 1960s. Hip-hop aesthetes and critical race theorists had to confront intellectual "segregation," which kept the contributions and experiences of African Americans and other historically marginalized groups outside of the nation's classrooms, museums, historical monuments, and legal doctrines. In this cultural context, African American cultural workers questioned who "owns" American cultural history and how minority voices should participate in contemporary cultural dialogues.

This chapter seeks to build a bridge between the Civil Rights and hip-hop generations through close readings of Toni Morrison's *Beloved* and Adrian Piper's *Vanilla Nightmare* series, texts produced in the late 1980s. These works, by two artists whose careers span the end of the Civil Rights era and the flowering of hip-hop, explore the politics surrounding property and cultural ownership and thus link Civil Rights era hopes to the reformulation (not simply a redistribution) of property rights. Neither Morrison nor Piper is generally considered part of the hip-hop generation, for good reasons, and it would be folly to view them solely in this vein. However, their work shares basic elements of hip-hop aesthetics (sampling, layering, rhythmic flows/asymmetry, and irony) and consistently questions what "ownership" means. Both authors also examine the problems African Americans still encounter when claiming ownership over themselves and their cultural heritage. Placing Morrison and Piper into dialogue with the hip-hop culture that Bronx youth created in the 1970s and 1980s allows an exploration of the connection between popular and "high" cultural forms. This conversation transforms hip-hop aesthetics from a potentially isolated artifact of youth culture to a response to broader concerns and ongoing difficulties in the post–Civil Rights era. It also acknowledges the pervasive shift from civil rights to property rights rhetoric within social and legal discourse. Morrison and Piper, along with other hip-hop aesthetes, anticipate the centrality of intellectual property law in contemporary debates about American culture because they foresee how the ownership of cultural texts and cultural memory remains an open question.

Through Morrison's and Piper's work, we can explore how claiming ownership in the post–Civil Rights era has been transformed by and through hip-hop aesthetics. Their works assume a critical attitude toward dominant legal theories of property. Legal decisions, much more so than scholarly writing on the topic, tend to presume that owners and appropriators share status and power.[2] African American writers, painters, and musicians tend to rely on an alternative assumption: racialized power shapes the existing distribution of property ownership, including rights in intellectual properties. Hip-hop aesthetics constitutes a primary strategy for African Americans to articulate ownership over the public sphere, even if legal discourse has already distributed the ownership rights over some of the texts, objects, sounds, and images of that "public" sphere. To understand how Morrison's *Beloved* and Piper's *Vanilla Nightmare* series participate in this ongoing conversation, one must attend to their examinations of property within the contexts of literary and visual culture.

## Claiming Ownership of Literature

> Freeing yourself was one thing; claiming ownership of that freed self was another.
> —Toni Morrison, *Beloved*

To link Morrison and her award-wining novel *Beloved* with hip-hop aesthetics may appear problematic because the novel does not reference hip-hop explicitly, nor has Morrison identified such a connection. In a number of interviews, though, she has linked this and her other works to the social, economic, and political crises that fueled the growth of hip-hop in the 1980s.[3] Literary or cultural studies scholars have generally considered her work through music, with blues- or jazz-based paradigms the norm, and with good reason.[4] However, I will argue that Morrison's *Beloved* and its trope of rememory constitute a metaphysical inquiry into the ironies of self-ownership in the post–Civil Rights era, especially as the ghosts of racism and racialization undermine the realization of the previous era's social activism. This focus on property, combined with Morrison's blend of Modernist and postmodernist writing strategies, suggest a number of affinities with hip-hop aesthetics.[5]

Many critics have identified the unusual structure and rhythmic flow of the novel and struggled to find an adequate paradigm to contain or represent it. For example, Linda Krumholz offers a fairly compelling and accurate characterization of *Beloved*:

> To make the novel work as a ritual, Morrison adapts techniques from modernist novels, such as the fragmentation of the plot and a shifting narrative voice, to compel the reader to actively construct an interpretive framework. In *Beloved*, the reader's process of reconstructing the fragmented story parallels Sethe's [the novel's main character] psychological recovery: repressed fragments of the (fictionalized) personal and historical past are retrieved and reconstructed. Morrison also introduces oral narrative techniques—repetition, the blending of voices, a shifting narrative voice, and an episodic framework.[6]

I have quoted Krumholz's description at length to reveal the conceptual difficulties talented and insightful scholars have encountered with the novel. Bernard Bell, an astute and influential critic, has similarly struggled to describe Morrison's text:

> In her multivocal remembrances of things past, Morrison probes the awesome will to live of her characters to celebrate the truth and resiliency of the complex double consciousness of their humanity. What she has wrought in *Beloved* is an extremely Gothic blend of postmodern realism and romance as well as of racial and sexual politics.[7]

To better capture the aesthetic structure of *Beloved* and its theme of how to "own the self," I propose the then-burgeoning hip-hop aesthetic—which features sampling, layering, rhythmic flows/asymmetry, and irony—as the principle that can unify this sprawling and seemingly disjointed text. Hip-hop aesthetics supplies both a poetic and a historical referent for *Beloved.* As a forerunner of hip-hop aesthetics, Morrison's novel captures the cultural tensions of the 1980s, when 1950s and 1960s activism had ebbed, and African Americans and other historically marginalized people reflected on the strengths and limits of Civil Rights strategies. Rememory, *Beloved*'s central trope, offers an alternative name for the processes by which sampling, layering, rhythmic flows/asymmetries, and irony provide emotional renewal despite the persistence of race, racism, and racialization. *Beloved* is not a hip-hop novel, but it responds to some of the same artistic and political challenges, especially as experienced by young African American artists.[8]

Morrison's *Beloved* relates the stories of a family and a community in the period leading up to and following the Civil War. Although the novel portrays a wide range of characters, its narrative center revolves around Sethe, who escaped from slavery; Denver, Sethe's daughter who survived the escape; Paul D, a friend who located Sethe several years after the war; Baby Suggs, Sethe's mother-in-law; and Beloved, the ghost of Sethe's daughter whom she killed in order to protect her from slavery. The novel constantly moves back and forth between the 1850s and the 1870s, suggesting how sampled bits of historical memory, not the events themselves, shape the present lives of her characters. The novel's shocking element, which some have termed tragic, is that upon being cornered by slave catchers in Ohio, Sethe kills one child and begins attacking the others. By killing her own offspring, Sethe "wins" her freedom. Beloved is the ghost of the killed girl, who has returned to demand Sethe's attention and love. The community, which once found warmth and self-love through Baby Suggs's preaching and hospitality, ultimately shuns Baby Suggs, Sethe, and her children. Writing initially in the voice of an omniscient author, Morrison moves toward a series of first-person narratives that alternate among characters.[9] Ultimately, through the help of the community, Sethe is able to exorcize the ghost of Beloved.

As my brief summary implies, the novel does not offer a simple chronological account of a singular event or a particular character's development. Rather, it is comprised of a complex web of voices, events, memories, and characters. Although few (if any) scholars have drawn such a comparison,

*Beloved* progresses through a relentless array of samples. Sampling is not simply the reshaping and reuse of a recorded text, but a method of textual production, in this case writing, that proceeds by listening for and incorporating discrete parts, rather than completed wholes, and constructing an aesthetically satisfying text out of them.[10] In recent years, hip-hop music producers have been forced, because of the difficulty and cost of clearing samples, to hide their samples by reworking them or cutting them into smaller and smaller pieces. As is well-known, Morrison first learned of Margaret Garner, the historical figure on whom Sethe is based, when completing research for *The Black Book*.[11] However, as Steven Weisenburger has demonstrated in *Modern Medea*, where he explores the historical events that led up to Garner's attempt to murder multiple children and her being forced to return to slavery, Garner's real story is more complicated than Morrison's version suggests, because the slave owner apparently fathered a number of the murdered children. The murders thus constituted a "rebellion against the whole patriarchal system of American Slavery," as Garner attacked not only her children but her master's property as well.[12] Moreover, unlike Sethe, whose violent actions freed her from slavery, Margaret Garner's actions did not result in her freedom, but fated her to being sold down the river. But Morrison does not aim to tell a historically accurate version.[13] Rather, she reworks the historical details to better fit a story, presumably one relevant to the 1980s situation that Morrison herself confronted.

Morrison's use of samples can be seen in her serialized description of Sethe's violence against her children after Schoolteacher, his nephew, the slave catcher, and the Sheriff—whom Morrison calls the "four horsemen"—descend upon Baby Suggs's house. The chapter opens with an unidentified narrator who describes the events based on the view of an 1850s slave owner or proponent of slavery. Through this sampled voice, Morrison "borrows" or "appropriates" a perspective not generally discussed or presented in the rest of the text. Rather than narrating the entire story through a singular narrator, Morrison relies at strategic moments on such sampled voices to represent the epistemological conflicts that continue to haunt American culture. For example, a nameless, ostensibly white narrator observes: "Caught red-handed, so to speak, they [African American slaves] would seem to recognize the futility of outsmarting a whiteman and the hopelessness of outrunning a rifle. . . . The very nigger with his head hanging and a little jelly-jar smile on his face could all of a sudden roar, like a bull or some such, and commence to do disbelievable things."[14]

In this passage, Morrison potentially shocks the reader because this voice has been muted or absent from the text and emphasizes the ideological context for Sethe's actions. It is irrelevant whether Sethe "knows" this particular articulation of racism because she is responding to a social structure and a systemic ideology, in which these comments are ubiquitous. This sampled voice allows Morrison to foreshadow and explain the unspeakable thing that Sethe will do.

The nameless narrator, however, does not tell the whole story, only one aspect of it. Baby Suggs takes over the narrative and describes the immediate aftermath of Sethe's deed. This second sample works against the first and offers a second perspective from which to view the spectacle. If the first narrator emphasizes the "danger" presented by African Americans, Suggs demonstrates the kindness and love as she attempts to take care of Sethe's children.[15] Baby Suggs possesses a keen eye for details that the white narrator omits: after Beloved's initial murder, Denver nurses from Sethe's breast, mixing mother's milk and Beloved's blood. This sampled image, only accessible through Baby Suggs's eyes, suggests the implicit tension for African Americans in claiming self-ownership after slavery. Any attempt to possess oneself requires coming to terms with how slavery and segregation destroyed and disfigured families and cultural traditions. There is no "pure" or "authentic" inheritance that is not tainted with the blood of ancestors. Contra Baby Suggs's exhortations before Sethe's actions, it is not enough merely to love one's hands and flesh.[16] Any attempt to claim self-ownership, especially in the post–Civil Rights era, is necessarily ironic because the flesh or the hands always exist within a historical or cultural context.[17] Sethe's desperate attack to save her children by killing them reinserts the violence endemic to making any kind of property claim, a violence that Baby Suggs's approach to healing had failed to consider.

Morrison's text, however, is not merely content to provide two accounts. Morrison also includes bits and pieces of Stamp Paid's and Sethe's memories, combined with Paul D's reaction upon learning of Sethe's actions. For Paul D, Sethe's "love is too thick." Sethe counters, "Love is or it ain't. Thin love ain't love at all."[18] She then asks Paul D if her love for her children required that she and her children return to slavery. At this point, the conversation between them breaks down, and Paul D hurls an insult at Sethe. Her choice reminds him, and ultimately the entire African American community, of the danger implicit to claiming ownership of and loving the self when emotional and psychic health are intertwined with property law. The dissonance between these two discursive regimes produces social,

cultural, and psychic conflict because the demands of law and family cannot be reconciled easily. Property law does not attempt to address the psychological aspects of ownership, even though it takes precedence over psychological discourses within American culture. By describing multiple
perspectives about the realities of slavery, Morrison shows the limits of romantic or tragic accounts that emphasize one view over all others and
highlights the ironies implicit within any claim of self-ownership.[19]

As a number of commentators have noted, *Beloved* and other novels
such as *Dessa Rose* (1986) and *Corregidora* (1975) constitute "neo-slave narratives [which revisit] an era marked by immense faith in the emancipatory
promise of print literacy."[20] However, this return to the slave narrative is
not a simple recapitulation of an older style in which contemporary writers
resurrect a previous generation's faith in America's promise of freedom
through literacy. Rather, Lovalerie King argues, "a neo-slave narrative
brings to light information subjugated by the privileging of certain narratives over others, Toni Morrison's *Beloved* exists as a form of alternative discourse and, thus, takes its place in a continuing tradition of resistance."[21]
Morrison offers multiple perspectives on the novel's events to illustrate the
generic limits, including those of the slave narrative, to describing social
reality and liberating individuals and communities. Although there is no
one slave narrative that Morrison samples particularly, *Beloved* writes
against this entire genre, as the novel only offers bits and pieces of potential slave narratives that could have been written by Sethe, Paul D,
Beloved, Baby Suggs, Halle, and others. As should be clear, however, their
stories have been omitted from the genre and thus American literary history because of illiteracy (in the cases of Sethe, Paul D, and Baby Suggs) or
because they did not survive the journey toward freedom (in the case of
Halle and Beloved). *Beloved*, as a text produced in the 1980s, attempts to
evoke enough of these slave narratives, via sampling, to demonstrate their
inadequacy as historical representations. At this moment in post–Civil
Rights era history, Morrison and other hip-hop aesthetes must rely on
sampling in order to show the limits of the received versions of history and
to claim ownership over it by reworking it.[22]

Sampling alone, however, cannot effectively assert the kinds of ownership claims that Morrison wishes to make. Sampling is not another word
for rememory. Rather, samples must be given new levels of meaning by
their deployment in new patterns. Rememory is the pattern, not the recol-
lections themselves, because certain moments stand out against the background and repeat themselves in the unfolding of chronological time. Like

a strip quilt, a nonlinear or asymmetrical pattern must be pieced together from the remnants of American literary history. By reshaping the debris of Margaret Garner's story and reorganizing it, Morrison creates a text that describes the historical trauma of slavery and property law while attempting to find a method to heal that pain. Layering is the art of creating productive tension.[23] For any historically marginalized community to claim ownership over American literary history, productive tensions must be revealed. In a moment when the comic meets the deadly serious, Morrison uses the voice of Sixo to signify on the limits of the property law and to emphasize its discursive authority to shape cultural relations. In an oft-quoted section, Sixo receives a beating from Schoolteacher for stealing and "to show him that definitions belonged to the definers—not the defined."[24] While scholars have tended to view this moment as a critique of Western epistemology or the Enlightenment, they have neglected or downplayed its ironic critique of property and the law of evidence, as Schoolteacher's methods of cross-examination force Sixo to testify against himself. When Schoolteacher claims that Sixo has stolen food, Sixo does not classify his actions as theft. Rather, he states that he has been "improving your [Schoolteacher's] property."[25] Sixo's response exemplifies signifyin', illustrates hip-hop's attitude toward intellectual property law, and highlights how property law itself has always struggled to distinguish among the layers of ownership. Reading this fictional conversation within the cultural context of when Morrison wrote *Beloved*, in the 1980s, Sixo can be understood as asking who owns the sample from a text that gets transformed through layering or a later act of consumption/production.

Morrison's textual response to this dilemma can be found a few sections later. As the story comes to a close, the novel's layers of samples begin to fall in on themselves, not merging into a unified voice but producing what Tricia Rose calls the "Black Noise" of hip-hop aesthetics. After rewriting the biblical "Song of Songs" and its heart-wrenching tale of lost love in a paragraph, Morrison weaves together the interior monologues of Sethe, Denver, and Beloved to show both the similarities and the differences between their personal and social desires. Rather than presenting distinct voices, the text makes clear how their respective identities are produced socially: "Beloved / You are my sister / You are my daughter / You are my face; You are me / I have found you again; you have come back to me."[26] In these lines, it is clear that Sethe, Denver, and Beloved are engaged in an unconscious dialogue about how to order their relationships to one another. Textually, Morrison represents this struggle for order by layering their voices. However, she does not portray their voices in fully drawn narratives. Rather, she samples their voices and then shapes the meaning of these samples by layering them in asymmetrical patterns. Sethe, Denver, and Beloved form a triangle in which desires and responsibilities do not fall evenly or symmetrically upon one another. Instead, their demands may be incommensurate, meaning that realizing one desire may necessarily frustrate a second desire.

The tension that layered samples produce comes to a climax in this section's conclusion, "You are mine / You are mine / You are mine," in which Sethe, Beloved, and Denver assert contrasting ownership claims. Layering their voices and placing these statements next to one another allows Morrison to interrogate the foundations of property law, in which there is an object and individuals with claims of varying strength. Rather than providing a neat or ready solution to conflict, property law must always navigate conflicting desires and choose one set of interests over another. Even as they struggle, as individuals and as symbols of a communal struggle, with the aftermath of slavery and the legacy of being "owned," Sethe, Denver, and Beloved continue to make ownership claims. Ironically, it is because their claims are too strong—or, in the words of Paul D, their love is "too thick"—that their desires for ownership come to "own" them. Only when the community returns to 124 can this trio be saved from their excessive internalization of property law's assumptions.[27]

According to the logic of *Beloved*, African Americans can only find freedom by balancing personal and communal claims of ownership. Excessive reliance on property law transforms too much into objects to be owned, while forgoing the logic of ownership creates its own problems. The choice to present the intertwined stories of *Beloved* through layered samples enables Morrison to depict the partial views of American history that literature provides. It also allows her to assert a certain ownership over that history, even if dominant groups already believe they own that history or literature. Morrison's strategic use of layered samples implies that property rights do not simply bind a text/object to particular individuals but are constructed by social and textual networks. Ownership rights can be created by producing something de novo or constructing new meaning within a social/textual framework—the primary tool of hip-hop aesthetics. Reading rememory and Sethe's violent acts through this aesthetic principle reveals that Sethe's crime shattered the fragile networks of signification that this newly freed community had created. The "art" of layered sampling thus hinges on the ability to invoke memory, but not be controlled by it, to assert ownership over literary and cultural history in order to reveal the "unspeakable thoughts, unspoken."[28] In one of the novel's multiple's endings, Morrison writes that "he [Paul D] wants to put his story next to hers."[29] Paul D's desire, in effect, articulates hip-hop's strategy of layering as a method to bring together what dominant society seeks to keep apart.

The aesthetic structure of *Beloved* does not simply rely on layered samples, but layers these samples in rhythmic patterns that defy traditional narrative and representational modes. Morrison's approach to storytelling in the novel swirls through time, jumping up and back, instead of moving forward in linear, chronological time. Organizing the novel's events proves difficult because Morrison seeks not to emphasize historical or representational accuracy, but to capture the experience of living in an age saturated with historical narratives and cultural icons. As many scholars have observed, *Beloved* attempts to show how the absences created by the African Diaspora have reinscribed themselves as presences or "ghosts" within contemporary African American cultural relations.[30] Unlike postmodern theorists who posit the emptiness of these historical and cultural signs, contemporary African American writers and artists struggle against their weight and oversaturation with meaning. The rhythmic flows and asymmetries of hip-hop aesthetics fashion these samples into pulsing, living texts, which do not simply haunt the reader but allow her to experience the past and unequal cultural relations viscerally. In the novel, the ghost of Beloved returns to life. She moves from being an invisible presence to returning to life to being exorcized. Paradoxically, Morrison suggests that in order to find healing from contemporary social problems, the haunting nature of existing narratives, icons, and symbols must be uncovered. If the chronological time of most narratives orders and thus protects us from experience, the discontinuities of hip-hop rhythmic flows and asymmetries draw readers/viewers/listeners into texts even as they frequently shift directions and open as many questions as they answer.

Critics have identified *Beloved* and other novels from the same period as neoslave narratives and have explored why writers chose to revise this genre during the post–Civil Rights era. According to Paul Gilroy, "Morrison and others are drawing upon and reconstructing the resources supplied to them by earlier generations of black writers who allowed the confluence of racism, rationality, and systematic terror to configure both their disenchantment with modernity and their aspirations for its fulfillment."[31] I would argue that the discontinuities within these neoslave narratives anticipate the growth of hip-hop aesthetics. The rhythmic flows and asymmetries of these contemporary slave narratives reveal the gaping silences within the original slave narratives. Most slave narratives operate within linear, chronological time, characteristic of Enlightenment epistemology. Even if the slave narratives do not describe every life stage or event, they move forward through time to demonstrate the transition from bondage to freedom as a fairly neat movement, without psychological remainder. Morrison fills her text, however, with gaps between samples, stories, and even historical periods. Instead of moving through time, the narrative moves *across* time, the characters' memories reorganizing the supposedly regular pattern of chronology as they, unlike the self-created heroes of the traditional slave narrative, are haunted by what they have experienced. *Beloved* refuses to draw rigid boundaries between the 1850s and the 1870s because those periods coexist within the present time of the characters' minds.

Morrison's approach to temporality shares hip-hop's rhythmic flows and asymmetries. I am not, however, suggesting that Morrison borrowed from the music or patterned her writing style from it. Rather, Morrison has interrogated the temporality of African American literature and cultural criticism since the early 1970s in *The Bluest Eye* and *Sula*. *Beloved*'s repetitions, gaps, and silences constitute a fulfillment of Morrison's initial approach to writing, in which she consciously created breaks or asymmetries in her texts so as to undermine the tragic or romantic vision proposed by canonical American authors.[32] Following a trajectory similar to that of hip-hop deejays, Morrison increasingly focuses her attention on the rhythmic undertow of American literary and cultural production, especially in those textual moments critics have typically overlooked. In *Playing in the Dark*, Morrison argues that American literary critics have "manage[d] *not* to see meaning in the thunderous, theatrical presence of black surrogacy—an informing, stabilizing, and disturbing element—in the literature they do study."[33] In order to make this haunting presence visible, Morrison ultimately decides to display the temporal limits of American literary history. The breaks among characters, settings, and dates within *Beloved* and her other novels require the reader or critic to piece together the connections that could have been otherwise overlooked. This novel displays the "cracks" that have always existed but have only become the subject of literary criticism in the post–Civil Rights era. Morrison's juxtaposition of flowing descriptions and tightly drawn dialogues with awkward gaps and silences depicts how race-conscious rules of etiquette limited public dialogue about race at the very moment when America should have been liberated to engage in wide-ranging and transformative interracial and intraracial conversations about race. The pacing of Morrison's novels plays with and frustrates settled expectations. The rhythmic flows and asymmetries invoke racial difference and mark ownership claims over public discourse by representing racialized contexts and narratives and by breaking down the unspoken or unconscious elements of those representations.

Although *Beloved* has been widely praised and taught as *the* exemplar of "multicultural literature," does this high regard for the novel follow from a faulty reading of its narrative mode? As this chapter argues, *Beloved* falls within the paradigm of hip-hop aesthetics because it relies on layered samples, rhythmic flows/asymmetries, and an ironic recounting of African American cultural history. Despite an absence of heroes and heroic actions, characters who are beaten down and haunted from the beginning, and an ambiguous ending, scholars and critics tend to understand the novel as either racial tragedy or racial romance. To read the novel as a romance requires a hero who overcomes a crisis. Most often, those who wish to read *Beloved* romantically transform either Sethe or Denver into a hero. Ashraf Rushdy, for example, argues that Denver is transformed by her experiences with Beloved and by her action to get the community's help to protect Sethe from the ghost.[34] Barbara Christian argues that the novel promotes healing and thus narrates an unsentimental but nonetheless romantic overcoming of the crisis of slavery and second-class citizenship.[35] Both readings place Morrison's text within a tradition of social and cultural uplift. Through this lens, *Beloved* appears as a story of one family's and one community's attempt to heal and claim ownership over themselves. Jon-Christian Suggs has argued that *Beloved* exemplifies the neoromantic impulses within contemporary African American literature and signals a break from the historical concerns of African American textual production in the post–Civil Rights era.[36]

Not all view *Beloved* as romance. In a well-known and frequently criticized essay, Stanley Crouch observes: "For *Beloved* above all else, is a blackface holocaust novel. It seems to have been written in order to enter American slavery into the big-time martyr ratings contest." He continues: "That Morrison chose to set the Afro-American experience in the framework of collective tragedy is fine, of course. But she lacks a true sense of the tragic."[37] Even though Morrison critics tend to dismiss Crouch's appraisal, Crouch's sense that the novel fails to realize the standards of romance is a telling one. For Crouch, *Beloved* constitutes a tragic text because it emphasizes the horrors of slavery and the general failure of Emancipation to liberate the novel's characters. He also rightly detects a "pulp style" that undercuts the tragic impulse, because individuals lack control over their fates, and perceives a lack of subtlety in the novel's overstatements and melodramatic moments of cultural and historical criticism.[38] To Crouch, all of these failings derive from Morrison's sentimentality and her attempt to transform the African American experience into a "martyr contest." Crouch's reading of *Beloved* suggests how a reader could mistake irony for tragedy.

For Morrison, "language can never live up to life once and for all. Nor should it. Language can never 'pin down' slavery, genocide, war."[39] Rather, *Beloved* offers an ironic and ambiguous account.[40] Two moments stand out as ironic narratives. The first is the aforementioned discussion of Sethe's attempt to claim ownership over her children by killing them both figuratively and psychologically. Morrison narrates this event from at least four points of view. Instead of directly stating the authoritative version of the events, Morrison chooses to let her characters present possible ways of reading this moment. In this manner, she provides a realistic account of the events and their aftermath without placing them within any one narrative. The result of Sethe's violent acts, however, is clearly ironic. Sethe wins her physical freedom by killing or psychologically maiming her offspring. Within the logic of the novel, this action frees Sethe because she is no longer deemed suitable for slavery As many have noted, *Beloved* is not designed simply to address historical concerns, but to engage contemporary cultural disputes. For Morrison, the central question of the post–Civil Rights era is: can African Americans claim ownership over themselves *and* provide a nourishing and hopeful environment for African American youth?[41] Can the Civil Rights generation free themselves without forcing their psychological scars onto their children? Sethe's story illustrates the ambiguous effects of major social changes. Contra romantic renderings of the novel, historical forces and cultural relations influence Sethe's actions and the community's response to them. Unlike Crouch's reading of *Beloved*, which finds the tidal waves of history and culture structuring the individual's experience, an ironic reading of the novel centers on the unintended consequences of Sethe's actions. Sethe's choice to claim ownership over her children and liberate them from slavery by killing them demonstrates not only the hand of history but her own importance in shaping the future. Crouch's tragic reading omits Sethe's role in shaping the future, while the romantic version neglects the very real power of history and social relations.

*Beloved*'s conclusion presents the second significant ironic moment, with its assertion that "this is not a story to pass on."[42] This sentence holds two apparently contradictory meanings simultaneously. First, the passage denotes that readers should not "pass on" or transmit this story to future generations. The historical trauma of slavery, segregation, and racism must be ended. However, the second meaning suggests that the story, as a chronicle of past psychological states and cultural inheritance, cannot be "passed on" and missed. Creating the necessary conditions for long-term hope and success for African Americans requires understanding and overcoming historical trauma. These alternate ways of reading this one expression could be synthesized and translated so that Sethe's claim for self- and familial ownership must be remembered, but not relived. Because slave narratives were written for public consumption and thus cautious about what they revealed, Morrison reminds her readers that "only the act of imagination can help" reconstruct the interior lives of enslaved men and women.[43] At its heart, the question of "passing on" the story or not invokes the laws of cultural inheritance and, by implication, property law.

Through *Beloved*, the question Morrison asks is not so much how Sethe or her contemporaries can heal themselves, but what the post–Civil Rights generation should inherit from their parents and how their experiences should be understood. In her speech accepting the Nobel Prize, Morrison asks this very question through a parable about the young children who ask the blind griot whether the bird in one of their hands is alive or dead. The griot answers, "I don't know whether the bird you are holding is dead or alive, but what I do know is that it is in your hands."[44] Later in the speech, Morrison explains that the future is in the hands of children.[45] In much the same way, *Beloved* articulates the choices African Americans face but ultimately allows future generations to choose their path. I identify this closing challenge as irony because the passage's brevity contains multiple possible readings. The book ends without an ending. If Sethe seeks finality and closure, *Beloved* refuses any simplistic endings (tragic or romantic) and offers ambiguity and irony instead.

## Claiming Ownership of Visual Culture

Completed in the same year as *Beloved*, Adrian Piper's *Vanilla Nightmare* series, examines questions of ownership in visual and popular cultures. Unlike Morrison, who has become the exemplar of post–Civil Rights era

African American literary production, Piper occupies a less-defined place in African American art.[46] As Kobena Mercer argues, Piper is more closely identified with Conceptualism and Minimalism, movements that seem relatively far removed from developments within African American art and art criticism.[47] Even though her work engages issues of identity and racial politics, its tendency toward abstraction and its reliance on canonical philosophy, especially Immanuel Kant, has frequently pushed her work outside African American art's boundaries. Moreover, her art pieces and performances, which use funk and R & B to explore identity and racial politics, have received less critical notice. These factors have shaped an uncertain legacy around Piper. Her work is relatively well-known, but it does not quite fit the categories used to understand and promote African American art. Piper's interventions into racial identity exude ambiguity and irony. Like Morrison, Piper neither romanticizes nor demonizes race but examines how it structures contemporary culture and shapes social relations.[48]

In *Beloved* and her other historically based fictions, Morrison suggests that contemporary racialization and racism result from history and its traumatic memories. Piper, however, suggests an alternative but equally compelling case for the persistence of racial discourses: visual culture. Jean Fisher offers an insightful observation on the assumptions underlying Piper's work: "Racism is a pathology first of the visual register. . . . Piper's work may be thought of as the development of strategies that would expose and disarm this gaze by deflecting visuality into other modalities—text with image, music, and the immediacy of bodily encounter."[49] In this account, race constitutes a spectacle that then shapes other discourses. By contrasting *Beloved* with the *Vanilla Nightmare* series, I do not mean to suggest that Morrison overlooks or neglects visual culture, as Margaret Garner's actions were memorialized in Thomas Satterwhite Noble's *Modern Medea*, an image that Morrison helped reprint in *The Black Book*. Rather, I argue that Morrison and Piper can be read in a complementary fashion in which both history and visual culture must be reclaimed. Their shared emphasis on layered sampling, flow, and irony reveals the limited vision of legal discourse, which attempts to produce a stable meaning from dynamic texts.

Long central to intellectual property law (although increasingly less so) is the idea/expression dichotomy, which states that specific expressions can be owned but that ideas, which can be articulated in many ways, exist within the public domain. The central premise of this idea is that an expression has a singular or relatively stable meaning. But what if, per Piper and Morrison, the words, notes, or images that comprise texts lack a stable meaning? What if these expressions change with their context? Morrison's intervention into the structures of meaning is primarily temporal. Her novels typically unravel how memory haunts the contemporary era. Her characters cannot escape the pull of history, even as they attempt to create a better future. For Piper, the challenge of racism is not so much temporal as it is spatial and visual. In the *Vanilla Nightmare* series, Piper interrogates how a newspaper, the *New York Times*, and its advertising conceal as much as they reveal. By sampling representative articles and advertisements and then layering images, especially raced and sexual ones, Piper questions the version of reality described by the *New York Times* and seeks to master and rework its racialized representations.

Perhaps even more than Morrison's, Piper's work has shifted dramatically from its early Minimalism and Conceptualism to share an aesthetic terrain with hip-hop culture.[50] From its very beginning, her work experimented with sampling, one of the key elements of hip-hop aesthetics. Piper's provocative statements about her theory of art echo hip-hop's concerns with American culture, especially intellectual property and the circulation and dissemination of ideas, symbols, and sounds. In addition, her work appears to have become increasingly focused on identity and racialization through the 1970s and 1980s. Writing in 1981 about one of her earliest pieces, *Meat into Meat* (1968), in which she photographed her then-boyfriend preparing and eating four hamburgers at certain time intervals, Piper explores why such a project ought to be considered art. Piper's answer is revealing because it explores the very meaning of originality and genius, which intellectual property regulates, especially vis-à-vis hip-hop culture. Piper writes that her "objectified perceptions became art by being registered deliberately as the product of an aesthetically informed consciousness. Thus, I [Piper] functioned as an active Art Selector, conferring Art status on certain objects in the environment (including human ones) by virtue of my Art Consciousness. . . . As artist, I use my art awareness as a tool for 'discovering' art."[51] In this explanation of her methods as a conceptual artist, Piper attempts, in effect, to defend the processes of sampling and layering. The language she deploys of "discovering art" within preexisting objects echoes hip-hop producers' claims that sampling requires hearing differently, not simply copying.[52]

In an interview in 1991, at a time when courts were first examining hip-hop sampling, Piper adamantly insists that she does not "appropriate images." She claims that "as a result of my Afro-American experiences, I see appropriation as an excuse for ripping off other people and not giving them credit. To me, it represents a certain kind of moral degeneration."[53] She adopts this position because she understands how Western artists have long sampled without permission from minority cultures: "We find the original styles and idioms the cubits, fauvists, surrealists, pattern painters, arte povera, performance artists, and neograffitists, among others have plagiarized without acknowledgment—under the ethically disingenuous, postmodernist rubric of 'appropriation.'"[54] Piper simultaneously condemns biting or stealing another's style or look even as her attempts to regain ownership over visual culture requires a certain amount of borrowing in order to criticize the racialized nature of American visual culture. Apparently reversing course in 1992, Piper defends her use of sampled music in her performance piece *Funk Lesson*, from the early 1980s:

> I had been trained as an art student in the late 1960s and was given to understand that I could appropriate from popular culture into a high-culture context just as Andy Warhol had done. I found that when I attempted to appropriate black working-class culture, in particular the music and the dance, that medium of artistic expression was universally condemned and misunderstood.[55]

Because of the conceptual nature of her work, Piper has argued both for and against using sampling or appropriation within her work. Although her critique of appropriation centers on the economic losses that African Americans have experienced due to cultural theft, her own work, especially *Funk Lesson*, borrows freely from African American cultural traditions.[56]

In the *Vanilla Nightmares* series, Adrian Piper freely samples from American popular culture. Despite her apparent ambivalence about appropriation art, she clearly samples from the *New York Times* and its advertisements. However, her own description of this work skips over words such as *appropriation* and *sampling* in favor of *selected* or *chosen*. Piper describes her artistic process as follows:

> The *Vanilla Nightmares* illuminate manuscripts selected from *The New York Times*. The manuscripts are chosen for their racially loaded content, their graphic imagery, their subliminal connotations, and the objective declarative voice in which they purport to speak. . . . With charcoal and oil crayon, I draw in the subauthoritarian news that's not fit to print.[57]

Much like hip-hop producers, Piper samples images and texts because they possess a truth not quite accessible to their creators. In the case of hip-hop music, producers and deejays liberate bass and drum lines lost under banal melodies. The original artists had missed the best or most interesting parts of their recordings, and copyright law imprisons these sections because it requires almost all samples—even brief ones—to be licensed. Sometimes deejays displayed their anger and/or comedic skills by establishing aural links that had gone unnoticed. Similarly, Piper attempts to show the un-spoken or unconscious images and narratives that allow dominant culture to make sense of these racialized images. Although stylistically distinct from graffiti art, the *Vanilla Nightmares* series operates much like graffiti because it disrupts the intended messages the advertisers and newspaper tried to convey. Graffiti art forces its viewers to recognize the ownership claims being made by historically marginalized people and acknowledge the stunning artistry of its practitioners. Piper's work functions similarly because it attempts to interrogate the nature of Western standards of beauty and demand a visual and narrative space within the *New York Times*.

*Vanilla Nightmares #18* (1987) provides an exemplary instance of Piper's reliance on sampling. In contrast to other drawings in the series, this image relies primarily on one sample: a print advertisement for American Express from the March 6, 1986, edition of the *New York Times*. This advertisement consists of a full page of white newsprint with the words "membership has its privileges" in large, capital letters, centered on the page. In small print, the advertisement states: "It is the privilege of knowing that, even though there is a number on the card, you will never be treated like a number by anyone at American Express." On top of this sampled image, Piper has drawn a crowd of bald, dark, male faces peering out at American Express's target audience. Despite some similarity among the faces, Piper has drawn subtle differences in bone structure, color, expression, and head shape in order to represent the faces as part of an undifferentiated mass for those who quickly view her image and as distinct individuals for those who care-fully scrutinize her work. Her drawings also feature a number of open hands that shield the dark faces from the brightness of the page, while also indicating these people's desire to be selected for membership. In the bot-tom right corner of the page, Piper does not simply sign her name but as-serts her ownership over the revised American Express advertisement and the *New York Times* by including the copyright sign next to her signature, much like Basquiat. The underlying political message of this artwork re-quires that the viewer knows that the advertisement is a real one that has been sampled, not a fake or a substitute one. Piper literally writes over both the *New York Times*, then the most prestigious paper in the United States, and American Express, then the most prestigious credit card. In both cases, Piper attempts to show that these institutions' very cultural importance follows from the subtle and unspoken ways that they continue to marginalize African American faces and voices from their products. Like Toni Morrison's and Anna Deavere Smith's, Piper's methodology requires sampling in order to challenge the unconscious racialization of American culture. Despite generic differences among literature, drama, and art, each relies on the same aesthetic structure to demand that her audience recognize the subtlety, intelligence, and humanity of African Americans. Interestingly, they all have chosen to sample others' stories or voices to articulate an African American perspective in the post–Civil Rights era.

Even though *Vanilla Nightmares #18* only relies on one sample, it nonetheless is a deeply layered image. Other pieces from the series include a variety of news stories and/or images. *Vanilla Nightmares #18*, however, only *appears* relatively thin because the sampled image and Piper's revision of it actually reveal the many layers of unconscious cultural narratives that shape the advertisement's meaning. The sampled image is actually a double sample. It is not simply an American Express advertisement, but one that appears at a particular spatial-temporal location in the most highly esteemed newspaper in the country. As her frequent analysis of the "indexical present" suggests, Piper "wanted to explore objects that can refer both to concepts and ideas beyond themselves and their standard functions, as well as to themselves."[58] In this instance, Piper clearly emphasizes the sample's original date, clearly within the post–Civil Rights era, and its location, the *New York Times*, by taking great care not to mark over these items as she did the rest of the page. By stressing its location within the *New York Times*, she suggests the tension between the articles this newspaper prints and the advertisements that support it. In this case, the supposedly liberal slant of the newspaper's coverage is undermined by its participation in the marketplace. Piper thus creates a certain ambiguity about the text from which she is sampling. On a second level, the image appears to provide a modern retelling of Plato's "Allegory of the Cave." As a Continental philosopher, Piper is clearly aware of this founding allegory of philosophy within Plato's *The Republic*, in which Plato describes how philosophy can enlighten those who seek the truth. In her contemporary revision of it, Piper depicts the seekers of knowledge as Diasporic Africans seeking to learn the truth of their condition. Ironically, they exit the cave of illusions when they see the

American Express advertisement, which "enlightens" them to their true position in society. Third, the mass of African American faces might connote to some viewers the Middle Passage and the continued disenfranchisement of African Americans during the current era. Although ostensibly only sampling one advertisement, Piper carefully layers historical, cultural, and philosophical arguments within her image to represent and critique the racialized nature of contemporary visual and popular cultures.

Piper's work not only contains layered samples but relies on rhythmic flows and asymmetries to further her ironic commentary on the *New York Times* and American Express. In *Vanilla Nightmares #18*, the appropriated or sampled image and her drawings on top of that image are interwoven, flowing almost seamlessly together even as they move in a jarring or asymmetrical way between mass culture and Piper's critique of that mass culture. The drawing requires this double effect or reading because it invokes multiple subjectivities that, according to Piper, necessarily conflict when they encounter the same object. Piper attempts to represent both flow and asymmetry simultaneously through her drawings because the viewer must be reminded of the original text and provided an avenue to see that text through new eyes. Like hip-hop music, this methodology enables the artist to produce new meanings out of extant and clichéd texts. As Schloss describes in his discussion of musical producers, Piper's approach allows her audience to hear and see according to the aesthetics of hip-hop. *Vanilla Nightmares #18* revels in the breaks between and among her revisionist drawing of the Middle Passage, the American Express advertisement, and the *New York Times*. Implicitly, she asks where the *New York Times* ends and her drawings begin and who can claim ownership over the unspoken but all too real relationship between American Express's advertising campaign and the continuing exclusion of many, if not most, African Americans from the American Dream.

Piper's answer, like Morrison's, is an ironic one. Although legal discourse suggests that the distinctions between competing property rights can be clearly delineated, Piper's entire corpus of art increasingly interrogates the spatial and temporal constraints that specify a text's meaning and its boundaries. Through the 1970s and 1980s, Piper explores the ambiguity of identity and property within her *Mythic Being* projects (1974–75); her installation work, *Art for the Art-World Surface Pattern* (1976); *Aspects of the Liberal Dilemma* (1978) and *Four Intruders Plus Alarm System* (1980); her performance piece *Funk Lessons* (1983); and the continuing *Vanilla Nightmares* series (1986–87). Drawing on her scholarly work on Immanuel Kant and merging it with her approach to art, Piper disrupts the conventional idea that an image possesses a distinct or singular meaning:

> I believe that in the case of any image the possibilities for interpretation are infinite. One way of directing the interpretation of an image is to rule out certain interpretations as being inadequate in various ways. I guess my sense is that it has to be, as I suggested earlier, based on the specifics of the particular, concrete situation that is occurring between two people who are interacting in the indexical present. One cannot prescribe such things as a general policy. . . . Political art presents the extra challenge of presenting content that is accessible, on the one hand, but sophisticated or ironic, on the other.[59]

Although her commitment to ambiguity and irony exemplifies postmodernism's impact on art and its critique of representation, this quotation highlights how Piper's commitment to racial justice and antiracism has caused her to develop methods or strategies that only appear to be postmodern. Piper, however, is critical of postmodernism for its ethical shortcomings[60] and because it enables white intellectuals to reify cultural difference as the *one* theory to explain social and cultural relations.[61]

Piper's art from this same period, however, exemplifies how concerns about racism's effects created the conditions for postmodern, postrepresentational, ironic art. Her installation *Four Intruders Plus Alarm Systems* attempts to exemplify, through sampled or appropriated language, the possible responses to images of black men. In it, the audience views images of African Americans and hears recordings of clichéd opinions (redneck, liberal, appropriative, etc.) about these images. Instead of "prescrib[ing] the politically correct one," Piper "delineates, and holds up for ridicule, what most black Americans agree are wrong (alienating, condescending, ignorant) responses."[62] *Four Intruders* thus constitutes an ironic narrative because it does not identify the moral failing that causes racism or the key trait to eradicate it. Rather, illustrating Deleuze's and Hutcheon's approaches to irony, Piper's art relies on ironic repetition to make racial difference visible by highlighting how a text's meaning is unstable and relies on the viewer to be completed. Commenting on her entire oeuvre, Robert Storr argues that Piper eschews tragic and romantic narratives to describe the condition of African Americans. Rather, she acknowledges that "the cruel givens of the collective situation in which we involuntarily share are not the work of the fates but the direct result of our illusions. If it is not en-

tirely within the grasp of logic to change the world, changing consciousness, which is the locus and origin of our crippling misperceptions, is."[63]
Storr identifies Piper's primary mode of narration as ironic precisely because it opens the possibility for reinscribing cultural history based on the
experiences of historically marginalized people.

Through her *Mythic Being* character and other strategies, Piper has
transformed her own person(a) into an art object that can criticize social
and cultural relations. Her *Self-Portrait Exaggerating My Negroid Features*
(1981) and *Self-Portrait as a Nice White Lady* (1995) reveal the "visual
pathology" of race by altering her appearance in subtle ways in order to
transform its racial meaning. Recounting the process behind her *Self-Portrait*, Piper offers:

> I sat in front of a mirror and drew myself, making certain key deci-
> sions at certain points of representation, so as to heighten certain
> features that are often associated with one's common image of what
> a black person looks like. I personally think there is no black person
> who corresponds to any stereotype about what Africans or African
> Americans look like.[64]

At one level, Piper makes clear that surface appearances, including her
own, do not possess a determinate meaning. At a second level, she aims to
implicate the viewer's preconceived ideas in shaping a text's meaning.

Lucy Lippard classifies Piper as a multicultural artist whose art emphasizes "turning around," or what I call irony. Lippard argues that "the effective turnaround is a doubling back rather than a collusion or a dispersion.
. . . Transformation of the self and society is finally the aim of all this mo-
bile work that spins the status quo around. While irony, with its tinge of
bitterness as well as humor, is the prevalent instrument, another is healing,
in which the artist, as neo-shaman, heals her or himself, as a microcosm of
the society."[65] Lippard's analysis makes clear that Piper's appropriations
constitute not just social criticism or deconstruction of social relations, but
an attempt to promote social transformation. This social transformation
begins with herself and the objects she works with in her art because healing herself requires claiming ownership over these representations. Piper's
ironic use of appropriated material both performs difference, as it reveals
hidden layers of meaning, and complicates the viewer's understanding of
consumer culture. Her work suggests how historically marginalized communities use and make meaning out of popular culture's imagery. Irony

empowers Piper because it allows her to deconstruct her cultural reality by revealing the ambiguity of texts, objects, and bodies. In addition, her work uncovers the unconscious influences shaping that social reality without reifying them into an irresistible force. Unlike tragic or romantic narrative modes, irony provides agency and autonomy precisely because its meaning cannot be fixed. Irony, like race itself, always signifies a double meaning, rejecting the rigid boundaries of either/or classifications that identity, art, and law have traditionally attempted to provide. Revealing these ambiguities provides Piper the imaginative space to revise dominant narratives and thus reclaim the right to "own" herself.

Reading *Beloved* and the *Vanilla Nightmare* series as complementary interventions into the cultural wars of the post–Civil Rights era suggests that claiming self- and cultural ownership, even after the Civil Rights Movement, requires African American textual producers to rewrite American history and visual culture. Although the NAACP's legal strategy ultimately led to court decisions and legislation that outlawed intentional discrimination in housing, employment, and other areas of life, Morrison's and Piper's work explores, in terms of both subject matter and aesthetics, how dominant white interests continued to claim American cultural discourses as de facto private property. A basic assumption of copyright law is that unowned texts remain in the public domain and can be reused and recycled as needed. African American activists, however, soon learned that the newly reconstituted legal discourse did not challenge extant cultural narratives that maintained cultural barriers, even as legal, political, and social ones had dismantled formal inequality. The post–Civil Rights era has made it apparent that the imaginary domain remains segregated, private property despite the legal victories of previous decades. African American writers, artists, musicians, and intellectuals have frequently relied on irony to show how color-blind rhetoric, the favored strategy of legal and cultural discourses, actually possesses a double meaning, in which racial hierarchy remains "hidden."

K. J. Greene, Olufunmilayo Arewa, Keith Aoki, and Stephen Best have recently examined how these "hidden" forms of racism or racialization constitute part of the foundation of copyright and trademark law. K. J. Greene observes that "an underlying assumption of race-neutrality pervades copyright scholarship. However, not all creators of intellectual property are similarly situated in a race-stratified society and culture. The history of Black music in America demonstrates the significant inequality of protection in the 'race-neutral' copyright regime."[66] Greene explores how inequalities in bargaining power and pervasive societal discrimination left most African American jazz, blues, and increasingly hip-hop musicians powerless to claim complete ownership of their creations. Record companies and producers found that a combination of contract and intellectual property law supplied them with the legal means to strip musicians of their ownership interests. Greene also claims that copyright law, due to its requirement that protected items be written or tangible texts, privileges Western forms of creativity, emphasizing composition over African American forms that tend to emphasize orality, improvisation, and performance. He suggests that African American cultural production follows different patterns and thus receives less protection from intellectual property law. Following Greene's analysis, Arewa shows how George Gershwin and his heirs could "own" his version of African American stylings in *Porgy and Bess* and other songs because his creativity focused on composing scores.[67] For Greene and Arewa, it is not simply formal legal doctrines but the social structure that produces the unequal distribution of ownership interests.

*Beloved* and the *Vanilla Nightmare* series anticipate these criticisms as they reveal how African Americans have entered property law too frequently as property to be owned or as trespassers to be excluded, rather than as owners. For Sethe, legal discourse, social institutions, and cultural relations come together to undermine any attempt to claim ownership over herself and her family. Baby Suggs, Sethe, Paul D, and even Denver disagree about exactly what kind of property claims they should make and what those claims might mean. Legal discourse provides little guidance for African Americans about claiming ownership rights, either through contract or through intellectual property law, primarily because they had little ability to participate in the crafting of official doctrine. Their experiences, institutions, and cultural traditions do not shape property law's normative assumptions. For Piper and today's hip-hop aesthetes, law continues to recognize the ownership of raced properties. Copyrights and trademarks still confer ownership rights over racialized images, texts, logos, and sounds. Hip-hop texts do not assume that racism or racialization has withered away or that legal discourse operates in a color-blind fashion. Rather, hip-hop aesthetics reveals how postmodernism's play and ambiguity stem from its reliance on the unconscious mapping of racism onto social relations. These samples recontextualize and thus make obvious what intellectual property law erases or hides. Thus, Piper completes the American Express advertisement by depicting the unspoken fear behind the company's famous slogan.

Providing a more thorough theoretical critique, Best argues that the long journey from an economic system based in slavery to one based in intellectual property rights reflects the ongoing conceptual problem of defining the relationships among the body, personhood, and property.[68] Over the course of the nineteenth and twentieth centuries—from the slavery that Morrison describes to the image culture of today, upon which Piper "draws" and comments—the theoretical elusiveness of defining personhood has evolved into new forms but remains tethered to property rights. For Best, a literary critic, the ambiguous relationship between bodies and authorial voice presents the challenge of speaking or writing authentically and establishing ownership of the self, its representations, and its expressions. As legal discourse frees legal personhood from particular bodies, their labor—both physical and mental—becomes increasingly available for commodification. As an example of his thesis, Best provocatively demonstrates how blackface minstrelsy becomes the trademarked act of T. D. Rice, a white performer in blackface, precisely because he mimics or copies "authentic" African American dancing practices, thereby breaking the link between a movement or ritual and its original performers.[69] Rice becomes the de facto owner precisely because he has transformed a communal ritual, based in shared knowledge and experience, into an easily consumed and commodified form. Racialized slavery is fundamental to capitalism's development and the legal infrastructure the country developed, Best argues, because it is the pervasive fiction of race that permits the distinction between legal persons and actual physical bodies. Best's analysis suggests a provocative explanation for Sethe's incomprehensible actions: she is not trying simply to save her children from slavery's horrors but to demonstrate their humanity despite the law's attempt to transform them and her into a commodity, thus refusing to acknowledge their legal personhood.

Best's study only examines property law through the *Plessy v. Ferguson* (1896) decision, but Best offers some provocative conclusions about how intellectual property law has become the contemporary battleground for distinguishing actual minds and bodies from legal persons possessing rights.[70] He also suggests that equality jurisprudence has followed property law's assumptions by distinguishing between persons and bodies. By doing so, equality has proven to be an empty standard for improving the conditions of those African Americans because its reliance on legal personhood rather than bodies has "made the world safer for commodified personhood than for universal freedom."[71] In her study about law and culture, Jane Gaines lays the groundwork for Best's conclusion. She argues that establishing property rights in cultural products constitutes the first step toward a de facto loss of ownership of those products for a cultural group.[72] Adrian Piper, in effect, illustrates Best's and Gaines's analysis by juxtaposing the trademarked slogan of American Express, a disembodied corporate entity but nonetheless a legal person, and images of African American men. Although Piper herself has never been directly sued over *Vanilla Nightmares #18*, American Express threatened to sue a publisher if it chose to use the image as the cover art for a book. In response, the publisher chose to include the image within the book, and American Express did not file suit.[73] Despite the drawing's imagery, the unconscious racialized fears upon which American Express's slogan plays have most likely affected many more people than Piper's revision of it has. As per Bent's argument, property law in effect preordains this outcome because the legal personhood conferred to American Express establishes its priority over the real bodies of African Americans, Adrian Piper, or the men depicted in her art. Piper, the philosopher and the artist, clearly understands the property implications in both her art and American culture because she signs this work with a copyright symbol, thereby attempting to assert her property rights over a racialized image and trademarked slogan. Despite recent efforts by African American cultural workers, such as Morrison and Piper, to speak the language of property rights, Best is skeptical. *The Fugitive's Properties* culminates with this final sentence: "To that extent, it seems reasonable to conclude, in matters of property as well as matters of right, that there are no rules."[74] The history of property discourses, according to Best, has developed increasingly abstract concepts of legal personhood, which fortify the distinction between legal subjects and actual bodies, thus furthering the marginalization of the disempowered.

In spite of Best's pessimism about the efficacy of property rights for fostering greater equality, African American artists have frequently asserted property claims within the post–Civil Rights era. The culture wars of the 1980s can be understood as a battle for ownership of and control over the intellectual domain from which individual people and the American people as a whole imagine themselves.[75] CRT, the primary response from legal scholars and activists of color during this period, appears more ambivalent about property law's potential. Like Morrison and Piper, CRT writers tend to adopt a cautious yet optimistic attitude that social change can happen even though the Civil Rights Movement did not realize all of its aims. Rather than suggesting a clean break with the Civil Rights Movement, critical race theorists and hip-hop aesthetes have learned from the

NAACP's overreliance on litigation as the key to social transformation. Increasingly, they have shifted their approach from legislative efforts to addressing the persistence of economic inequalities.

Responding to the same cultural dynamics that informed Morrison and Piper, Patricia Williams and other critical race theorists began embedding their legal criticisms within the forms of autobiography, fiction, and dialogue. Unlike their Civil Rights era precursors, they explicitly examine the relationships among cultural narratives, normative assumptions, and legal doctrines. Rather than adopt the more deconstructive tone of CLS, CRT attempts to "probe, mock, displace, jar, or reconstruct the dominant tale or narrative" in order to reconstruct these cultural assumptions and reconstruct legal discourse so that it might more effectively respond to those inequalities the Civil Rights Movement failed to address.[76] In *The Alchemy of Race and Rights*, Patricia Williams explores how Civil Rights era court decisions and legislation no longer provide sufficient remedies to the operation of racial hierarchy during the post–Civil Rights era. Irony proves to be a central feature of its critique. Seeking both to represent difference through repetition and to show how the experiences of minorities shape their social perspective, CRT demonstrates how putatively color-blind decisions and actions constitute de facto, unconscious, and discursive racism. These "new" forms of racism have replaced the intentional and legally enforced racism of earlier periods.

Similar to *Beloved* and the *Vanilla Nightmare* series, *Alchemy* sutures together a range of perspective issues and time periods within a single work. Williams also anticipates Stephen Best's focus on the shifting relations among body, personhood, and property. She uses a variety of anecdotes about ordinary events—what I have been labeling layered samples—as entry points to explore racialization and racism as quotidian phenomena that occur within well-trodden paths laid down by legal discourse, rather than as deviations from American culture. Williams's text moves from "what may have been the contract of sale for [her] great-great-grandmother" to her exclusion from a Benetton store, then engaged in an aggressive multicultural advertising campaign, and her difficulty in writing about this experience for law journals, to her reconstruction of a founding case in property law to demonstrate how cultural narratives influence notions of legal personhood and ultimately shape legal doctrine.[77] In each of these instances, the cultural fiction of race organizes social relations even if its influence remains unseen to most (white) people. Because the Civil Rights Movement focused primarily on voting rights, public accommodations, and housing issues, interventions into the construction of (intellectual) property discourses tended to fall outside its parameters. The Civil Rights Movement reviewed existing legal doctrines for their suitability for redeployment within its litigation strategy, not as racist artifacts to be modified or destroyed. To demonstrate the injustice of segregation and racism, the Civil Rights Movement displayed a tragic or romantic facade in which African Americans, especially of the middle class, existed as living saints, suffering hardships heroically. Because of this strategy, legal discourse and American culture more broadly accepted some changes in race relations so that those African Americans who proved themselves worthy could enter into dominant culture. Williams, however, specifically repudiates such romantic or tragic renderings of African American history or culture because she is attempting to create the discursive openings to reconstruct legal discourse for the daily struggles, both heroic and pedestrian, that ordinary folks face.

Not to diminish voting rights, housing segregation, or job discrimination, Williams attempts to show how race shapes nearly every interaction or contract, no matter how big or small, in which most African Americans engage with white people. To demonstrate the banality of race, Williams compares her attempt to rent an apartment in New York City with that of Peter Gabel, a white colleague and founder of CLS.[78] In the 1980s, when she writes, formal housing segregation is prohibited, and there are no longer designated white or black neighborhoods. Rather, individuals must make individual contracts to secure housing. Although there is no grand social policy driving residential patterns, race still shapes where and how people live. Gabel, as an adherent of CLS, believes that contract law impedes his effort to develop a mutually enriching agreement with a landlord and thus eschews a formal arrangement with clear rights. Williams, however, is skeptical of this approach because Gabel's trust in property law forgets or neglects how property law has tended to frame African Americans as anything but legitimate bearers of rights for more than two hundred years. Contrasting her experience with Gabel's and recounting their ongoing dialogue about it, she writes: "For blacks, then, the battle is not deconstructing rights, in a world of no rights; nor of constructing statements of need, in a world of abundantly apparent need. Rather, the goal is to find a political mechanism that can confront the *denial* of need."[79] For Williams, property law will necessarily play a significant role in the continued liberation of African Americans, but legal discourse will need to confront the violence against African Americans upon which it was built. Switching terminology, as CLS suggests, is unlikely to produce a real change in the material conditions of African Americans. Nor is it enough to say, as law and economics tend to suggest, that racism is inefficient in the long run because the skills of creative and hard-working people and money-making opportunities will be lost or underutilized, so the market will ultimately persuade all but the most racist individuals to stop discriminating. This might be true if current property and contract law had developed strategies "to become multilingual in the semantics of evaluating race" or to recognize irony.[80] However, because property law operates in a fairly abstract manner, it favors abstracted legal persons who are disinterested, who operate in transactions at arm's length, and who tend to follow Anglo-American cultural traditions. Claiming rights within the public sphere requires not only access to that sphere, which stands as the primary achievement of the Civil Rights Movement, but a reconstruction of the imaginary resources available within it and greater freedom in how those resources may be deployed. The Civil Rights Movement laid the foundation for including foundational texts about the African American experience and presenting a less idealized representations of black life. Hip-hop aesthetes have sought to complete this reconstruction of the imaginary domain. The resulting texts, as a result, frequently examine the meaning of ownership and the distribution of property rights

One goal of post–Civil Rights era cultural production, such as Morrison's, Piper's, and Williams's, is to represent these varied histories and traditions and suggest how existing institutional and discursive frameworks elide the experiences of historically marginalized people. Although the Civil Rights Movement achieved its greatest success when making claims based on abstract moral principles, contemporary artists, writers, and intellectuals have adopted a less idealistic and more realistic tone in order to demonstrate the relative failures of settled legal doctrines. Contemporary African American cultural production increasingly focuses on materialism, despite its connection with immorality, because abstract rights without material consequences constitute empty promises. Patricia Williams concludes *The Alchemy of Race and Rights* by reflecting on the relationship between rights and power:

> In the law, rights are islands of empowerment. To be unrighted is to be disempowered, and the line between rights and no-rights is most often the line between dominators and [the] oppressed. Rights contain images of power and manipulating those images, either visually

or linguistically, is central in the making and maintenance of rights. In principle, therefore, the more dizzyingly diverse the images that are propagated, the more empowered we will be as a society.[81]

For Williams, the creation of any property regime relies, either consciously or unconsciously, on a distinct configuration of language and images. Although she makes no mention of either Morrison or Piper, Williams articulates the stakes in their efforts to claim ownership over a portion of visual and literary culture. In addition to sharing a historical moment and some aesthetic characteristics, these works engage with and provide alternative lenses for viewing law's influence on contemporary culture.

In reading *Beloved* against the *Vanilla Nightmare* series in the context of CRT, the causes of the 1980s culture wars become clearer. The imaginative resources of literary, visual, and even legal culture had become implicated in the social reconstruction project begun during the Civil Rights Movement, and the political and social changes necessitated a cultural transformation. As Morrison noted just after publishing *Beloved*: "Canon building is Empire building. Canon defense is national defense. Canon debate, whatever the terrain, nature and range . . . is the clash of cultures. And *all* of the interests are vested."[82] In this frequently cited essay, Morrison specifically frames debates about culture as debates about property discourse. According to Morrison, critics, especially white and male ones, have neglected the hidden African American presence in canonical literature in order to claim exclusive ownership in American literature. Her task in this essay and in her fiction is to reveal that ghostly presence and examine how it has disfigured the American cultural imagination. Similarly, Henry Louis Gates views the culture wars as a battle between those who wish to see the canon as personal property and those who can imagine a pluralist alternative of shared ownership. Gates argues that "pluralism sees culture as porous, dynamic, and interactive, rather than as the fixed property of particular ethnic groups."[83]

Despite modernity's attempt to distinguish realms of knowledge as discrete disciplines, African American cultural workers have used similar forms to break these discursive boundaries down and show how disciplinary structures form an interlocking framework for creating and maintaining racial and cultural hierarchy. Hip-hop aesthetics, rather than ing a break from the Civil Rights Movement, may be its cul because perhaps the only way to realize the movement's social an

goals is through a cultural transformation that necessitates a reconstruction of the property concept. By examining ownership in literature and visual culture, Morrison and Piper contribute to the development of aesthetic practices that might engage productively with the turn from civil to
property rights within dominant legal discourse. Their attempts to claim
ownership reveal the normative assumptions that have long dominated
property law. As Gates suggests, the pluralist conception of culture views
tradition and extant texts as inspirational and as the raw materials for future
innovations. Of course, this pluralist approach has come into increasing
conflict with how intellectual property law has structured the rules for fair-
use copying and secondary uses. Not unsurprisingly, the next generation of
artists, writers, and musicians is grappling with these questions.

## CHAPTER 5

# "Fair Use" and the Circulation
# of Racialized Texts

It was white theft of black culture that most moved the group
to anger and eventually to action.

—Derrick Bell, *Gospel Choirs*

In his groundbreaking *Harvard Law Review* article examining post–Civil
Rights era Supreme Court decisions, Derrick Bell challenges the normative assumptions of legal discourse.[1] Anticipating concerns articulated by
participants from the first CRT workshop, Bell predicts that CLS's deconstruction of rights discourse will prove insufficient to challenge the racism
and racialization of the post–Civil Rights era. Even though Bell began his
career within the Civil Rights Movement, he argues that conservative (and
even some liberal) responses to the NAACP's legal victories necessitate a
revised strategy for transforming social and cultural relations. To illustrate
the limits of existing civil rights legislation, Bell creates fictitious inter-
locutors, such as Geneva Crenshaw and Jesse Semple, who show the limited improvement in the material conditions of ordinary or average African
Americans. These writings layer disparate voices into conversations that
ebb and flow to reveal an ironic reading of legal discourse.

Bell's characters examine the violence and inequalities that found
American jurisprudence. In the opening chapter of *And We Are Not Saved*
(1987), Bell relies on a science fiction device to transport Geneva Cren-

shaw, a movement lawyer who now questions the NAACP's litigation strategy, back to the Constitutional Convention of 1787. Her journey's purpose is to convince the delegates to remove the document's implicit acceptance of slavery.[2] The dialogue between Crenshaw and the founders explores how traditional doctrinal remedies to racism respond to the symptoms of inequalities, not their causes. Bell's writings suggest that the founders' commitment to property rights undermined the constitutional promise of freedom and equality. The fictional Crenshaw asks the founders: "Do you not mind that your slogans of liberty and individual rights are basically guarantees that neither a strong government nor the masses will be able to interfere with your property rights and those of your class?"[3] In Bell's retelling, the founders cannot conceive of any way to create a constitutional structure that could deracialize property law and also provide for a stable government.[4] This decision, according to Bell, created a permanent disadvantage for African Americans and placed property law above civil rights law within American legal discourse. Throughout his provocative writings, Bell returns to property rights and economic inequalities as the fundamental challenge of the post–Civil Rights era.[5]

For Bell, cultural products, whether music, art, or literature, document and serve as catalysts in the African American struggle for political and economic equality. In *Gospel Choirs* (1996), Bell relies on gospel music to anchor his legal critique and demonstrate how this musical form continues to provide spiritual sustenance. Bell does not, however, ignore hip-hop's importance to the post–Civil Rights generation.[6] As one element of the book's thought experiment, Bell imagines in the chapter "Racial Royalties" that a group of "talented scientists and computer programmers" have been passed over for promotions in favor of "less impressive white co-workers."[7] These African Americans "devise a means of metering the greater society's use of cultural expressions of subordinated peoples of color" and then charge a royalty fee for companies that borrow cultural styles without licensing or attributing them.[8] These programmers and scientists then distribute these royalties to advocacy groups, cultural centers, and not-for-profit agencies. Pretty quickly, corporations notice the loss of revenue because many of their profits derive from the commodification of African American styles. The group produces a documentary to defend their actions and demand legal change:

> "This nation has long urged people of color to lift themselves by their own bootstraps," one of the group reminded the audience.

"Such admonitions were repeated even when the nation knew, or should have known, that the boots of many of those people were nailed to the floor by poverty, by lack of education, by racial hatred. We have simply done as society urged, and we have done it on terms that, based on history, society should recognize—the involuntary taking of property. As victims of such takings throughout this country's history, we find it amusing that the nation now calls us thieves and condemns us."[9]

The early 1990s copyright cases about the legality of hip-hop sampling constitute the unspoken context of Bell's thought experiment for returning ownership over African American cultural products to the African American community. *Gospel Choirs* insists that established property law doctrines, especially copyright and trademark, continue to benefit the white majority. Bell's interest convergence thesis, developed throughout his writings, argues that the Civil Rights Movement succeeded in making changes when the interests of blacks and whites converged. In practice, this has meant that those policies that benefited whites tended to become law, but that those that would have helped African Americans and other minorities exclusively languished.[10]

"Racial Royalties" anticipates recent concerns about the dilution of copyright's approach to fair use. It also implicitly questions whether law's normative assumption of doctrinal color-blindness has ever existed, especially within copyright law. In particular, "Racial Royalties" wonders about what exactly has constituted "fair" about "fair use" for African American cultural workers. As a metaphor to describe the relationship between initial creators and later artists, copyright law has generally treated African American musicians poorly. Bell's "Chronicle of the Constitutional Contradiction" depicts the difficulty African American critics and artists face in redressing long-standing racism and racialization. In Bell's fictive account of the Constitutional Convention, a founder asks Crenshaw, "How dare you insert yourself in these deliberations?"[11] In effect, the delegate argues that Bell's reuse of the Constitutional Convention is unfair because it alters *his* understanding of the event's purpose and meaning. Although it is not the direct subject of that chronicle, Bell inaugurates a critique of "fair use" by sampling speeches, characters, and songs in his work. In his rendering, fair use constitutes both an aesthetic principle, in which tradition is rewoven, and a doctrinal problem involving competing racial and cultural subjectivities.

This chapter examines Colson Whitehead's *John Henry Days* and the paintings of Michael Ray Charles to evaluate how hip-hop aesthetes deconstruct "fair-use" appropriations of racialized imaginative properties. Whitehead's and Charles's work questions how property law distributes ownership rights over copyrighted or trademarked material and seeks to reveal how fair use itself constitutes a racialized doctrine, which courts apply in a racially conscious manner even as they claim to engage in a universal and color-blind analysis.[12] This deconstruction and reconstruction of fair use criticizes the simplistic theories about textual meaning and creativity underlying intellectual property law. For hip-hop aesthetes, intellectual property law cannot easily regulate such meanings without reifying a text's racialized meaning, thus creating a false-origins myth to legitimate a particular distribution of property rights. Contemporary African American cultural workers demand, ironically, stronger intellectual property rights to protect African American culture even as they question copyright's historic complicity with racism, racialization, and racial hierarchy.

## Fair Use

Copyright law regulates who can reproduce, distribute, or authorize a copy or a derivative text.[13] However, because intellectual property law provides only a limited monopoly—not the exclusive ownership of chattel or real property—common law and federal legislation permit fair-use copying under certain conditions. The U.S. Code offers a four-factor test to determine fair use that examines:

(1) the purpose and character of the use, including whether such use is of a commercial nature or is for nonprofit educational purposes;

(2) the nature of the copyrighted work;

(3) the amount and substantiality of the portion used in relation to the copyrighted work as a whole; and

(4) the effect of the use upon the potential market for or value of the copyrighted work.[14]

There is not a single rule for determining whether a particular use is fair. Rather, courts must balance these various factors. Reviewing cases decided by appellate courts between 1994 and 2002, David Nimmer argues that "courts tend first to make a judgment that the ultimate disposition is fair use or unfair use, and then align the four factors to fit that result as best they can."[15] He also concludes that positive findings about factors 1 and 3 slightly increased the likelihood of a fair-use determination, but that a party did not need to prevail on a majority of factors to win their claim.[16] Because Nimmer's analysis includes cases whose controversies extend beyond the scope of this study, his results do not speak directly to either the racialization of intellectual properties or legal discourse's attitude toward hip-hop aesthetics. They do, however, make clear the ambiguous nature of fair-use doctrine and its potential complicity in further empowering those with greater cultural and economic capital. Nimmer's study does not capture how the ambiguity of fair-use doctrine shapes the decisions of artists, agents, publishing companies, gallery owners, and music companies. It is quite likely that copyright law's ambiguity chills some protected artistic activity because people fear litigation. This is especially true for many African American artists, writers, and musicians who historically and still overwhelmingly lack sufficient cultural and economic capital to bargain effectively with either distribution companies or copyright owners.

Many legal commentators have suggested revisions to fair use to better balance the rights of creators and the public and to further democratic dialogue about social, political, economic, and cultural issues. For example, Julie Cohen has argued that the concept of the user has been underdeveloped within copyright law, overemphasizing the owner as the primary focus of legislation and doctrine. In an attempt to remedy this deficit, Cohen has theorized about the "situated user" (as opposed to the economic, romantic, or postmodern user) who "appropriates cultural goods found within her immediate environment for four primary purposes: consumption, communication, self-development, and creative play."[17] In her provocative analysis, the situated user provides a counterweight against copyright's focus on the owner. Cohen recognizes that the public incorporates cultural texts into their own lives, shaping their identities and their worldviews.[18] She argues that this should be permitted because it "fosters collective progress."[19]

Similarly, Laura Bradford suggests that courts apply insights from cognitive research to copyright jurisprudence. Attempting to create a brighter line rule regarding secondary uses, instead of what fair-use doctrine currently offers, and one that better protects users' rights, Bradford develops a legal doctrine based on psychology's insight that "our general attitudes toward iconic works, which are most often the subject of disputes, are resistant to change."[20] Rather than the current four-factor test, Bradford suggests that courts should evaluate secondary uses based upon (1) attitude resistance, (2) source effects, (3) frequency effects, and (4) processing hierarchy.[21] Within this framework, the likelihood that a copy would change a user's attitude based on the secondary source's credibility, the frequency with which the user would encounter the secondary copy, and the amount of time it takes to process the copied item would all affect the outcome of the fair-use inquiry. The quicker a user could process the copy, the more an infringing use would be suggested. Bradford's approach attempts to evaluate how the viewer's perception of the original text is changed by the copying.[22]

In their attempts to find a better balance between owners and users within fair-use doctrine, Cohen and Bradford create legal doctrine based upon a more robust conception of the user. Their frameworks would constitute significant improvements over current legal analysis because they portray individuals not as passive receptacles but as active agents shaping their world. Despite their proposals' strengths, they still tend to conceive of the user as an ahistorical agent, who exists independently of the copyrighted and trademarked texts, images, and sounds that populate cultural life. Cohen and Bradford suggest that individual users can deploy intangible properties however they wish. Contra this assumption, this book attempts to demonstrate how some users layer samples in literary, audio, and visual texts in rhythmic patterns and breaks, based on their understanding of hip-hop aesthetics, an extant cultural practice. While individuals certainly make distinct choices to improvise from and revise the underlying aesthetic paradigm, cultural boundaries appear to play a greater role than either Cohen or Bradford suggests. Although both recognize the increasing importance that imaginative properties play in allowing people to develop self-identities, they neglect how such texts, images, and sounds colonize people's bodies, regardless of people's attempts at self-definition. Much contemporary African American cultural production conceives of American culture not as an imaginative commons or public domain where individuals can fashion an identity for themselves without outside interference, but as a prison where freedom can be found only by resisting social conventions. While Cohen and Bradford appear to liberate and legalize certain kinds of copying, Regina Austin argues that hip-hop finds freedom precisely because it "flaunt[s] the laws of private property."[23] Austin is not arguing that all hip-hop devotees constitute criminals, but that the aesthetic demands of hip-hop rely for their very meaning on breaking certain stylistic and/or legal boundaries. Hip-hop aesthetics—especially as explored by Colson Whitehead and Michael Ray Charles—assumes a more ambivalent user than the one posited by Cohen and Bradford. Whitehead and Charles examine how extant copyrighted and trademarked properties shape raced individuals and seek to reconstruct the unfair uses that have furthered the racialization of the imaginative realm. In their critical reworking, fair use may constitute a problematic metaphor because it assumes that identity and subjectivity exist prior to property relations.

## John Henry Days

Colson Whitehead's *John Henry Days* begins with a prologue that arranges a series of samples from scholarly works that explore the origins of the folk song "John Henry." The song details a steel-driving contest between an African American worker and a newly invented machine. John Henry wins the contest but then dies, suggesting that a machine-driven modernity is destroying what is precious about humanity. Whitehead's novel then describes, in hilarious fashion, the efforts of J. Sutter, the novel's protagonist and a modern-day John Henry, a son of Striver's Row in Harlem, to secure receipts to pad his reimbursements from publishing and advertising outlets. The novel proceeds to narrate J. Sutter's visit to Talcott, West Virginia, as part of a public relations junket to write a story for an Internet site about the town's John Henry festival, which coincides with the U.S. Post Office's release of a John Henry stamp. Over the course of the book, Whitehead introduces his readers to various fragments in the John Henry myth's journey, from Henry's thoughts before his famous battle with the machine, to the composer who copyrighted his version of the song, to Paul Robeson's failed play about the hero. He also explores the world of publicists, stamp collectors, and freelance writers. J. Sutter also encounters and begins a romantic relationship with Pamela Street, the ambivalent heir to her father's collection of John Henry memorabilia. Street, a New Yorker like J. Sutter, is considering selling her inheritance to the town so that she can unload this unwanted legacy.

In addition to its other intersecting plotlines, the novel focuses on J. Sutter's thought process as he endeavors to break the record for nonstop junketeering, a contemporary analogue to John Henry's competition with a machine. Sutter must negotiate the demands of the information age, the

Internet, and intellectual property law, in which man continues to battle for his humanity against the increasing commodification of information and culture. Unlike John Henry, however, Sutter decides to opt out of his own battle with intellectual death, or what the novel describes as being "devoured by pop," after journeying with Pamela Street to the supposed location of John Henry's original battle with the machine. They also visit Henry's likely grave atop a local mountain where the railroad company buried the bodies of African American workers who died during the construction of the Big Bend Tunnel, the site of the mythical battle between John Henry and the machine. Street buries the ashes of her father there and decides to sell the town her father's collection. Sutter and Street then disappear into an indescribable future, as they have apparently shed history's weight. The novel ends when Sutter and Street leave the festival before it reaches its ceremonial height. Through a series of hints, Whitehead suggests that the planned apogee in this celebration of John Henry goes awry when Alphonse Miggs, a collector specializing in railroad stamps, decides to use this occasion to shoot himself and an unspecified number of those attending the gathering. The novel thus does not provide a clear resolution to its main conflicts but implies that the cultural logic underlying the John Henry myth must be transcended so that the main characters can find real freedom and escape the ubiquitous and pernicious influence of popular culture.

Although the novel provides a kaleidoscopic view of American history and culture, Whitehead devotes considerable narrative attention to the intellectual property issues that the information age has provoked. Like Smith's *Twilight—Los Angeles, 1992*, Morrison's *Beloved*, and Piper's *Vanilla Nightmares* series, *John Henry Days* displays the signs of hip-hop aesthetics: layered samples, rhythmic flows and asymmetries, and an ironic narrative mode. Beyond claiming ownership over imaginative properties, including John Henry, Whitehead reflects upon how such texts get transformed as they move through American culture. Regardless of the original intent or meaning behind his story, African Americans and cultural outsiders have used John Henry as a cultural resource to explore what it means to be human—for some what it means to be a raced being—in both the industrial and the information ages. In this hip-hop and postmodern version, John Henry the steel-driving man constitutes a familiar rhythm or narrative that has become cliché or stale. Writers and artists must deconstruct and reconstruct this tale to carve out narrative space to capture the challenges and choices of contemporary life.[24] By laying down sampled versions of

John Henry as the basis of his hip-hop revisionist version, Whitehead implicitly criticizes copyright's fair-use doctrine because it fails to account for how texts, especially racialized ones, produce cultural memory, influence future creative activity, and shape individual identities. Whitehead also reminds legislators and judges that limited copyright protections proved more than sufficient motivation or incentive for the hundreds of musicians, storytellers, playwrights, and visual artists who fashioned their own John Henrys, even if those rules limited the ownership rights of these cultural workers in their creations. His critique of copyright suggests that a narrowly constructed fair-use doctrine would impede, if not prohibit, certain cultural forms and the critical conversation around those forms.[25]

The novel documents how the circulation of the John Henry myth through several genres enriched American culture, writ large, even as it failed to alleviate the relative economic poverty of African Americans. Whitehead never states that fair use and the distribution of ownership interests within copyright or property law constitutes a primary theme of *John Henry Days*, but the circulation of imaginative properties and the economic effects of that movement always remain central to the novel's narrative trajectory. Since Reconstruction, or the putative 1872 contest between John Henry and the machine, intellectual property laws have consistently favored those white individuals who wrote down, composed, drew, or marketed the story over those African American individuals who lived or experienced it.[26] Whitehead sprinkles evidence of this redistribution of ownership rights over the American imaginary domain throughout the novel. In what appeared to some initial reviewers as extraneous material, Whitehead attempts to illustrate the many ways that African American creativity got transformed into other people's intellectual property, owned by fictional individuals such as Jack Rose, who copyrighted his version of the song after overhearing a pedestrian humming a version, or Andrew Goodman, who offered to record a traveling bluesman's version of the song.[27] A nameless participant in the writing of the John Henry folk song opines: "Like a dollar bill it changes hands. Others will hear it and add a verse, goose the rhythm, slow it down to fit their mood . . . . This is his own John Henry."[28] In a humorous rant by Dave Brown, one of the senior statesmen among the junketeers, Whitehead reminds his readers how the Rolling Stones began their careers by borrowing riffs and lyrics from Mississippi bluesmen.[29]

In addition to these individual actions whereby specific white creators appropriate and profit from African American culture, Whitehead emphasizes time and again how institutions and corporations borrow select images of African American life whenever it's convenient. One of the junke-teers, Tiny, remembers that his elementary school read kindergartners a version of John Henry after the local school board determined that *Little Black Sambo* contained negative imagery about African Americans.[30] The U.S. Post Office's use of folk heroes most obviously exemplifies this at-tempt to circulate a popular image of African American life,[31] even if this event attracted relatively few African Americans.[32] Pamela Street and J. Sutter even encounter and reflect upon a John Henry statue designed and built by Talcott's Ruritan club after they persuaded Johnny Cash to donate money for their statue because he mistakenly identified Beckley, West Vir-ginia, as John Henry's home.[33] Pamela muses after viewing the statue: "He is open to interpretation. Talking out of both sides of his mouth. You hear what you want to hear." Whitehead then adds that Pamela "is confusing the statue before her with the man, and the man with her conception of the man."[34] To further the irony, J. recognizes this particular John Henry statue because Jim Beam licensed from Ruritan the use of this image for one of its whiskey bottles.[35] Whitehead deploys these textual moments to demonstrate how cultural properties circulate far beyond copyright's as-sumptions about the flow of cultural materials.

*John Henry Days* also serves as an intellectual property ghost story on at least two levels. First, Josie, one of the white owners of the Talcott Motor Lodge, where J. Sutter, Pamela Street, and the junketeers stay, knows that a ghost haunts the motel and the region. Through her, Whitehead relates: "The first ghost any child of the region hears of is John Henry. Each time a train leaves the Talcott station and rushes into Big Bend Tunnel, the en-gineer blows the whistle for old John Henry, poor John Henry."[36] Josie, however, is convinced that there is a ghost, apparently John Henry's, living in the hotel and disturbing guests. She is concerned about the weekend of the John Henry festival because they have booked all of the rooms, mean-ing that the ghost will likely inhabit a guest's room. After searching for some clues, she suspects that the ghost will haunt room 27, J. Sutter's room.[37] Of course, the ghost shares a room with J. Sutter, as he constitutes a contemporary analog for John Henry. Second, the ghost of John Henry haunts Pamela Street as an ambivalent inheritance. For Pamela, the novel details her attempt to heal the wounds associated with her father's obses-sion with John Henry memorabilia, a bizarre contest of his own construc-tion in which he pitted his own commitment to the folk hero against the world's neglect and misunderstanding.[38] Her father filled Pamela's child-hood home with the ghostly presence of John Henry. The memorabilia crowded out her needs and snuffed out Pamela's and her mother's dreams for the future because of her father's obsession with John Henry and the past. In both instances, the ghost of John Henry constitutes an unwanted paradigm for perseverance in a racialized world as Pamela and J. Sutter seek freedom from historical limitations endured by their parents and grandparents. By selecting John Henry and the many iterations of his story as a primary metaphor for the historical legacy inherited by African Americans, Whitehead fuses the common theme of historical racism with more contemporary concerns about intellectual property law.

Whitehead's exploration of John Henry's legacy offers a surprisingly rich cultural matrix from which to explore the efficiency and ethics of fair-use doctrine. As discussed above, intellectual property law relies on four factors (purpose, nature, amount, and market effect) to determine whether a particular instance of copying constitutes infringement. Enacted in 1976, this legislation was passed by Congress to codify fair-use doctrine because a conflicting body of case law had emerged. The legislative history suggests the many concerns, from educational use to parody, that shaped the specific language adopted. The linked concepts of culture, cultural matrix, and/or cultural formations, however, are conspicuously absent, because in 1976 few American scholars had yet adopted cultural studies as a primary method for understanding texts. As many others have noted, copyright law generally reflects a romantic conception of authorship in which a genius creates in isolation with full consciousness and knowledge about her creation. Fair-use doctrine generally shares these assumptions, even if later scholarly investigations of cultural and imaginative texts by the Birmingham school and their American progeny question this founding truth of intellectual property law. Given the many powerful criticisms of the romantic model of authorship, it would be redundant to simply add *John Henry Days* to the already long list of works that rebut this theory due to liberal use and refashioning of extant cultural objects and texts.

Rather, Whitehead's engagement with cultural icons reflects a more specific criticism of fair use: how copyright confers ownership rights in racialized and often stereotyped images that dominate popular memory and shape individual identities. Examined through the lens of racialization and the long history of racial caricatures within American culture, the appropriation of images, whether moving the characters from Harriet Beecher Stowe's *Uncle Tom's Cabin* into minstrel shows or Public Enemy's satirical rendering of *Driving Miss Daisy* in "Burn, Hollywood, Burn," illustrates the false binaries that fair-use doctrine arranges because it ignores the racialized nature of imaginative properties. The 1976 congressional codification of fair-use doctrine addressed neither the systematic redistribution of ownership rights over African American cultural forms nor the complicity of culture industries' perpetuation of racial hierarchy. Rather, it sought to provide clearer guidance for institutional and corporate actors as commerce in intellectual properties burgeoned. In this context, cultural influences or effects had little relevance to Congress's deliberations, even if the unacknowledged circulation of racialized texts frequently creates the very value intellectual property owners wish to capture. Racialized images, characters, and sounds possess meaning and thus market value precisely because they trade on the preexisting recognition of stereotypes and caricatures.

Fair use's first factor divides potential uses into two categories: commercial purposes or nonprofit educational purposes.[39] While courts tend not to apply this as a strict binary and recognize that these categories overlap, the concepts of culture, cultural memory, and cultural formation are conspicuously absent. Although scholars, intellectuals, and activists have vigorously debated its meaning recently, culture cannot be reduced to merely commerce, education, or some synthesis of the two. Rather, culture involves shared ideologies, habits, rituals, objects, practices, beliefs, values, and/or communal attitudes toward texts and textuality. Most cultural critics conceive of these items as public-domain property, in effect, because they form the basis of public communication, understanding, and social institutions. Susan Scafidi, Michael Brown, and others have attempted to develop concepts of communal ownership for cultural properties in order to enrich indigenous and minority cultures whose knowledge, artistic products, and rituals have become prized commodities by outsiders. This approach, however, privileges traditional practices and knowledge over ongoing developments and the vibrant expressions of living cultural groups. In October 2005, the United Nations Educational, Scientific, and Cultural Organization (UNESCO) adopted a convention in which it ratified the importance of fostering a diversity of cultural expression and urged states to protect, maintain, and promote diverse cultural expressions.[40] The UNESCO convention illustrates the limitations of the commerce-education binary offered by the first factor in fair-use analysis. It suggests that a third purpose should guide fair-use inquiries: the promotion of diverse cultural expressions. Whitehead's deployment of John Henry illustrates the importance of constructing a fair-use doctrine that validates and promotes a rich cultural imaginary in which potentially copyrighted texts, images, and sounds can be recrafted to speak to contemporary dilemmas.

Even though *John Henry Days* clearly possesses a commercial purpose, it explores and creates an imaginative universe that reveals the shifting tensions facing African Americans specifically and all Americans more generally. The segregation and intentional racism of the Industrial Revolution have morphed into the putatively color-blind but nonetheless racialized information age. In its own way, *John Henry Days* educates its audience about changing conditions of economic production and organization. However, it can be best understood as part of an ongoing cultural dialogue both within the African American community and across racial lines. Although Whitehead could have written about these ideas without reference to John Henry, the transformation of this mythic tale and moral fable for contemporary readers provides a particularly compelling and revealing articulation of current economic, cultural, social, political, and psychological challenges. As the ambiguous ending suggests, some images must become museum relics so that specific individuals can be liberated from the cruel hand of history. Any "fair-use" analysis must engage with the commercialization of cultural products by outsiders, the racialized effects of protected images, and the continuing need to refashion symbols and metaphors based on contemporary events and challenges. Because the fair-use doctrine does not specifically or consciously explore the effects of protected texts, images, and sounds, it neglects the very conditions and structures that give cultural objects meaning and importance.

The second factor of fair-use analysis explores the nature of the copyrighted work.[41] Arguably, this allows courts to explore the cultural relations a specific text invokes. For example, the U.S. Supreme Court found that 2 Live Crew's "Pretty Woman" constituted a parody of Roy Orbison's song and thereby needed to copy substantial portions of it to perform its satiric function. The predictable result of this decision has been that parodies receive considerable latitude in fair-use decisions when compared to other genres or forms. The court's decision in this case, however, distinguished parody from other satiric forms, arguing that satire alone does not provide license to copy material because the articulated criticism does not specifically address or is limited to the appropriated text.[42] Analyzing this decision, David Sanjek concludes that Judge David Souter's opinion implicitly permits artists to refashion texts for criticism and transformative uses.[43] In this decision, Judge Souter makes it quite clear that "this is not, of course, to say that anyone who calls himself a parodist can skim the cream and get away scot free."[44] For Souter, what permits 2 Live Crew's appropriation of Roy Orbison's song is not that it transforms the song from romance to irony but that it effects a parody, a distinct form within the ironic mode.

Courts typically rely on the second factor of the fair-use test to determine whether a work is fiction or nonfiction and quickly move onto the third factor. In determining a text's nature, courts tend to rely on common-sense approaches even if there exists considerable scholarly debate about how best to classify a given text. For example, in *SunTrust Bank v. Houghton Mifflin*, the court determined that *Gone With the Wind* was fiction and that it required a high level of protection.[45] Hip-hop aesthetics, however, suggests that a text's meaning is invariably related to its context and its narrative mode. The *SunTrust* court acknowledged that Alice Randall's *The Wind Done Gone* "de-mystified" and "stripped the romanticism" from Margaret Mitchell's *Gone With the Wind*.[46] Although both parties offered considerable expert testimony about the nature of Randall's work and whether it was parody, signifyin', or just plain copying, neither party needed to present testimony about the nature of Mitchell's novel. Because the two differed in narrative mode (romance vs. irony/satire), the texts operate in necessarily conflicting ways. The court's final decision, however, tended to omit the considerable academic debate about the relationship between the two works in favor of a common-sense perspective. The court cautioned that "literary relevance [or meaning] is a highly subjective analysis ill-suited for judicial inquiry."[47] The court reluctantly concluded that when copyright-infringement claims and defenses invoke aesthetic interpretations, legal discourse cannot easily render clear and efficient guidance.

In *John Henry Days*, Whitehead contributes to ongoing discussions about fair use by examining the relationships among texts, their predecessors, and the cultural relations that give those texts meaning. By charting the many renderings of John Henry, Whitehead suggests that cultural context defines the nature of a copyrighted text. Because particular cultural sensibilities are crystallized in songs, images, and stories, their very existence hinges upon their relationship to an interpretative community. Whitehead explores how the relationship between text and context determines a work's meaning. For example, Pamela Street's father's museum, as a private collection, fails to attract visitors and eventually estranges him from his family because the objects and songs lack a clear narrative context other than his own obsession.[48] Mr. Street's museum that lacks visitors illustrates the dangers of severing a text from its cultural moorings. Street's collection of John Henry memorabilia has become disconnected from the cultural formations that gave the song its initial meaning. Street desperately wanted to absorb the romantic/tragic myth associated with early versions of the song. However, Whitehead makes all too clear that these narrative modes no longer speak to contemporary sensibilities. Instead, he frequently invokes irony to depict contemporary culture.[49] For this reason, John Henry achieves considerable popularity as postmodern pastiche, a postage stamp, and the inspiration for a town's marketing plan.

Contemporary ironic appropriations of John Henry differ qualitatively from earlier borrowings because they alter our understanding and attitude toward the original folk tale and its cultural meaning. In these iterations, corporate actors have refashioned or reconstructed John Henry into a new object, related to but distinct from earlier versions. By contrast, Whitehead's fictional Jake Rose, the Tin Pan Alley–style composer, simply wrote down the melody and lyrics he overheard sung by a nameless African American on the street.[50] Earlier in the novel, Whitehead describes the creative process of a nameless singer/songwriter who is developing his own John Henry. The musician reflects upon his efforts in crafting his version of the song: "He's practically stealing the song today; it's not his but he's got his fingers on it and that's half the battle."[51] A page later, this nameless composer acknowledges that his is just one version in which each artist struggles to fashion a John Henry that represents his or her experience.[52] Jake Rose does not seek to bare his soul. He does not care why a song is popular. Rather, he just wants to get a start in the music business by whatever means necessary.[53] For legal discourse, the difference between these two composers may be difficult, if not impossible, to distinguish. However, in the realm of creation and cultural expression, such distinctions allow one artist to be viewed as real, while another will be viewed as a fraud. Even if law cannot detect these fine differences, many audiences can. For African American artists, the problem has been that white singers and songwriters, who appropriate their styles, have had greater access to the recording and music-publishing industry and thus could pass themselves off as originals even when they present pale imitations of African American cultural forms. In this context, the second factor for fair use needs to get beyond the sheet music, image, or written word and account for the creative and cultural processes that generate particular copyrighted texts. Failure to do so produces an arbitrary but nonetheless raced distribution of intellectual property rights in which those who have the greatest access to copyright and contract lawyers, not the greatest amount of creativity, will ultimately come to own a greater share of the imaginary domain. This situation furthers romantic conceptions of authorship because these copyright owners appear to have created texts, songs, and images out of thin air, as their intellectual properties may have little connection to their own cultural practices. The existence of a fairly weak approach to a text's nature, which emphasizes genre over cultural connections, only furthers the redistribution of intellectual property ownership rights from marginalized communities to dominant corporate interests.[54]

The third fair-use factor examines the "amount and substantiality of the portion used in relation to the copyrighted work as a whole."[55] The amount and substantiality test explores how much the second text borrows from the first and how central the borrowed element is to the meaning of that first text.[56] This factor considers the borrowed portion only in relation to the first text. Courts will examine what percentage of the original or first text is used in the later text and whether the appropriated material constitutes the central message or artistic sensibility of that first text. In applying this factor, the only significant analytic distinctions involve the original meaning or operation of the sampled portion, not *how* a second text reworks it or reshapes its meaning. Legal discourse thus implicitly assumes that the borrowed material will function and signify in a similar or identical fashion in later texts as it did in its original setting.

Olufunmilayo Arewa argues that because courts tend to emphasize melody, as opposed to rhythm and percussion, in their fair-use analysis of music, they neglect how context determines the meaning or significance of notes and pitches. For Arewa, hip-hop and other music created in the African Diaspora emphasize orality and linguistic play as central features, rather than textuality or composition.[57] Courts, however, simply listen to the music and apparently determine if there is any kind of literal or fragmented similarity between the putative original and the alleged copy.[58] Although Arewa points out that "orality and linguistic play are . . . not sufficiently considered in analysis of hip hop," her system to license samples, however, returns to a test of recognizability, which would apparently require legal actors and courts to return to the very forms of analysis she criticizes.[59] Despite this limitation, Arewa's approach goes beyond current legal doctrine because it would require courts to attend not only to the appropriated text but to how a secondary user deploys the borrowed material. Arewa encourages courts to go beyond simplistic applications of the third fair-use factor and examines how the meaning of words, images, and sounds changes as their context does. Such an approach offers copyright law, which has become increasingly significant as an arbiter or regulator of multicultural exchange, a richer model of culture.

In its incessant critique of how marketing and public relations have re-shaped the contours of cultural life, Whitehead's *John Henry Days* implic-itly provides a corrective to fair-use doctrine's romantic approach to textu-ality. Arewa's analysis of fair use's failings interrogates copyright discourse's grounding assumption that creators write and produce their work as com-pleted wholes, free from historical and contemporary popular culture influences. For the John Henry myth, partial and unlicensed borrowings or appropriations have allowed the story to develop and suit its message to a wide range of audiences. Although this is not explicitly stated, Arewa ap-pears to rely on post-structuralism and performance theory to criticize le-gal discourse's tendency toward ahistorical understandings of particular texts. Her analysis allows judges and scholars to transcend narrow spa-tial/temporal boundaries and determine the relationships among the cre-ator's likely initial intent, the text's probable initial social meaning, and later appropriations of that text. Whitehead's novel attempts a genealogi-cal reconstruction of John Henry's myth. Weaving together diverse strands of the tale, Whitehead demonstrates that cultural texts can quickly take on a life of their own, regardless of their creators' intent. John Henry quickly became part of a de facto public domain, and musicians, playwrights, mar-keters, and even the U.S. Post Office drew on John Henry's iconic status to articulate their own hopes and dreams or to appropriate some of his signi-fying power for their own purposes.

Although both Pamela Street, through her father's collection, and J. Sutter, due to his attempt to break the nonstop junketeering record, pos-sess forms of ownership over the John Henry myth, the novel culminates abruptly with the pair apparently leaving the festivities early. In what would be unthinkable, or at least highly unlikely, within legal discourse, J. Sutter and Pamela Street simply relinquish control and ownership over the John Henry myth once they realize its pernicious effect on their lives. Even as it excavates the origins of John Henry, the novel also reveals Sutter's and Street's dawning consciousness of how the John Henry myth has ensnared them and shaped their life choices. Much like his earlier *The Intuitionist*, with its ironic deconstruction of uplift metaphors within African American culture, Whitehead's *John Henry Days* reflects upon the limits of received myths and narratives for the ultimate liberation of African Americans. The novel deploys sampled elements from and about John Henry in order to produce a rupture with the past. Echoing Paul Gilroy's examination of black vernacular uses of futurology, *John Henry Days* encourages readers to liberate their imaginations and free themselves from stories that leave

African Americans trapped in a racialized and white-supremacist past.[60] John Henry thus appears to constitute a narrative or myth whose existence has outlasted its political utility. What remains is merely a text ripe for sampled appropriations and other derivative uses. The novel's ambivalent ending suggests that, despite the importance of remembering history, especially the horror of racial hierarchy, African Americans need to generate new myths. As the novel's numerous hints suggest, the continued celebration of the John Henry myth will produce sometimes violent effects. Whitehead's novel thus implies that even though derivative uses of John Henry can proliferate and constitute new texts in and of themselves, which his own novel clearly exemplifies, overreliance on historical narratives can result in an unconscious reproduction of racial stereotypes.

The final factor that influences fair-use determinations considers the "effect of the use upon the potential market for or value of the copyrighted work."[61] This element of fair-use analysis connects recent copyright discourse with its founding concern about piracy. The fourth factor asks courts to consider whether the derivative use will serve as a market substitute for the appropriated text. In other words, will the borrowing of sounds, images, or words result in the earlier writer, artist, or composer losing sales or profits? The 2001 Napster litigation, for example, focused on whether the music-sharing service caused fewer college students to purchase music and impeded the recording industry's efforts to create new markets for music.[62] The court concluded that although time- or space-shifting can operate within the parameters of fair use, Napster's customers exceeded those limits.[63] This decision, along with others, makes clear that this fourth factor contemplates whether the copying serves as mere duplication and thus negatively impacts the sales of the earlier version. Conversely, recent litigation involving Google's search engine examined whether its use of cached images constituted copyright infringement. The U.S. District Court for Nevada held that such copying leaned toward a finding of fair use because it did not impact the potential market for the claimant's works.[64] In *Ty v. Publications International Limited*, the Seventh Circuit differentiated between complementary and substitutional uses. The *Ty* court held that only substitutional uses violate copyright law.[65] In these fair-use decisions, courts establish fairly clear rules to determine permissible kinds of appropriation and differentiate them from prohibited forms of copying.

Copyright law, however, permits criticism of earlier works even if it persuades consumers not to purchase the initial text. Critical appropriations differ from pirating because the resulting text incorporates previous material and shapes it into something that exceeds the original. In *Sun-Trust*, the court held that while its commentary might affect the sales of *Gone With the Wind*, *The Wind Done Gone* constituted a fair-use appropriation of Margaret Mitchell's book. The court noted in a footnote that the publication of *The Wind Done Gone* did not curtail or limit the sales of *Gone With the Wind*.[66] Judge Marcus, in his concurring opinion, noted that the two books "aim at different readerships; to the extent that there is any overlap between these respective markets, further factfinding [*sic*] may well reveal that these two books will act as complements rather than substitutes."[67] The court clarified the meaning and scope of this fourth factor to limit this category of copying that adds little to the original but only harms the ability of the copyright holder to realize income from that intellectual property. It appears as if Margaret Mitchell's heirs sought to use copyright law as a shield against any criticism of *Gone With the Wind*, which might affect sales. The *SunTrust* court, however, held that copyright infringement occurs only when that diminution of value occurs through blatant piracy, not critical rewritings.

Whitehead's novel charts the various rewritings, reworkings, and reuses of the John Henry name and myth. Within *John Henry Days*, the activities of and references to the eponymous hero generate considerable revenue for the various songwriters, performers, marketers, and advertisers. The endless repetition of the John Henry sign does not appear to diminish its value. Rather, the John Henry myth appears to be an inexhaustible cultural resource that retains its value, no matter how many people tap or mine its power, even if these various uses transform its initial meaning. Over the novel's course, Whitehead suggests that any attempt to trace the mysterious origins of John Henry will be partial and incomplete. Whether it focuses on the future or on the past, the book deconstructs the myth that John Henry is the product of a particular creator or that any one person can control its meaning. The novel, for example, identifies two failed scholarly (one black and one white) attempts to locate the myth's origin. The novel also exposes how the song appeared to take on a cultural life of its own, jumping from composer to composer, writer to writer, advertiser to marketer, and picking up steam all along the way. Echoing Rosemary Coombe's argument in *The Cultural Life of Intellectual Properties*, John Henry appears to possess a cultural life of its own, irrespective of its creators. Through acts of appropriation and recontextualization, John Henry becomes a textual space where democracy gets articulated and rearticulated.

Perhaps ironically, John Henry's transformation into American myth and the basis for democratic dialogue requires Pamela Street and J. Sutter to abandon this cultural inheritance. The nation's adoption of an African American folk story, in effect, "dispossesses" African Americans of the story and severs the link between them and the story. The commodification of John Henry elides the very historical subjectivity the story initially articulated and thus effects a revision of American racial history. Both the town and the U.S. Post Office participate in this racial myth-making in their attempt to demonstrate their multicultural values. Although Street and Sutter struggle with abandoning the myth and the many artifacts it has generated, the novel's ending suggests that they ultimately escape the John Henry celebration's concluding violence precisely because they have renounced the myth before it has been completely commodified. Within the novel's twisted logic, John Henry's value grows as songwriters, advertisers, and marketers use the myth for their own ends. In terms of the fourth fair-use factor, the deployments of John Henry do not hurt its *economic* value even as they transform its *cultural* value.

*John Henry Days* invites a range of questions about intellectual property, fair use, and post–Civil Rights era African American culture. It examines whether multiculturalism's attempt to broaden the boundaries of American culture has effected a dispossession of African American cultural memory. Whitehead skillfully notes the irony that copyright law, which has limited or impeded hip-hop's development of sampling, has proven quite receptive to corporate attempts to appropriate African American culture, such as Talcott's and the U.S. Post Office's efforts.[68] He illustrates that the very diversification or "multiculturalization" of post–Civil Rights America has required that African Americans give up ownership rights over their history and folk culture so that it, too, may become incorporated into commodity culture. Ironically, the demand to transform African American folk or popular culture into a broader or multicultural vision of American culture, writ large, coincides with what Phillip Richards has termed the rise of the "signifiers," a group of literary and cultural critics who "seek to convert this rhetorical method . . . into a literary institution embodying black culture."[69] Richards persuasively argues that their work posits a false and troubling romanticization of vernacular culture because it omits or elides the very real ways that African Americans have always drawn on European forms to articulate cultural, social, legal, and political criticisms. The turn toward vernacular forms within African American studies at this historical moment romanticizes folk culture, including hip-hop, and frames it as a proxy for racial authenticity precisely when intellectual property law enables and protects corporate uses of such materials. Sutter and Street's exit from the John Henry festival at the novel's conclusion suggests that once folk culture possesses significant economic value, it is no longer folk culture. Thus, the critical effort to locate signifyin' or any other folk protégé at the center of African American culture, ironically, transforms the very rituals they seek to protect.

Whitehead affirms the importance of signifyin' to African American culture and the need for legal discourse to recognize the latent creativity in such methods even as he suggests that the search for authenticity, which frequently underlies the critical support for signifyin', will ultimately prove futile. Exemplifying a post-structuralist sensibility, *John Henry Days* ultimately questions whether any return to the romanticized past is possible or whether folk culture can ultimately ground African American cultural identity.[70] The growing public interest in John Henry, which the novel explores, appears to reflect nostalgia for a past that never existed. Instead of the romantic version proposed by marketers, John Henry, as cultural inheritance, haunts individuals such as Sutter and Street. As a result, the novel offers an ambiguous, perhaps slightly negative conclusion about intellectual property law's role in distributing ownership interests in African American folk culture and history. While Whitehead is quite clear that copyright plays a disproportionate role in shaping cultural relations, the novel expresses considerable doubt about who benefits from subsequent uses of the John Henry story. The transition from folk culture to intellectual property, whether in the guise of popular music or academic theory, presents numerous challenges and dangers. It is unclear, within the novel's universe, whether continued ownership over the myth would improve the lives of African Americans. *John Henry Days* thus presents as many questions as it answers about copyright and fair use.

## Fair Use and Racist Images from (African American) Popular Culture

Not all ownership claims regarding folk culture involve romantic figures or myths, such as John Henry, nor do they all fall within the purview of copyright law. The circulation of putatively racist images and words has become a central concern within post–Civil Rights era African American culture. For example, a diverse group of African Americans, from Damon Wayans to Randall Kennedy, have attempted to reclaim ownership over the term *nigger* or *nigga*, despite its tremendously negative meaning within American culture in general.[71] The use of the word and its variants are common within hip hop-lyrics. Depending on the context, the speaker, and the audience, the N-word can denote either an insult of an African American or a recognition of friendship and group affiliation.[72] Comedians such as Chris Rock and Dave Chappelle use the word both critically and affirmatively in their routines. In his film *Bamboozled*, Spike Lee explores a middle-class African American's attempt to use the N-word and other racial stereotypes ironically. Lee, however, has criticized Quentin Tarantino, a white filmmaker whose work has frequently paid homage to blaxploitation films and their directors, for using the N-word. In his analysis of the Lee-Tarantino controversy, Randall Kennedy argues that Lee, and others like him, want to "cast a protectionist pall" over the word and so limit the ability for American culture to rehabilitate the word and thus repair one of the most damaging legacies of racism.[73] While I maintain my skepticism about the efficacy or logic behind his argument, Kennedy's position is shared by numerous African American cultural workers even as others within the community criticize the use of the N-word in equally strident terms. Within the context of intellectual property law, the debate over the N-word and other inflammatory words and imagery presents a question of fair use: who can use the term and in what ways? Put otherwise, who has the right to claim ownership over or register a trademark for the N-word?[74]

Unlike the constitutional foundation for copyright and patent law, trademark law developed through the common law, and Congress eventually codified it in 1946. Copyright and patent originate in a "bargain" between inventors and society in which the public gives creators a limited monopoly in their inventions as an incentive to engage in creative work.[75] Trademark, however, does not rely on a contract between the trademark holder and society. Rather, trademarks protect consumers by minimizing public confusion about the origin of a particular product.[76] The Lanham Act defines a trademark as "any word, name, symbol, or device, or any combination thereof—used by a person . . . to identify and distinguish his or her goods, including a unique product, from those manufactured or sold by others."[77] According to Sheldon Halpern, courts developed methods, such as the *Abercrombie* factors, to determine the distinctiveness of a particular trademark or trade dress and decide whether a particular mark seemed merely descriptive or generic, and thus undeserving of protection, or arbitrary and fanciful enough to be properly considered a trademark.[78] For Halpern and other scholars, trademarks and trade dress operate as a stamp of authenticity, informing consumers that the product or service is the "real thing."

Both post–World War II trademark jurisprudence and the Black Arts Movement[79] shared a concern with protecting consumers from inauthentic or counterfeit goods—no matter whether they are ordinary commodities or ones that hold particular racial or class significance. The turn toward vernacular criticism and the signifyin' school of cultural criticism, according to Phillip Richards, sought to identify the essential artistic differences between white and black artists so that authentic black voices could be nourished and developed. Skeptical of this project, Richards argues that establishing one's credentials as a complete or genuine African American artist or critic caused African Americans to minimize Anglo-American influences and broke down necessary dialogues between the humanities and the social sciences and between African Americans and other ethnic/racial groups, including whites.[80] Both the Black Arts Movement and hip-hop culture rely extensively on the logic of trademarked identities even if not all of the goods, symbols, and icons are registered with the U.S. Patent and Trademark Office. R. A. T. Judy argues that "rap becomes an authentic African American cultural form" precisely to the extent to which it "adapts to the force of commodification."[81] For Judy, hip-hop and other cultural-nationalist forms rely on the logic of authentic human experience within a world of hypercapitalism.[82] Hip-hop aesthetics, in effect, serves as an "anti-trademark," recuperating the very authenticity lost due to the commodification of African American cultural styles. If the Black Arts Movement tended to deploy such identity trademarks romantically by associating them with an uncompromised racial identity, hip-hop deploys trademarks ironically or with ambivalence.

Perhaps the best example illustrating this faux ownership, or parody of ownership, might be the life and career of Jean-Michel Basquiat. Basquiat began his career as a graffiti artist, known for his trademark tag "SAMO," or "same old shit," and then transformed himself into a high-culture painter who deployed hip-hop methods to "dismantle [his] historical precedents by showing mastery over their techniques and styles and [put] them to new uses, in which the new becomes the final product layered over the past."[83] The "typical" Basquiat canvas includes multiple misspellings; copyright symbols;[84] scratched-out phrases; crude or faux-primitive drawings; ambiguous allusions; and liberal borrowings of trademarked figures, especially superheroes and famous personas. The images intentionally invite comparisons with primitivism, even though Basquiat's work clearly subverts and mocks Modernist appropriations of primitivism. Following the long trajectory of African American Modernist experimentation, Basquiat relies on the interplay between text and orality to deconstruct the stereotype that African Americans rely solely on oral culture. Frequently, Basquiat's images depend on textual literacy in order to decode the putatively primitive writing. For example, in his 1982 painting *Natives Carrying Some Guns, Bibles, Amorites on Safari*, Basquiat twice connects the words "TUSK$" and "$KIN$" with arrows. Within the context of the painting's stated theme of exploring colonization, this repetitive blending of letters and symbols requires viewers to "read" the painting at least twice because it is unclear whether the blend of symbols and letters refers to the relationship among tusks, skins, and money or tusks, kins, and money. Analogous to hip-hop's use of misspellings or neologisms for lyrics and names, Basquiat's paintings play with the slippage between oral and textual cultures. Analyzing experimental and avant-garde African American literature of the post–World War II era, Aldon Nielsen argues that an African American tradition, in which "orality and textuality were not opposed to one another and did not exist in any simple or simplistic opposition to modernity or postmodernity," had been well-developed by the time Basquiat began painting.[85] Basquiat transformed this textual and oral wordplay by consciously merging avant-garde African American styles with putatively "working-class" or "street" styles, thereby forging a synthesis of both popular and high-culture aesthetics. This blended approach deconstructs essentialized or essentializing approaches to identity, where a person's authenticity as an African American appears directly correlated with her connection to street life.[86] Oddly prescient, Basquiat predicts white America's fascination with gangsta rap and thug life.[87] Basquiat's mapping of the complex relationship between mimicry and authenticity, ostensibly regulated by copyright and trademark law respectively, provides a ready reminder that authenticity remains the primary or dominant criterion for evaluating and rating African American cultural production. Consequently, trademark—the legal device that regulates authenticity—has proven an inescapable but unspoken analytic within contemporary African American cultural criticism.

Within this context, it appears that the debate over who can or cannot use the N-word in comedy, film, music, clothing, and literature increasingly presents a question of authenticity and cultural capital—the primary concern of trademark law. The discussion among Chris Rock, Spike Lee, Quentin Tarantino, Randall Kennedy, and others fundamentally involves determining the relationship between the word and its speaker. If the speaker possesses the requisite "blackness," he or she can recast an apparently racist phrase into a more positive identity claim. Todd Anten argues that self-disparaging trademarks, such Wayan's attempt to trademark "Nigga" for his clothing line, can promote social change and that the U.S. Patent and Trademark Office ought to allow them if a member of the referenced community puts forth the trademark petition.[88] This argument mimics trademark's underlying logic because the producer's identity determines the authenticity or the quality/meaning of the good. Such trademark claims would enable African Americans to commodify their racial identity and permit further consumption of racialized goods and services.

Anten's logic for supporting self-disparaging trademarked terms and the probable cause for their contemporary popularity relies on the implicit irony within the dialectical relationship between body and text/word. Recent debates about the N-word echo Rosemary Coombe's application of Foucault's conception of the author-function to trademarks:

> Although trademarks are not conventionally understood to have "authors" because they require no necessary genius, originality, or creativity, the legal recognition that trademark "owners" have a proprietary interest in marketing signs increasingly relies upon a reenactment of the author-function described by Foucault. This is evident in judicial acceptance of the belief that through investment, labor, and strategic dissemination, the holder of a trademark creates a set of unique meanings in the minds of consumers.[89]

Coombe does not specifically or systematically apply this insight to potentially contradictory uses of such self-disparaging trademarks within African-American art and literature. Such self-disparaging terms and trademarks provide authors and artists the means by which to assert themselves as raced authors even as they aim to deconstruct and/or interrogate the very logic of race. Trademark, especially in the context of hip-hop aesthetics, allows cultural workers to transform their labor and creativity into ownership rights over the very illusion of authenticity hip-hop offers.

Distinct from copyright law, trademark has developed its own approach to fair use. Traditionally, trademark law permitted "fair use of a famous mark by another person in comparative commercial advertising or promotion to identify the competing goods or services of the owner of the famous mark." Only in 2006 did Congress amend the Lanham Act to allow parodies of trademarked logos.[90] Stephanie Greene argues that promoting free speech, within the framework of "preventing consumer confusion and protecting the goodwill of the trademark holder," has guided the development of trademark's approach to fair use.[91] Courts, however, have split upon the best method for applying fair use to trademark disputes. Greene suggests that the current statutory scheme provides fairly clear guidance for resolving disputes, especially in limiting the rights of descriptive marks (i.e., trademark names that provide a generic description of the item rather than arbitrary or fanciful names, unrelated to the item's function), while permitting "an appropriate balance between consumer confusion and competition."[92] She contends that trademark law cannot prohibit or enjoin all potential confusion, but only that customer confusion that would cause uncertainty about a particular product's origin. Her reading of trademark's approach to fair use contemplates that some comparative uses of a trademarked name might cause consumers to decide against purchasing the other trademarked name. This, according to Greene, is analytically distinct from the problem when one commodity borrows the reputation of another, thereby diluting the value of the original trademarked name and/or free-riding on another's good name. Unlike copyright law, which has expanded the scope and duration of copyrights, Halpern and Doellinger argue that recent court decisions have limited trademark rights, especially to promote free speech.[93]

While copyright law has received considerable notice from hip-hop aesthetes and their critics, much less attention has been focused on fair use within trademark law. Certain cases, such as Damon Wayans's trademark application for the term "Nigga," have received general public notice, but it has been fairly disconnected from research in contemporary African American art, literature, and music. By connecting Whitehead's *John Henry Days* and the artwork of Michael Ray Charles, this chapter seeks to explore how African American cultural workers have represented and criticized the ongoing circulation of raced imaginative properties. Unlike legal discourse, with its historically clear boundaries, which Moffat argues appear to be eroding with the increased demand for overlapping forms of protection for all forms of intellectual property, between trademark and copyright, African American creativity and critical analyses of imaginative properties have adopted their own discursive framework for analyzing and regulating imaginative properties.[94] *John Henry Days* presents the problem of how the transformation of folk culture into intellectual property creates a disenabling cultural inheritance for post–Civil Rights era African Americans, such as J. Sutter and Pamela Street. Whitehead apparently concludes that the only way to free oneself from the history of racism is to alienate or abandon stultifying cultural traditions or narratives. The artwork of Michael Ray Charles has adopted a much more controversial style by reworking established trademarks (even though he uses copyright symbols liberally in his work, like and/or in homage to Jean-Michel Basquiat). Ignoring the subtle legal distinctions between copyright and trademark, Charles promotes his own version of "fair use" of racist caricatures in order to liberate himself from their power. No less than Whitehead, Charles illustrates how intellectual property law, especially trademark law, has created raced property interests that operate through racist stereotypes and that have effected the transfer of ownership rights of the American cultural imagination to white people and the corporations they own.[95]

Drawing on advertisements from the nineteenth and early twentieth centuries, Charles has created scores of paintings that illuminate the racial fictions that structure popular culture's imagery. Central to his critical project is the ongoing deconstruction of unconsciously (and sometimes consciously) raced trademarks and trademarked styles. Everything from the Pillsbury Dough Boy and Aunt Jemima to Wonder Woman and Clorox Bleach has become subject to Charles's critical eye. Charles even reworks images that have become trademark signatures of other artists, such as Grant Wood's *American Gothic* and Norman Rockwell's *Saturday Evening Post* imagery. In working with and through popular-culture icons and trademarks, Michael Ray Charles draws on strategies developed by earlier African American artists, especially their use of Aunt Jemima. As Michael Harris ably demonstrates by collecting dozens of artworks including and/or commenting on Aunt Jemima, artists during the 1960s and 1970s "manipulated them for effect, deconstructing the visual sign, questioning Aunt Jemima's role as a popular trademark, and giving voice and humanity to all the black women aggrieved by the stereotypical representation of Aunt Jemima and the mammy image."[96] Calvin Reid also notes the influence of Robert Colescott and David Hammons and their use of appropriation on Charles's work.[97]

Charles's approach to such trademark images, however, diverges from that of earlier artists because his work condemns the stereotypes less clearly. Unlike his Black Art predecessors, Charles presents a more ambiguous attitude toward these trademarked images. He typically relies on hip-hop aesthetics to stylize his representations of African Americans and develop a sociopolitical critique of African American cultural life. *(Forever Free) Aneminentevaluation* (1995) displays the same sampling, layering, rhythmic flow/asymmetry, and irony as other hip-hop-influenced texts. The painting depicts three stereotypical minstrel-style men tearing through a two-dimensional image of a Clorox bottle. Two of the figures smile broadly and sport patriotic neckties, while the third figure gestures to the viewer to be quiet. All three figures wear minstrel gloves and possess hair that sticks up in all directions. On the left side, the words "DISTRIB-UTED BY LIBERTY PERM PRODUCTS" are printed. On the right side, the painter's signature doubles as a copyright sign: "MICHAEL RAY ©HARLES '95." Across the bottom, Charles has painted "ANEMINEN-TEVALUATION."

At the most basic level, the painting samples the trademarked image of a Clorox bottle and classical minstrel figures. Layered on top of these images, Charles offers an allusion to Ralph Ellison's *Invisible Man*. In the novel, the invisible narrator forgets his name after an industrial accident at Liberty Paints when a coworker sabotages one of the machines because the narrator has tainted the company's Optic White paint and appears sympathetic to union organizers.[98] This layered allusion deepens the significance of the Clorox bottle when paired with the marginal note that the image itself is distributed by Liberty Perm Products, a fictional company common to many of Charles's paintings. The minstrel figures have apparently infiltrated the most known and trusted bleaching/whitening agent in American culture. Like Ellison's fictional Lucius Brockway, the minstrel figures seem to have commandeered the purported "bleaching" action of Clorox and shifted the product's real effects. Offering an analogy to the influence of African Americans on American popular culture, the minstrels appear to have penetrated the heart of American culture despite the best efforts to "bleach" it and many of its citizens white.

Beyond its use of layered samples, *Aneminentevaluation* revels in rhythmic flow and rupture. Obviously, the words in the title flow together into a single word, thereby rupturing the viewer's initial expectation when searching for the painting's title. The viewer must locate the "breaks" themselves because Charles has blended the words, much like a hip-hop deejay weaves tracks and beats together to form a looped beat. On a deeper level, the title suggests that someone or something will be evaluated, but it is unclear whether the minstrel figures or a bleached American culture will be the subject of that evaluation. In addition, "eminent evaluation" evokes the legal procedure of eminent domain by which government takes private property for a public purpose. The slippage between the painting's title and this feature of modern property law suggests that the minstrel figures have invaded the Clorox trademarked image in order to remedy the violence associated with the history of "bleaching" American culture. In addition to the title's flow/rupture, the image itself depicts a rupture within American culture. The painting disrupts how viewers consume advertising images of Clorox without considering historic inequalities in the job market or the metaphorical significance of this very ordinary cleaning product. By juxtaposing the trademarked Clorox bottle with the white gloves and dark faces of the minstrel figures, the painting forces the viewer to consider how such trademarked images conceal the real work African Americans have done, because such marketing campaigns have rarely exalted the labor of African Americans, and how such menial labor has rarely translated into greater cultural or economic capital.

By offering several critical commentaries on cultural bleaching and eminent domain/evaluation within his series *Forever Free*, Charles produces an ironic vision of contemporary American culture. The putative freedom the series explores ultimately seems both less liberating and more ominous than the term initially suggests. It appears as if Charles concludes that freedom in the contemporary era involves resisting the stereotypes offered by popular culture and refashioning this imaginary domain. Charles describes his project in the following terms:

> I'm choosing to speak about the African-American experience in a different way. By talking about what we have been calling the negative. By trying to speak about the invisible image, the invisible reality. I don't think that we can speak about the black experience and not conjure up all the stuff about stereotypes. I think a lot of art that is being done in that vein is real safe. I think my work has the same feel, but I've just decided to take more risks.[99]

For Charles, his work seeks to reclaim ownership over what American culture has bleached out or made invisible. By evoking the negative images of the past, Charles necessarily engages in an ironic project because he aims both to remind his audiences of what they have chosen to forget and to offer these stereotyped figures as potentially ambiguous and thus potentially reconstructable.

Trademarks and their fair use constitute linchpins to understanding

Charles's imagery. As a legal symbol denoting authenticity, the trademark allows its owner to control the public image of its products and build good-will with customers. Dilution—harming a product's good name—and free-riding—when a competitor selects a name close enough to an existing trademark to cause confusion—present potential threats to the holders of trademarks because they create ambiguity about the item's identity and worth where none existed before. Trademark protects against these harms because it assumes that any reputation was gained honestly and that com-petitors must compete fairly, not merely foster confusion. Charles's art-work questions these basic assumptions and suggests that the apparent sta-bility of trademarks constitutes more of a problem than their ambiguity. Without a thorough examination of the invisible racial history they con-ceal, trademarks can further both material and imaginative disadvantages for African Americans. In particular, they can create a stereotypical world-view where African Americans are reduced to hackneyed clichés such as mammies or minstrel figures. For Charles and other hip-hop aesthetes, "fair use" ought to permit cultural workers the opportunity to create am-biguity and transform the meaning of objects or texts central to the Amer-ican cultural imagination. Hip-hop aesthetics asks what is "fair" about copyright and trademark doctrines that permit the continued circulation of racist or racialized caricatures in American culture or hide racial inequality. Obviously, this is one instance where official legal discourse and African American culture conflict. Until now, legal discourse has persisted in rely-ing on the metaphor of fair use, even though the doctrine appears to priv-ilege one cultural perspective over another. In effect, Michael Ray Charles's deconstruction of trademarked images seeks to highlight the conflict between these competing norms.

Although generally critical of Charles's work, Michael Harris argues that Charles's most effective "critiques may be those of NBA basketball players, athletes he lampoons as coons acting out stereotypical behaviors and showing little responsibility."[100] In *(Forever Free) The NBA* (1995), Charles reworks the logo of the National Basketball Association (NBA). Instead of the ostensibly white athlete on the original trademarked logo,[101] Charles paints a blackface player, replete with white gloves and the wild hair characteristic of Golliwog dolls. In the painting, Charles includes the echo of minstrelsy by replacing the word *Fantastic* in the NBA's slogan ("The NBA is Fantastic") with *Tantastic*, another minstrel reference. The figure also displays a price tag with seven dollar signs, suggesting that the millions of dollars most players earn merely confirm racial stereotypes. By inverting the popular trademark and logo of the NBA, Charles notes the irony that many African American youths dream the sport will lift them out of poverty despite the ways the sport commodifies a particular form of blackness that stereotypes and pigeonholes other African Americans. For Charles, this constitutes an "unfair use" of racial stereotypes. By turning the basketball player in the NBA logo into a minstrel figure, Charles suggests that basketball, despite the success and fame of Michael Jordan and others, has been transformed into a modern-day minstrel show. Basketball has long been a "raced" sports spectacle in which racial identity stereotypically confers certain stylistic and physical advantages on a player's game. In its contemporary form, the NBA increasingly gravitates toward an African American aesthetic, a development that both fascinates and horrifies various segments of its white audience.

Because Charles relies on imagery with historically racist associations, his critics argue that his "recycling of stereotypes is insulting and degrading and should not be exhibited. They also feel that the artists [such as Charles] are making their reputations off of their own people's suffering."[102] Although his critics suggest that Charles cannot control his explosive imagery, his work rebuts this assumption by revealing unspoken or invisible relations between his subject matter and African Americans from many different walks of life. For example, in *(Forever Free) Servin with a Smile* (1994), Charles paints the Pillsbury Doughboy in the style of a black minstrel figure. This "unfair use" of Pillsbury's trademark offers a reminder that historically African Americans cooked for white folks and that the famous icon's smile makes invisible the inequalities experienced by house slaves and domestic servants.[103] I reference Charles's appropriation of this logo as an "unfair use" not because it causes consumer confusion or dilutes the value of Pillsbury's trademark, but because it suggests the power of racialized icons. For Charles, such racialized imagined properties operate unfairly or discriminate, whether they intend to do so or not. The very metaphor of "fair use" implies a racial subjectivity. The copyright or trademark holder presumptively engages in fair use of their intellectual property because no existing doctrine has proven consistently effective in prohibiting or sanctioning racist or discriminatory uses. In many cases, logos or trademarked images operate at a subconscious level to make racial hierarchy invisible.

In *(Forever Free) The NBA*, Charles draws an analogy between artists and basketball players in which artists must produce art within the same racist or racialized culture that converts basketball players into well-worn stereotypes. The painter, no less than the athlete, must grin and play the minstrel figure, according to Charles. In a relatively ubiquitous picture accompanying many of his shows, Michael Ray Charles has been photographed with a penny in his mouth, echoing the very blackface images to which his work frequently refers.[104] The catalog for his 1997 show at the Baffler Gallery at the Art Museum of the University of Houston has a penny affixed to the back cover. Charles also frequently uses the markings from copper pennies to produce his blackface or minstrel-inspired images. In an interview, Charles explained his use of the penny:

> All the other coins are silver and reflect. And they are all facing one direction. The only coin of color, with Lincoln on its face, supposedly the Great Emancipator, is looking the other way. I made a painting entitled *Quota Piece* and it was after hearing Jesse Jackson speak. I was looking for something to balance the composition. The penny came to me as a token, a token coin. I balanced the composition between a Sambo image and the penny. . . . So I began signing my paintings with it as a trademark, as a cosignature. Every product has a trademark. It was my acknowledgement of tokenism.[105]

Through his strategic use of pennies, Charles suggests that the very images contemporary African American visual and basketball artists create must satisfy American consumer culture's demands for familiar imagery. The penny, which is seen as virtually worthless, frequently appears next to a copyright symbol in his work and offers an ironic commentary on its status as Charles's trademark.

Charles's decision to fuse trademarked images from Norman Rockwell's *Saturday Evening Post* and Disney with minstrel-era racist imagery illustrates an ongoing conundrum: how can African Americans and other historically marginalized groups contest such racialized imagery when those icons are privately owned? Obviously, Charles answers this question by engaging in what I have termed unfair use to make vivid the racist underpinnings or connotations of such trademarked icons or copyrighted images. This deconstruction of racist imagery, however, has not been embraced by everyone, especially other African Americans. They question his choice of subject matter and argue that it appears to merely recapitulate racist messages and provide only negative stereotypes for African American youth.[106] Exploring the recent trend toward examining minstrel and other racist imagery, Michele Wallace argues that work like Charles's is attempting to recuperate authentic African American culture from a lost era, whose racist advertising images constitute an abundant and integral part of American cultural mythology.[107] For Wallace, it is the relative absence of cultural memory that has fostered interest in racist imagery because these images offer a unique lens through which to view the genealogy of African American culture. Echoing Wallace's claim, Charles suggests that the Sambo image "was a tool used by blacks to survive—to escape lashings, etc."[108] Charles culminates this interview by suggesting how he and Whitehead share a view about copyrighted and trademarked images: "I'm most interested in the evolution of images, ideas, and people. Despite the presence of these images and the stereotypes, blacks continue to strive."[109]

In their tracing of the "evolution of images, ideas, and people," Whitehead and Charles share critical race theory's shift from race and racism to the racialization of American culture. In a fascinating 1996 law review article, Alex Johnson Jr. argues that racial classifications, especially within the black-white binary, have functioned like trademarks.[110] Johnson accepts Richard Posner's law-and-economics rationale for trademarks in which he posits that trademarks guarantee customers uniform product quality and thus minimize the consumer cost of evaluating or inspecting each individual product for flaws.[111] Johnson then lists a set of racist assumptions that have historically been associated with black racial identity: intellectual inferiority, athletic prowess, sexual superiority or excessive sexual libido, laziness, and violence.[112] He argues that African Americans, like a trademarked product, are assumed to possess these characteristics unless or until a particular African American demonstrates that they possess different attributes.[113] This "showing" does not dispel such racial stereotypes; rather, it simply releases one lucky person from their punishing grip. Johnson concludes that race, due to its binary structure in American culture, maintains racial hierarchy and continues to "preserve the economic status of the white community."[114] The only way to dismantle racism, according to Johnson, is to "destabilize" racial trademarks, "(1) by improving the quality of the mark, or (2) through the process of shade confusion."[115] Historically, the Black Arts and Black Power movements sought primarily to "improve the quality" of black identity. Johnson supplements this strategy and argues that we must also create market confusion by replacing our primarily binary racial classification scheme with one that is multivalent and thus less efficient for creating and sustaining stereotypes.[116] Johnson turns to ethnicity as a positive identification system that is passively ascribed but must be actively maintained. Such classifications, because they are based in history and cultural rites, require much greater research to ascribe than the passing glance associated with race. While this destabilization of race as a trademarked identity may make current affirmative-action and other antidiscrimination programs difficult to administer, Johnson argues that such strategies show signs of having decreased utility.[117] Preserving race as the identity category for these programs would be a poor strategy. Rather, Johnson argues that the trademark exclusivity of black and white racial identities, even if race is still used as a basis for some community actions or cultural traditions, must be abolished. In other words, the idea that race denotes uniform identity or behavior must be destabilized. While Johnson admits that there may be short-term confusion or backsliding, the ultimate gains from dismantling racial trademarks as proxies for behaviors and identity characteristics would clearly outweigh any intermediate growing pains.[118]

Johnson's article, which appeared at the same moment that both Colson Whitehead and Michael Ray Charles emerged on the literary and art scenes, captures the challenge against which post–Civil Rights era activists struggle in resisting new/persisting forms of racism and racialized thinking. It grapples with how race finds a refuge within trademark rights. Further developing Johnson's argument, David Troutt has created a wonderful hypothetical exploring the tension between trademark law and racism during the post–Civil Rights era. For Troutt, any trademarked identity, whether positively or negatively charged, necessarily limits human flourishing.[119] As part of his analysis, Troutt observes that "it is no great surprise that a discourse on commodification and signification in a consumption-based society should be able to draw on the example of so many African American men," including Martin Luther King, Kareem Abdul-Jabbar, Tiger Woods, and Bobby Seale, all of whom have been involved in trademark and publicity-rights cases and controversies.[120] He also notes that much cultural studies scholarship has lavished an equal amount of attention on the commodified images of African Americans, such as Michael Jackson, Michael Jordan, Tupac Shakur, and other hip-hop stars. Troutt's observations about the interrelationships among trademark law, commodification, and race reveal the ongoing economic value of black identity within the marketplace. Despite or because of the love/hate relationship white America appears to have with stereotyped assumptions about African Americans, corporations want their products associated with African Americans as long as it titillates white audiences. If, however, the product becomes too "black," it will likely fail or have a limited market. African American endorsers can mark a product as cool, or they can just as easily mark a product as exclusively black and thus too dangerous or "low" class. In this context, the increasing commodification of black identity requires post–Civil Rights era intellectuals or hip-hop aesthetes to engage with and criticize the logic of the trademark, even if it has furthered racial stereotypes and limited the "human flourishing" of many African Americans.

Colson Whitehead's recent novel *Apex Hides the Hurt* narrates the story of a disabled nomenclature consultant who has been hired to select the name for an African American town that was named for a white business leader. The town adopted the name Winthrop after its only white businessman, who made a fortune selling barbed wire. A black entrepreneur, however, wants to change the town's name to "New Prospera" to improve its image and has thus hired the naming consultant. This name, however, does not impress the narrator, who sets out to find another one. The novel recounts the nomenclature consultant's exploration of the town, its history, and its current inhabitants and records his ruminations about the function and meaning of names in American culture. He learns of a deal between one of the town's African American founders and the white businessman that led to its current name of Winthrop. The African American community had earlier chosen the name Freedom over the other proposed name, Struggle. The narrator, ironically an unnamed African American man, thus inviting comparisons to Ellison's *Invisible Man*, ultimately concludes that the town ought to return to the name it originally spurned. The novel culminates with the nomenclature consultant wryly observing the absurd phrases that will become common to the town's inhabitants: "I was born in Struggle. I live in Struggle and come from Struggle. We crossed the border into Struggle. Before I came to Struggle. We found ourselves in Struggle. I will never leave Struggle. I will die in Struggle."[121] Like many contemporary African American novels and artworks, Whitehead's novel includes abundant references to African American people and their cultural history without offering explicit racial claims or arguments. The novel's end, like that of *John Henry Days*, offers an ambiguous conclusion about the current state of African American life. It refuses to depict African Americans in stereotypically positive ways, and Whitehead's characters, unlike those created by previous generations of writers, are not clearly "race" men or women. Moreover, their connection to African American history and culture seems less certain and more optional than ever before. The narrator's decision to impose, in effect, the name of struggle on the town suggests that the specter of race remains, even if the town wishes to adopt the more color-blind "New Prospera."

Paired with Michael Ray Charles's paintings, Whitehead's work testifies to the ongoing struggle contemporary African American artists and writers face in creating images and narratives as race has become a key element of trademarked identities. However, unlike earlier generations, they present and explore a wider range of artistic and life options for African Americans. Their work exemplifies the changing nature of property, from tangible to intangible goods, and how this new terrain offers a fundamental challenge to the ethos and activism that have historically underwritten African American cultural production. *John Henry Days, Apex Hides the Hurt,* and the *Forever Free* series focus almost exclusively on how African Americans struggle with and against racist and/or racialized narratives within the American cultural imagination, as opposed to the intentional and overt racism of previous generations.[122] Claiming ownership over oneself and one's representation in this imaginary domain requires engaging with the legal rules that govern its distribution and control. For Whitehead and Charles, the imaginary domain and, by implication, intellectual property law provide an entry into the tortured psyches of both whites and African Americans, who continue to be marked by racism and racialization even if *how* it shapes social life has changed. Their work, like much contemporary African American cultural production, examines and signifies upon the fair/unfair use of extant symbols, icons, and narratives. Hip-hop aesthetics provides an artistic and narrative framework to explore how race continues to influence American life even after the Civil Rights Movement. The shift from fighting segregation to interrogating the continued circulation of raced images has challenged social justice activists. Unlike those involved in earlier movements that focused primarily on material inequalities, today's intellectuals must find a way to blend those traditional concerns with the increasing appropriation of African American cultural sensibilities. Ironically, borrowing African American style and/or authenticity is considerably more marketable and valuable than developing long-standing corporate relationships with African American people or communities and their leaders. This dynamic has led to a perceived (and probably real) crisis in leadership within the African American community.[123]

The work of both Charles and Whitehead reflects these tensions and emphasizes how copyrighted texts and trademark icons produce social fragmentation because they have become the primary path for individuals to enter into an imagined community (as opposed to the church or Civil Rights organizations for African Americans from the 1950s and 1960s) and are simultaneously the source for racism and racialization. This ambiguity in signification cannot be easily understood through legal discourse, even if its structures and concepts define intellectual property law, because law tends to view texts as thin and univocal, rather than as layered, rhythmic objects located in a specific narrative trajectory. Artist and writers—no matter their racial, ethnic, or gender identity—have examined the effect of advertising and marketing on American culture. For white artists, trade-marked and copyrighted images tend to show the ubiquity and banality of American popular culture. Andy Warhol, for example, appropriated every-thing from his well-known Campbell soup cans to Mickey Mouse to Aunt Jemima. His work deployed trademarks' very repetition, fundamental to their value, as a metaphor for their corrosive influence on our interior lives. Warhol, however, traced the problem to their status as commodified im-ages. Feminist artists such as Sherrie Levine and Cindy Sherman have used repetition to comment upon the circulation of received images, demon-strating how their ubiquity reenacts certain gender and classed narratives and distinctions. Like other hip-hop aesthetes, Whitehead and Charles un-derstand such trademarked images and copyrighted texts as both constitu-tive of social being, and thus central to one's self-understanding, and per-petuating the circulation of racist myths and mythologies. Their work revels in the fair use of imagery from folk or popular culture even as it in-terprets that use as frequently anything but "fair."

The best example of the dual function of such imagery is Michael Ray Charles's attempt to recuperate Aunt Jemima, although it could just as eas-ily be applied to Whitehead's revision of John Henry. Black Arts–influenced painters, including Jeff Donaldson, Joe Overstreet, and Betye Saar, deployed Aunt Jemima's image to promote cultural nationalism during the 1960s and 1970s.[124] These earlier paintings sought to correct the injustice done by over one hundred years of stereotyped advertising[125] and depict Aunt Jemima in angry, defiant, and/or rebellious poses. By con-trast, Charles employs Aunt Jemima in a more ambiguous fashion to ex-plore and illustrate the contradictory effects of her continuing circulation, albeit in a recently updated form.[126] Marilyn Kern-Foxworth has identified a number of modified or improved Aunt Jemimas in Charles's work, in-cluding Aunt Jemima as Wonder Woman, Rosie the Riveter, a presidential candidate, a pin-up, the Statue of Liberty, a farmer's wife in a remake of Grant Wood's *American Gothic,* and Marilyn Monroe.[127]

In two related images, Charles's *For Women* paintings from the *Forever Free* series depict Aunt Jemima as a mammy and as a recently updated mid-dle-class woman. The words *For Women* also appear to reference Nina Simone's famous song "Four Women," in which she gives voice to the struggles of four ordinary African American women who encounter extraordinary difficulties due to racial, gender, and class inequalities. By connecting his images to Simone's song, Charles suggests that this image not only is dedicated to women but acts as a representation of their ongoing struggles as well. In *President* (1993), Aunt Jemima is represented in typical blackface manner. Her face is so dark that her bulging eyes and white teeth, outlined with dark red lips, provide the only contrast to her skin. In addition, her head is adorned with a bright red handkerchief with white spots. Echoing Norman Rockwell's *Saturday Evening Post* drawings, Charles places this Aunt Jemima on the yellowed and faded front cover of "The Forever Free Post." PRESIDENT is painted across the bottom, with the slogan "It's time for a clean sweep" printed underneath. In contrast to this faux-historical image, Charles also signifies on Aunt Jemima's most recent trademarked image in *Vote Black* (1993). In this companion painting, Aunt Jemima is portrayed as a successful middle-class woman with more fully developed features, replete with earrings and a professional hairstyle. The painting's setting has shifted from the front page of a newspaper to an election poster, encouraging the viewer to "ELECT" Aunt Jemima "FOR PRESIDENT" and to "VOTE BLACK." The poster redeploys the red-and-white handkerchief pattern as the top half of its background, with the bottom portion colored blue with white stars, thereby completing a flag motif. Even though much has changed between the respective creations of the two Aunt Jemima trademark logos, the tagline remains the same: "IT'S TIME FOR A CLEAN SWEEP."

In both versions, Charles is engaging in a fair/unfair use of Aunt Jemima's trademark image. Relying on and criticizing its historical and current iterations, these paintings interrogate the meaning and the effects of the trademarked image. On the one hand, Charles notes the ironic undertones of the original icon by reprinting it on the "Forever Free Post," thereby suggesting that any purported freedom for African Americans has existed within a racialized and racist American culture. On the other hand, Charles's second painting acknowledges that public perceptions and stereotypes have improved. However, the improvements still operate as stereotypes, just more positive ones. The older stereotypes lurk in the background, represented by the handkerchief transformed into a background print. The need for a "clean sweep" remains, even after the Civil Rights Movement. His copying of these trademarked symbols serves as a political and cultural commentary on the racialized ideas Aunt Jemima has fostered. They do not cause consumer confusion about the origin of his paintings. Thus, they would likely satisfy either copyright or trademark's definition of fair use. Charles implies that we must purify American culture, starting with the image of Aunt Jemima herself. But she remains, in a sanitized form. The idea that somehow Aunt Jemima, either the mammy or the middle-class version, could become president, while desirable, still seems a bit like a science fiction, even after the recent election of Barack Obama. From this angle of vision, Charles's Aunt Jemima represents what I call an unfair use because she reminds us that the very ownership interests that copyright and trademark confer continue to effectively disenfranchise African Americans by reducing them to minstrel figures, even in a new and improved form. Although consumers *elect* to purchase Aunt Jemima thousands of times a day, this consumer choice has not translated into all those consumers deciding to "vote black," as the painting suggests. The slippage between the two kinds of choices, consumption and representation, questions the recent corporate interest in channeling consumers to commodifying their dissent by purchasing particular products and/or services. Rather, the *For Women* series implicates the very structures of commodification in furthering racial stereotypes, even if they put a kinder and gentler face on them.

Through their deconstruction of popular icons, such as John Henry and Aunt Jemima, Whitehead and Charles use hip-hop aesthetics to demonstrate that even putatively fair use of intellectual properties, by rights holders and critics alike, can result in unfair or unjust effects on historically marginalized people. In its current, color-blind form, trademark and copyright law provides little recourse to challenging such representations without recirculating the offending images and texts. Fair use, as legal doctrine and cultural metaphor, ultimately offers an ironic reading of the relationship between African Americans and intellectual property law. Derrick Bell's fictional tale of "racial royalities" ultimately concludes that the American cultural imagination has appropriated African American styles and enriched many white Americans. Despite the fantastic mechanism described in his short story, legal doctrines and cultural interventions have proven only partially successful in remedying these historical wrongs. Critical race theorists and hip-hop aesthetes have sought to imagine alternative ways of conceiving of and distributing imaginative resources, but the ongoing circulation of raced images and texts has proven resistant to transformation. Although cases such as *Campbell* and *SunTrust* suggest that African American artists can deploy existing texts in either parodic or transformative ways, both rulings eschew race or racial subjectivity as an explicit component of legal doctrine. Rather, the rules they apply/announce continue the fiction of an unraced intellectual property law. Cases involving hip-hop music also avoid cultural explanations and have become increasingly confused and confusing regarding the state of sampling, fair use, and the de miminis defense. Despite the widespread popularity of sampling and appropriative borrowings within African American culture, intellectual property law still clings to a color-blind jurisprudence even as race and ethnicity frequently structure the unspoken subtext for these seemingly contradictory decisions.

## CHAPTER 6

# "Transformative Uses":
# Parody and Memory

Many scholars and activists have concluded that Civil Rights era reforms only affected a partial transformation of the American political, economical, and social structure. Recent multiculturalist and CRT activism seeks to emphasize culture as a key component in the continued fight for social justice. Drucilla Cornell, a postmodernist and a feminist, defines transformation as "change radical enough to so dramatically restructure any system—political, legal, or social—that the 'identity' of the system is itself altered." She explains further that transformation requires engaging the "question of what kind of individuals we would have to become in order to open ourselves to new worlds."[1] Homi Bhabha, a proponent of postcolonial theory, argues that transformation occurs through "the process of reinscription and negotiation" and "happens in the temporal break in-between the sign, deprived of subjectivity, in the realm of the intersubjective."[2] Moments of agency or articulation, for Bhabha, arise in the space between discourses when words, texts, icons, and logos gain a new meaning as they shed their old "skin" but before a new one limits their potential or softens their radical edge.

These feminist and postcolonial approaches build on and inform CRT and hip-hop approaches to transformation. In *Teaching Community: A Pedagogy of Hope*, bell hooks provides an extended meditation about social and cultural transformation. She insists that the concept of white supremacy, rather than racism, ought to be the focus of inquiry because it more fully describes the systematic and unconscious operation of race. Further, she observes that activists "once naively believed that if we could change the way people thought we would change their behavior." However, she also notes that "in a culture of domination almost everyone engages in behaviors that contradict their beliefs and values."[3] She concludes that this inconsistency between words and deeds suggests that American culture relies on a series of lies that blur fantasy and reality. In another book, hooks argues that "to break with the ruling hegemony that has a hold on images of the black male body [and African American culture], a revolutionary visual aesthetic must emerge that reappropriates, revises, and reinvents, giving everyone something new to look at."[4] Hooks reveals the difficulty of transforming social and cultural relations when legal discourse officially prohibits intentional racism but permits de facto racism. Existing racist imagery and stereotypes must be reworked; they cannot simply be ignored. Patricia Williams echoes hooks when she argues that antiracist activism now needs to focus on "creating a livable space between the poles of other people's imagination and the nice calm center of oneself where dignity resides."[5] For Williams, hooks, Cornell, and Bhabha, transformation is simultaneously the personal project of finding a safe space and the bigger project of helping historically marginalized people represent themselves in popular and political culture.

Lani Guinier, best known for her failed nomination as President Bill Clinton's assistant attorney general for civil rights, offered a series of proposals to reinvigorate democratic principles during the early 1990s. Her scholarship argues that our current emphasis on geographical districts and the idea of "one person, one vote" assumes "relative homogeneity within [a] district" and conflicts with the complex shifting of coalitions that influences most elections.[6] The voting system the United States currently follows—the winner-take-all approach—endures, Guinier argues, "because it promotes a two-party system that, accompanied by the high costs of campaigning, gives incumbents enormous power to retain their seats." This approach, she argues, is "ill-suited to the multiracial and polyethnic society of today because [it is] unable to fill the need for diverse debate and broad representation."[7] The rhetoric of "color-blindness," within election law among other discourses, has been a major impediment to transforming social, legal, political, and cultural relations. Supporters of color-blindness argue that a color-conscious jurisprudence would violate constitutional commitments to neutrality and fairness because such approaches rely on racial or ethnic calculations. Guinier counters that color-blindness is not a virtue "but a visual defect" and "not a solution to centuries of discrimination based on race."[8] To ignore the historical and current meaning of race in American culture is to blind oneself to the very real ways that majority interests and perspectives continue to structure the political landscape for their benefit.[9] Guinier's efforts to empower African Americans to gain political representation offer a compelling analog to the role of hip-hop aesthetics during the post–Civil Rights era.

Hip-hop aesthetics has allowed contemporary artists, musicians, and writers to articulate a demand for social, political, economic, and cultural transformation. The concept of representation links the multifaceted concerns articulated by the hip-hop generation because neither their voices nor their likenesses are readily seen or heard even in a media-dominated society. Rather, worn racial stereotypes continue to circulate, in part because intellectual property law doctrines permit the ownership of racialized images or texts. The emphasis on consumption within hip-hop has only intensified the racialization of texts, images, objects, and logos and furthered their role as identity markers and avenues for self-representation. Social, political, economic, and cultural transformation necessarily involves engaging with and claiming ownership over extant texts within the American cultural imagination—even if they are (always) already owned either officially, through intellectual property law, or unofficially, as members of the Western canon.[10] Given the skepticism of postmodern movements, including CRT and postcolonial theory, about grand narratives and universal ideals, the concept of transformation, however, presents a problem, what Derrida might term an *aporia*. While CRT and postcolonial theorists attempt to use theory and scholarship to improve the lives of marginalized people, they also realize that any solutions they offer will necessarily be culturally bound and thus partial and incomplete. Consequently, their approach to cultural transformation is deeply imbued with irony, questioning whether real change is possible.

Intellectual property law, as a mediator between the public good and private property, has historically negotiated precisely these kinds of questions, increasingly so with the burgeoning of digital culture. The doctrine of transformative use permits copying when, echoing Bhabha, it dislocates the original from its conceptual and theoretical moorings, thereby opening up a new perspective or critical commentary. Unlike fair use, transformative use allows the creator who appropriates a text, image, icon, sound, or symbol to receive a cognizable legal interest over his or her creation. A transformative work does create new property. However, this new property must also either license the right to copy any borrowed material or demonstrate that the copying constitutes a fair use.[11] In an influential law-review article from 1990, Judge Pierre Leval argues for a finding of transformative use when "the secondary use adds value to the original—if the quoted matter is used as raw material, transformed in the creation of new information, new aesthetics, new insights and understandings—this is the very type of activity that the fair use doctrine intends to protect for the enrichment of society."[12] The boundary or borderline between derivative copying, which simply borrows elements from an earlier text, and transformative copying, which "adds value" to the original, appears to vary based on the court engaged in the review. Recent commentators have begun to articulate the concern that transformation has crept into fair-use analysis, changing the reserved public right to make copies in certain situations to an implied requirement demonstrating creative or critical purpose in the copying.[13] Some scholars have noted that courts are considerably more receptive to transformative borrowings in certain art forms (i.e., literature and painting) than in others (i.e., hip-hop music).[14] By analyzing and comparing the aesthetic structures of Alice Randall's *The Wind Done Gone* and Fred Wilson's *Mining the Museum*, this chapter contrasts the legal definition of transformative use with the one offered by hip-hop aesthetics. This focus on transformation helps clarify the shared critique of representation offered by hip-hop aesthetics and CRT.

The status of "transformative use" is murky within copyright and trademark law, even if courts are increasingly requiring it in fair-use defenses. Not specifically defined in either statutory framework, transformative use alternatively has been categorized as a special kind of fair use, because it permits copying if it significantly alters or comments upon the original[15] or as a noninfringing activity that is therefore outside the scope of fair use.[16] *The Wind Done Gone*, as a parody and with its distinctive perspective, narrative, and style, was deemed a transformative use of Margaret Mitchell's *Gone With the Wind*.[17] Quoting from the *Campbell v. Acuff-Rose* decision, the Court of Appeals concluded that "the fact that a parody may impair the market for derivative uses by the very effectiveness of its critical commentary is no more relevant under copyright than the like threat to the original market."[18] In his concurring opinion, Judge Stanley Marcus emphasized both free-market and free-speech concerns, arguing that the "two books will act as complements rather than substitutes" and that Randall's version of parody is "a vital commodity in the marketplace of ideas."[19]

Many legal and cultural critics viewed the litigation as an opportunity to highlight how current intellectual property law regulates and stifles freedom.[20] Jeb Rubenfeld, Alice Randall's legal counsel, characterized the case as one involving the "freedom of imagination" and argued that "no one [ought to] be penalized for imagining or for communicating what he imagines."[21] By recasting the First Amendment around the freedom of imagination, Rubenfeld attempted to develop constitutional protections for "readers, viewers, and listeners as well" as speakers, artists, and writers to invigorate democracy, free speech, and creativity.[22] His approach was endorsed neither by the *SunTrust* court nor by other courts. Rather, they viewed the case through the lens of transformative use. My reading of copyright law suggests that it would not prohibit anyone from imagining or even producing a derivative musical, visual, or literary work, contrary to what Rubenfeld suggests. It is not communication or speaking that gives rise to a claim of infringement, but selling those expressions in the marketplace and creating a market substitute. Consequently, if hip-hop artists and aesthetes did not seek to "get paid" and merely enjoyed their music and art on their own, there would be an open question as to whether their fair use or transformative copying would violate intellectual property law.[23]

Transformative use, unlike some of the issues explored here, can be usefully approached by law and economics scholarship, a form of legal analysis that competed with CRT during the 1990s and promoted legal change based on economic theory.[24] Richard Posner, a founding member of the law and economics movement, argues that intellectual property law, because it provides monopolies, can stifle the flow of those imaginative resources by enabling unproductive owners to engage in rent-seeking behavior that charges exorbitant licensing fees.[25] Posner's concern about rent seeking, however, does not indicate that he argues intellectual property law needs a wholesale revision. Rather, he and William Landes find basic concepts in law and economics, such as the difference between complementary and substitutional copying,[26] to offer efficient solutions to the challenges brought about by the increased propertization of cultural life. For Landes and Posner, the transformative, complementary, or "productive use is one that lowers the cost of expression and thus tends to increase the number of original works, while reproductive use simply increases the number of copies of a given work, reduces the gross profits of the author, and reduces the incentives to create works."[27] They argue that intellectual property law ought to maximize the incentives for authors to produce new works without creating artificial barriers for newer artists; hence they criticized the Sonny Bono Copyright Term Extension Act of 1998 that lengthened the term of existing copyrights.[28] Referencing *The Wind Done Gone* and other works, Landes and Posner argue that because parody, by definition, occasionally attacks the original and its author, there are some instances in which the market is unlikely to arrive at an efficient agreement because the benefits of the transformative use accrue to society, not to the parodied artist. Fair and transformative uses, as result, promote creativity and timely criticism better than a strong property regime does.[29] Throughout their book, they make it clear that copying itself is not the problem. Rather, unproductive copying, which merely reproduces another text, disrupts the efficient operation of intellectual property law. This substitutive copying creates the problems of "free riders" who steal away the goodwill and originality of another. Ironically, their defense of copyright's fair-use doctrine borrows the idea of "consumer confusion" from trademark law. Rather than arguing that infringement primarily disrupts copyright's incentive structure, they blur boundaries between incentives for creativity and protecting the creator's goodwill.

Both Posner and Rubenfeld conceive of originality, fair use, and transformative use as transcultural and color-blind strategies to regulate the circulation of texts, including raced texts. Neither connects texts to specific genres, to cultural traditions, or to how popular culture's taste for Roy Orbison and *Gone With the Wind* derive, in part, from interaction with America's racial history. Although both agree that Randall's book constitutes a transformative use, they rely on the color-blind literary category of parody to define and limit its critical edge. To represent Randall's engagement with Mitchell's *Gone With the Wind* as parody alone severs the link between her work and African American culture, hip-hop aesthetics, and CRT. This characterization undermines Randall's critical impulse—displaying the racist narrative underlying Mitchell's novel—because it prematurely resolves the conflict between Mitchell's property rights in that narrative and efforts like Randall's to demonstrate the unconscious racial subjectivity that marks a putatively color-blind discourse.[30]

## Re/Writing History: *The Wind Done Gone*

*Gone With the Wind*, Margaret Mitchell's dramatic rendering of the South before the Civil War, has frequently been criticized by African American writers and cultural critics.[31] Mitchell's novel explores the antebellum South through the eyes of Scarlett O'Hara, the young daughter of a rich, white plantation owner. Determined to find love and wealth as the Civil War approaches, Scarlett interacts with many African American characters, who appear lazy, stupid, and childlike. Scarlett alone stands as a frustrated romantic hero who must overcome numerous obstacles, including the general ineptitude of her African American slaves and servants, as the South disintegrates following the war. Upon its release, the book and subsequent movie produced a wide range of responses—from adulation to disgust.[32] Although sixty years have elapsed between the release of the book and the movie and the present day, *Gone With the Wind*, in both movie and book form, still remains popular and constructs popular memory about antebellum Southern life, even as it depicts African Americans in stereotypical ways.[33]

Alice Randall's *The Wind Done Gone* takes the original and turns it on its head, perhaps following the paradigm offered by Margaret Walker's *Jubilee* (1966).[34] Randall appropriates the original's elements and reshapes them through her version of hip-hop aesthetics.[35] Randall's revision focuses on the viewpoints of the slaves on the plantation Tara. Unlike *Gone With the Wind*, which does not include any characters that suggest sexual liaisons between whites and blacks in the antebellum South, Randall creates a new narrative center for her retelling by developing a character—Cynara, the illegitimate daughter of Planter (Gerald O'Hara)—who was not present in Mitchell's version. Cynara's life is a direct contrast to Scarlett's and demonstrates the differences between black experiences and memories of that period and those described by Mitchell. Randall changes the character and place names. Scarlett is now named Other. Ashley Wilkes, the white gentleman after whom Scarlett pines, is named Dreamy Gentleman, and he is gay. Melanie Wilkes, Ashley's wife, is called Mealy Mouth in Randall's parody. Other changes include transforming the main plantation's name from Tara to Tata, Rhett Butler to R., and the plantation's nickname from Twelve Oaks to Twelve Slaves Strong as Trees.

The first half of *The Wind Done Gone* retells the basic plot of *Gone With the Wind* from an African American perspective, particularly that of a mixed-race child of a slave and her owner. Her owner/father sells Cynara to a friend, but at a discounted price and with the caveat that she should be spared hard labor.[36] Planter undertakes what he perceives as a benevolent act, but this separates Cynara from her mother and the African American community on the plantation. This also initiates a competition between Cynara and Planter's daughter, Other, over Mammy's affection and culminates in a battle for R.'s affection.[37] *The Wind Done Gone* narrates Other's sexuality as Mammy's calculated attempt to torment and torture white men, rather than as the product of Scarlett's inner strength, as portrayed by Mitchell.[38] Randall also reverses Mitchell's account of Gerald O'Hara's luck and hard work. For example, she describes how Garlic, Planter's trusted servant, arranged for Planter to win him and Tata at cards.[39] She also provides an alternative account of the plantation's construction and meaning. Randall relates that the African American slaves shaped the building's architecture, encoding themselves as the twelve pillars that cleared the land and constructed it. In their minds, the twelve slaves represented the twelve disciples.[40]

The second half of Randall's book follows the life of Cynara as she explores the upper echelons of African American society during Reconstruction, including a fictional party at Frederick Douglass's house in Washington, D.C. This second section departs significantly from the original. It narrates Cynara's thinking as she decides whether to marry an African American congressman, which would symbolize her identity as a race woman, or R., signifying her triumph over Other in their competition for affection. This choice causes Cynara to contemplate the meaning of her newly found freedom. She remarks: "It has nothing to do with politics or elections. It has to do with having many things you want and being free to choose between them or free not to choose and remaining safely the same."[41] In this passage, Randall blurs Reconstruction and post–Civil Rights era concerns. Echoing the law and economics movement and hip-hop culture, Randall argues that freedom follows from choosing between desires, not simply participating in elections or democracy. Within this framework, slavery and segregation limit the life choices for African Americans and thus stifle their freedom. The post–Civil Rights era, by contrast, emphasizes material and sexual satisfaction, for better or worse, as the ultimate *feeling* of freedom. Despite her own reflections on freedom, Cynara finds herself forced to select R. as her husband because he is what she names "my Debt."[42] R. constitutes her debt because she cannot escape her past, especially the emotional and psychological effects of being dispossessed by her father and mother. Later, Cynara tries to leave R. and resume her affair with the engaged congressman, Adam Conyers. She leaves R. and all his things but takes Other's prized family possessions because she feels that she should have inherited them, as Planter was her father too.[43] An African American doctor, who is examining her about a mysterious skin blotch, tells her that her role as a "Confederate's concubine" would taint Conyers within the African American community.[44] Cynara ultimately sells "Lady's earbobs [her retrieved inheritance] and [buys] a little house" with the proceeds.[45] The novel's closing intimates that Conyers's wife cannot bear children, but that Cynara, his lover, gives her child to them so that the boy can be liberated from her past and its racial-sexual trauma.

In addition to their respective endings, the two books differ in that Mitchell's possesses an omniscient narrator, who focuses primarily on developing Scarlett's subjectivity. Randall's book, by contrast, is a fictional diary that exclusively relates Cynara's point of view. This shift of perspectives is critical for understanding the transformative aspects of Randall's revision of Mitchell. In a key moment of the diary, Cynara writes: "It is not in the pigment of my skin that my Negressness lies. It is not the color of my skin. It is the color of my mind, and my mind is dark, dusky, like a beautiful night."[46] Anticipating the litigation surrounding her book, Randall emphasizes how subjectivity, both the writer's and the reader's, determines a text's meaning. Based on this reasoning, logic suggests that any revisionist account would most likely be a wholly new creation, as the later one reworks the earlier based on a particular viewpoint or perspective. However, as *The Wind Done Gone* also explores, establishing ownership over one's self and one's perceptions requires social recognition. About her relationship with R., Cynara observes: "Without mutuality, without empathy to join and precede sympathy, I am but a doll come to life. A pretty nigger doll dressed up in finery, hair pressed for play."[47] Although she desperately wants to establish a formally recognized relationship with R., she cannot do so without R. and society abandoning stereotypes and preconceptions around such interracial relationships.

As might be expected, Randall's *The Wind Done Gone* caused considerable controversy and resulted in a copyright infringement lawsuit, which threatened to enjoin publication of the novel. Many African American scholars, including Henry Louis Gates and Toni Morrison, supported Randall's right to publish the novel. They relied on two claims about how it transformed, or attempted to transform, the American cultural imagination. First, Gates asserted the role of parody in African American cultural production:

> Scholars have long established that parody is at the heart of African American expression, because it is a creative mechanism for the exercise of political speech, sentiment, and commentary on the part of people who feel themselves oppressed or maligned and wish to protest that condition of oppression or misrepresentation . . . and

*The Wind Done Gone* is only the most recent instance of a long and humorous tradition.[48]

Gates claims that Randall's reliance on and use of African American aesthetic forms, what I have termed hip-hop aesthetics in its contemporary iteration, enable her to protest social inequalities and racial stereotypes. Bridging politics, art, and literature, Gates suggests that artistic creations help foster fuller and more systematic forms of democratic representation. Randall's novel merges the political and the literary to dissent from current representational regimes, in which historical conditions and cultural hierarchy limit the democratic potential of either discourse alone. By locating Randall within a specific cultural tradition, rather than the universal category of literature or even parody, Gates implicitly suggests that legal discourse must engage in a color-conscious jurisprudence in order to understand the copyright and trademark claims brought forth by the litigation.

*The Wind Done Gone* litigation also provided an avenue for African American and copyright activists alike to expose how legal discourse ignores cultural context when applying intellectual property law doctrines. Toni Morrison articulated the second argument about how an African American novel could challenge its use of an extant text, written by a white author. She argued that the novel "imagine[s] and occup[ies] narrative spaces and silences never once touched upon nor conceived of in Mrs. Mitchell's novel: that is the interior lives of slaves and ex slaves, their alternative views; their different journey."[49] Echoing Bhabha's postcolonial articulation of "transformation" as negotiation and reinscription, Morrison insists that writers, artists, or musicians who engage questions of racial or ethnic difference frequently refashion artifacts of dominant culture to challenge the worldview encoded in those texts. Unlike Gates, who tends to omit or elide ownership questions, Morrison characterizes the entire litigation as an effort to determine the relation between property law and cultural memory: "Who controls how history is imagined?" and "Who gets to say what slavery was like for the slaves?"[50] For Morrison, such representations of history do not involve simply the past but the continued ownership of Mitchell's slaves for future generations. The extent to which Randall's text transforms Mitchell's hinges on Randall's ability to show the representational limits and blind spots in *Gone With the Wind*. Mitchell's omissions, which her heirs claim to own as much as they possess the actual text, reflect Mitchell's racial subjectivity and the copyrighted material that flows from it. According to Morrison, Randall must be free to create and own a counterversion of those events because the only way to transform the future is to present an alternative vision of the past. It would be ironic, however, to say the least, if Mitchell's heirs could demand ownership over and profit from an act intended to remedy the racist effects of her text. An appropriate analogy would be if a company dumped toxic chemicals that seeped onto their neighbor's land and then demanded to be compensated for the unlicensed use of the contaminating products because their neighbor sought to remove them. Racialized texts like Mitchell's should be viewed as environmental polluters, not the neutral or innocent victims that the fair-use doctrine suggests. Lovalerie King ingeniously notes that only the commercial success of *Gone With the Wind*, in part due to its racialized imagery, could later finance the Mitchell heirs' lawsuit against Alice Randall and Houghton Mifflin.[51]

Although her testimony does not engage with legal discourse at this level of specificity, Morrison implicitly questions both the distributive and the metaphorical effects of the fair-use doctrine. Fair use, in either its copyright or its trademark form, allows and perhaps reinforces the original ownership claim and forces artists, writers, musicians, and others to endorse earlier uses as "fair" even if they intend to engage in an "unfair" use that transforms the earlier text. The metaphor that permits cultural criticism thus undermines the very cultural or political claims these critics offer. Based on his review of property rhetoric in American culture and its racial effects, Stephen Best cynically concludes that the rhetoric of equality or neutrality within property discourses has always operated in a racist or racialized manner in which African American bodies, cultural practices, and ideas seem to regularly get transformed into property by whites and their corporate interests.[52] The fiction of fair use elides the very way this doctrine stabilizes the transformative potential of the radical utterances offered by hip-hop aesthetes because fair use does not fundamentally alter or redistribute property rights. Ongoing critical dialogues about whether "fair use" applies or ought to apply to a given situation cause antiracist activists to adopt a seemingly color-blind language. Although critics and scholars of African American literature and culture read the novel in ways outlined by Gates and Morrison, copyright law's doctrine affected how Houghton Mifflin marketed the book and how some consumers read the book. In response to the threat of litigation, Houghton Mifflin marketed *The Wind Done Gone* as a parody to augment its fair-use claim, and readers were encouraged to understand the book in this way once the cover described it as an "unauthorized parody." I would argue, however, that viewing the novel as an example of hip-hop aesthetics, although not a view adopted by either court during the litigation, might be more useful.

Like other texts that exemplify hip-hop aesthetics, Randall's relies on sampling, layering, rhythmic asymmetry, and irony to produce its metaphoric structure, tone, pace, and ultimately its overall effort at representing the subjectivity absent from Mitchell's novel. As the *SunTrust* court noted, Randall does not sample or appropriate the entire novel. Rather, she engages in what courts describe as "fragmented literal similarity" because she borrows elements almost exactly from the source but then creates a substantially different text.[53] The sampling is thus selective and tactical, deviating from the original frequently. Randall engages in layering, as she appropriates only key moments from Mitchell's text to present its racialized nature and then juxtaposes those samples in rapid succession to demonstrate how this textual foundation could have uncovered alternative subjective realms. Randall's use of staccato-like journal entries, instead of the flowing chapters employed by Mitchell, both reinforces the layered quality of her novel, because she provides an intentionally uneven and slightly disjointed narrative, and captures the tell-tale rhythmic flow and asymmetry of hip-hop music. Unlike Mitchell's novel, which appears encyclopedic and complete in its description of Southern plantation life, *The Wind Done Gone* highlights the novel's many "breaks." Through its structure, Randall's text reinforces its partial and subjective rendering of events, calling attention to silences and gaps. The foundational fiction upon which the novel rests—that it is the found journal of a forgotten hero—reflects the hip-hop ethic of digging in the crates to find "phat" beats that have gone unrecognized. These found sounds, however, serve as both a testament to the original and an opportunity for the listener/dancer to find something new in this material and display their own dancing skills or moves. The resulting rhythmic flow and asymmetry of Randall's text provide an opportunity for the reader to look inward and find his or her own truths, connecting and disrupting the reader to/from the historical events the novel describes.

Cynara's journey, unlike Scarlett's romantic transcendence of the Civil War and Reconstruction, offers a more ironic or ambiguous account of what the era and Mitchell's novel mean for contemporary African Americans. Exploring the inverse of Scarlett's struggle to maintain her identity despite the abolition of slavery, Cynara relates her struggle to claim ownership over herself during the failed effort at Reconstruction:

Everything about ownership is changing: land, people, money, gold into foreign currency back into foreign gold, and gold back into money in our banks. It doesn't seem in this time of hurricanes and storms and other acts of God, with winds of every sort of change in the air, that hearts would be any different. Why couldn't she who couldn't own, who now owned forty acres and a mule—if I could own a former plantation—could I not own a planter's heart?[54]

In this quotation, Cynara contemplates how newly freed African Americans must navigate numerous challenges after the Civil War. Fairly quickly, Cynara makes a transition from owning wealth to "owning" affection—suggesting the affective dimensions of ownership and commodification. Although property law traditionally understands its subject as regulating the relationship between people and things, this passage intentionally undermines these assumptions by characterizing love under the rubric of property rights. Cynara's reflections bring attention to how property rights, despite the law's stated intentions, regulate emotional and personal landscapes as much as physical ones. Randall's word choice also reminds readers that antebellum law offered white men the legal form to realize their desires, against the wishes of the objects of their affection.

Foreshadowing current debates over intellectual property law and the likelihood of being sued by Mitchell's heirs, Randall describes Cynara's reaction when R., without permission, reads her diary: "It is thrilling to be known even when the knowledge is stolen, stolen like rubies."[55] Once again, Randall frames personal, emotional, psychological, and cultural conflicts in the language of property law. However, her deployment of property rhetoric does not offer clear solutions to persistent legal problems. Property law necessarily appears as both a natural language for articulating such claims and wholly problematic because it transforms people and their emotions into commodities. R. ignores Cynara's ownership over the journal, and thus she is quite rightly outraged at his behavior. Despite this violation, Cynara nonetheless relishes the attention being paid to her. R.'s desire to read her diary in effect validates her worth because R. views it as something worthy of stealing, which is a perverse honor in its own right. Through this incident with the diary, Randall shows that the culture industries have treated African American culture like a colony with raw materials worth plundering. In the realm of copyright law, jazz and blues musicians frequently found themselves forced to sign bad contracts that transferred their rights to white producers. Having a bad recording contract was better than not having one.[56] Hip-hop musicians have seen how the Federal Communications Commission's decision to deregulate the airwaves during the 1990s has contributed to the overexposure of gangsta rap and the underexposure of other forms of hip-hop.[57]

For Randall, the prospect of enduring the wrath of the Mitchell estate presents a surprisingly analogous dynamic. The estate's copyright infringement lawsuit against Houghton Mifflin emphasized that Randall's book would limit its ability to authorize derivative works, even though its own guidelines for licensing such works specifically prohibited writers from exploring miscegenation or homosexuality.[58] It appears that through its lawsuit, the Mitchell estate recognized the suppressed subjectivities only to engage in an act of neocolonialism that retraumatizes African Americans by refusing them ownership rights to their very thoughts and imaginations. Because Randall's subject matter—race and sexuality—contradicts the Mitchell estate's wishes, Mitchell's heirs refused to even consider negotiating a license with Randall. What caused this conflict was a concern about race and sexuality, not the length of copyrights, the topic upon which many commentators focused. Intellectual property law merely proved an effective strategy for increasing the value of a copyrighted text and impeding social and cultural criticism of that product.

A CRT response to intellectual property must engage with how its central principles unconsciously invoke, evoke, and protect racism, racialization, and racist structures. Their transformation likely requires copying, dilution, and unfair use of existing images, texts, logos, and sounds. The challenge for antiracist activists will be to become knowledgeable about legal discourse even as they maintain sufficient grounding in other discursive spheres, including music, literature, art, and popular culture, to highlight the ruptures, ambiguities, and ironies in law's understanding and regulation of culture and vice versa. Increasingly, cultural practices and legal discourse regulate and write over one another. Hip-hop aesthetics, as articulated in and through Randall's *The Wind Done Gone*, suggest that the freedom to innovate, in either law or culture, will be found in the breaks or ruptures between sampled material.

## Fragments of Memory: *Mining the Museum*

Fred Wilson's 1992 show *Mining the Museum* captured the attention of audiences and institutions, causing even popular magazines such as *Rolling*

*Stone* and the *Economist* to review the show.[59] Drawing on the work of David Hammons, Betye Saar, Allison Saar, and others, Wilson's work takes ordinary objects, from both high and low culture, and examines the racialized nature of contemporary power relations within them. Wilson does not merely copy or appropriate but explores the possibility of transforming American culture. He juxtaposes objects to make explicit the filters or lenses that limit the American cultural imagination. In particular, Wilson makes vivid the artificial boundaries created by and reinforced through art galleries, museums, and curatorial practices. Like Alice Randall, Wilson helps clear the intellectual landscape so that alternative subjectivities and perspectives may be heard or seen. Implicitly applying insights from CRT and postcolonial theory, his installations challenge white supremacy, not simply as an ideological system but as an ongoing set of unconscious racialized and racist practices perpetuated by well-meaning people whose actions frequently frustrate their stated intentions or values.[60] Some of his most disquieting pieces demonstrate that apparently color-blind or neutral categories, such as cabinetmaking and woodworking, have helped maintain white supremacy in the United States.[61] If Whitehead and Charles question the fairness of particular images and texts, Wilson interrogates the operation of the entire institutional structure of art in the United States.

In *Mining the Museum* and other shows, Wilson waits until he is approached by a museum or institution and then builds a strong relationship with them.[62] Unlike Randall, who had to defend herself from a copyright infringement suit, Wilson receives permission to appropriate before beginning his installations. This method protects him from legal liability but limits his art to those institutions that permit him access. Even though he does not operate as a copyright or trademark outlaw, Wilson's pieces deploy hip-hop aesthetics to question how a museum collects and displays objects. Like other hip-hop aesthetes, Wilson deploys layered samples, borrowed from the museum, to create ruptures in the American cultural imagination and ironic commentaries on institutional practices. Wilson describes his own artistic process: "I appropriate, reuse, and combine things that already exist. I am guided by concerns that preclude painting, sculpture, and drawing as they are usually known."[63] Following Andy Warhol and many contemporary artists, Wilson deploys the museum collections into a critique of how those institutions aid and abet cultural hierarchy.[64]

Unlike other practitioners of museum-based art, Wilson seeks to demonstrate how the host museum perpetuates racism and racial hierarchy through its curatorial practices and processes.[65] He speaks with the museum's curatorial staff, docents, and local experts to deploy the museum's collection to show how race, racism, and racialization affect the museum's shows. Reviewing *Mining the Museum*, Maurice Berger concludes that the installation's "meaning . . . emerges out of this confluence of dialogues—between historical and newly created objects, between artifacts and fictional wall labels, between the codes and styles of exhibition and the objects they validate and define, between the artist and the institutions he critiques, between the spectator and the exhibition itself."[66] Lisa Corrin argues that Wilson's work "provides a strategy to reclaim the terrain of the museum for itself" and "to make cultural experiences 'mine' by participating in the process of writing and presenting history."[67] Somewhat surprisingly, neither Berger nor Corrin (nor other critics who have written on his work) has connected its aesthetic structure to any musical form, despite the tendency for such comparisons in African American cultural studies. While Wilson has casually mentioned that both Romare Bearden and Richard Hunt inspired him, few scholars have examined how African American art or music has influenced him.[68] His transformative use of museum materials displays the elements of hip-hop aesthetics, particularly as his work asserts a form of cultural-ownership claims over the host institution. Because he has received permission to sample the materials he uses, Wilson does not assert a direct property claim over the museum, but the right of African Americans to represent themselves within the museum.

For Wilson's work, the distinction between text and context is blurry if not nonexistent. Even the book associated with the *Mining the Museum* show contributes to this blurring by including comments from docents and visitors. This leads to the question of whether the docents and visitors, and their experiences, constitute part of the display.[69] Although critics and Wilson himself have identified his primary form as installation, Leslie King-Hammond suggests that this designation does not do justice to his art's complexity. Rather, she argues that "space arrangements may be more appropriate because part of your [Wilson's] process involves interpreting or reinterpreting or trying to define an experience within space."[70] This difficulty in defining the appropriate genre for Wilson's art reflects both its innovative nature and the limits of generic classifications. It also presents a challenge in describing and analyzing his work. Rather, per King-Hammond's and Berger's observations, his work's central features include its layered samples and its ideological ruptures that pierce the apparent flow of the museum.

Critics such as Irene Winter and Ira Berlin have analyzed or viewed

Wilson's museum installations primarily through the lens of postmodernism or as an application of Foucault's concept of genealogy. In their analyses, Wilson deploys documents, objects, and other texts to provide a counterhistory that explains how America arrived at its current ideological state. While their analysis provides much of the historical context of his exhibitions, they neglect the aesthetic dimension of his installations. Wilson deploys these items primarily as samples to be recontextualized into an alternative narrative, not as independent facts that can stand on their own merit. Wilson has even commented that he sees "beauty as a way of helping people to receive difficult or upsetting ideas."[71] Characteristic of hip-hop aesthetics, Wilson relies on the logic of the sample to quickly make a connection with the audience, only to rework the sample and transform its meaning.[72]

Perhaps the best examples of his use of sampled materials to visually convey an idea might be *Baby Carriage* and *Hood*, from his installation piece *Modes of Transport, 1770–1910*, in the *Mining the Museum* show. In a 1908 black baby carriage, Wilson placed a white hood, found in Maryland and presumably used by a member of the Ku Klux Klan. The explanatory cards accompanying the objects indicated that the makers of both were unknown. The hood was an "anonymous gift," a description that ironically comments on the owner's ambivalent relations to the hood and the ongoing anonymity surrounding racist activities in the United States. Wilson produced neither object; rather, he found them within the Maryland Historical Society's collection. Wilson did, however, write the explanatory note. His creativity, like that of Adrian Piper's conceptual art, consists in his ability to juxtapose the objects within a new framework that transforms their meaning and causes viewers to make new connections between the objects that had not been obvious but can no longer be denied. In his analysis of musical sampling, Joseph Schloss argues that the break beats sampled by hip-hop only come into existence as samples once the deejay hears and deploys them, thus creating the sample.[73] By analogy, the materials Wilson finds within the Maryland Historical Society's archives do not exist as museum objects (neither had been previously displayed) until he selects them for this installation, where they become linked. The connection between a black baby carriage and a Ku Klux Klan hood is by no means obvious or necessary. However, once joined, they become powerful symbols of the role African American slaves and domestics played in raising white children who ultimately became responsible for maintaining and promoting white supremacy. It also presents the irony that many African American women devoted disproportionate attention and care to white children who would likely grow up and engage in acts of racial violence against them, their families, and their community. For some viewers, their juxtaposition constituted the single most powerful moment of the entire exhibit.[74] Through these combined samples, Wilson represents the complex and intertwined relationship between raising children and fostering racial hatred. The sample thus becomes a key building block in producing the tensions and contradictions his work seeks to expose. It allows him to undermine the representational practices of museums through mimicry that takes the familiar and makes it unfamiliar.[75]

As the relationship between *Baby Carriage* and *Hood* suggests, it is not simply the use of sampled material but how the samples are layered that structures Wilson's artwork and differentiates it from other museum-based installations. For example, *Punt Gun* juxtaposes a gun with a series of posters advertising rewards for capturing runaway slaves. On the reward posters, Wilson highlights the frequent references to distinguishing marks or traits that resulted from the owner's violence against the African American slaves.[76] The posters, which could be found in both the North and the South, evidence how such signs and symbols were deeply embedded in American culture. Further illustrating the quotidian nature of white supremacy, Wilson uses not a rifle but a punt gun in this piece. Hunters used this gun and others like it for hunting ducks and other fowl, not chasing runaway slaves. Nonetheless, Wilson tries to demonstrate or jar the audience into considering how closely related such hunts were, even if today duck hunting is still commonly practiced and slavery is nearly universally condemned. Nearby, Wilson has posted a description of game hunting, offered by a white man, and the testimony of a former slave about how whites raised and trained dogs for tracking runaway slaves. Through this layering of objects and texts, Wilson's exhibit relies on the interaction between samples to raise questions and demonstrate how context determines the meaning and significance of the text or object.

Irene Winter argues that Wilson's museum installations force viewers to confront the contingent or plural histories possessed by artifacts.[77] For Winter, Wilson's installations undermine the assumption, adopted by fair-use doctrine, that a particular text possesses a singular and determinate meaning. Rather, Wilson's method of juxtaposing objects and texts suggests that museums regulate meaning, much like intellectual property law, by fixing or imprisoning art into a distinct context. By segregating the punt gun and the reward posters for runaway slaves, museums had in effect erased the social or cultural ethos of nineteenth-century white supremacy, even as they displayed or possessed the objects that told that story. According to Wilson, the context creates a text's or an object's meaning. Like intellectual property law, museums discourage transformative uses, as they tend to protect the expectations of audiences and adopt a "status quo" version of visual culture. They can operate more like copyright owners than like spaces fostering public dialogue because frequently they are heavily invested in the artwork they own and thus inclined to transform their holdings into icons, which conceal the darker side of American history. As institutions, they prefer stability or continuity to bold change so that they can purchase art with the confidence that their holdings' value, both economic and cultural, will remain high or increase.

The expectations of museums and other cultural institutions run directly counter to one aspect of African American creativity—signifyin'—especially as developed by hip-hop aesthetes. Signifiers can turn the meaning of any particular text or utterance upside down, depending on how it is employed or cited. Copyright and trademark law, in part, seek to regulate the context to which a particular text or mark can be applied. Hip-hop aesthetes and other African American cultural workers, however, assume that a primary artistic challenge is to show mastery over existing texts by reworking them. Wilson's creativity centers on the intangible intellectual and emotional bonds his work elicits, rather than on producing new objects or texts. The fair-use doctrine purportedly promotes free speech, but it does so at the cost of characterizing Wilson's methods as copying, albeit under the doctrine of fair use, rather than as signifyin' or some other cultural category, because legal discourse views such texts as static. Wilson's deployment of layering undermines this assumption by demonstrating how historical and cultural context shape a text's meaning. Layered samples provide an aesthetic structure to criticize how intellectual property law protects the status quo, especially in terms of the American cultural imagination. Because commodities, especially in copyrighted and trademarked forms, have become the focus of cultural struggle, efforts to articulate alternative or subaltern perspectives through those very commodities increasingly are regulated by intellectual property law and the fair-use doctrine.

Like other hip-hop texts, Wilson's installations operate through rhythmic flows and ruptures. By offering an elaborate mimicry of curatorial practices, Wilson's work deploys layered samples to defamiliarize the familiar.[78] Destabilizing both temporal and spatial dimensions, Wilson relies on the structure and feel of the museum precisely to demonstrate what these institutions consciously or unconsciously hide. In *Mining the Museum*, Wilson disrupts the flow of the Maryland Historical Society in numerous ways. In one room, he displays the busts of famous non-Marylanders owned by the museum and the absence of busts of famous African American Marylanders, such as Harriet Tubman, Frederick Douglass, and Benjamin Banneker. In another room, he displays a portrait by Henry Bebie with a rip in it, breaking the general museum practice of only showing undamaged paintings. Another gallery uses lights and recorded questions to draw viewers' attention to how eighteenth- and nineteenth-century painters used black figures to balance their compositions. The questions encourage viewers to consider the lost or hidden subjectivities of those African American figures. At other shows, Wilson has identified purportedly Native American skeletons as "Someone's Sister" or "Someone's Mother" in *Friendly Natives* (1991) and placed Egyptian-style heads on Greek statuary in *Panta Rhei: A Gallery of Ancient Classical Art* (1992). Like a skilled hip-hop deejay, Wilson's installation pieces create a particular flow or feeling only to deconstruct the very familiarity offered by that flow, thereby representing the historical gaps in art history.

These moments of rupture allow Wilson to interrogate the assumption of race-neutrality or color-blindness within art, culture, and law. In an interview with Martha Buskirk and elsewhere, Wilson explains that because contemporary art, especially its lineage from Duchamp and Warhol, successfully destroyed the barrier between high and low culture, the only way to create ruptures is "look at the museum itself and to pull out the relationships that are invisibly there and to make them visible."[79] Every element of the museum, for Wilson, reflects the history of race and racism. While Duchamp, Warhol, and others successfully demonstrated the class biases and ideology of museums, Wilson extends their critique to racism. Through his work, it has become clear that museums provide the intellectual space where legal, cultural, and art discourses converge to produce a racially encoded narrative about genius, creativity, and originality. In this narrative, individual artists, primarily from Europe, produce paintings purely from their imaginations based on their interpretation of or response to Western European culture. Within this narrative, African Americans and other racially or ethnically marked people produce naturalistic, utilitarian, or imitative work that lacks the imagination or creativity of Western Europeans. African or Asian influences on Western art tend to be downplayed, if not ignored. Museum staff and art historians also quietly elide the horrors Europeans inflicted on non-Western people by omitting that art from museums and keeping silent about the historical conditions that allowed Western museums to gain ownership of non-Western art. The art museum thus typically provides a history from above that not only refuses to acknowledge the experiences of ordinary citizens but also makes invisible colonialism, slavery, and their attendant horrors.

In his museum pieces, Wilson ruptures the unspoken narratives of racialized genius, elite patronage and ownership of the arts, and color-blind curatorial practices. Citing Homi Bhabha, Jennifer Gonzalez argues that Wilson's exhibit *The Other Museum* (1990) "present[s] a subaltern perspective on colonial conquest and the subsequent international trade in material goods, aesthetic artifacts, and people."[80] Like Randall's *Cynara*, Wilson's mining of the museum's archives allows him to reveal the stories hidden from dominant culture. Rather than acting as a neutral testament to artistic achievement, the museum enshrines a set of racialized hopes, fears, dreams, and aspirations. This unconscious racialized and class gaze appropriates and commodifies other cultures' artifacts and practices even as it devalues the creativity and genius of historically marginalized people. Gonzalez astutely notes that in *The Other Museum* the "objects were identified neither as the 'gift' of a particular donor, nor as having been anonymously 'acquired' by the museum, but rather as 'stolen from' a particular community or sacred burial site."[81] In this exhibition and others, such as *Guarded View* (1991) and *Friendly Natives* (1991), Wilson clarifies the regulative function of the explanatory card. Although frequently the size of a note card, these cards assert ownership and interpretative claims over the artwork they label and describe. By mimicking the structure/form of these cards, Wilson questions their banal and frequently color-blind description of provenance and historical context. This rupture reminds audiences that these cards seek to maintain the status quo and transform potentially dynamic artwork into static representations of white supremacy. By intervening in the ephemera associated with art, Wilson produces a break in art history discourses, as well as questioning the allocation and distribution of ownership rights over art.

Wilson's imaginative reworking of museum collections frequently results in irony and ambiguity.[82] In these works, Wilson deploys the artifacts not as unique objects, but as symptoms or effects of institutional practices and ideology. By making previously hidden curatorial decisions visible, Wilson offers an ironic reading of textual meaning. While Duchamp and Warhol used the museum space to criticize high culture's faux elitism and the growing influence of popular culture, Wilson's irony aims at the necessarily contradictory roles museums perform in contemporary culture. The museum, as George Stocking observes, possesses the twin goals of collecting (i.e., owning) art objects and of creating a public space to observe and discuss art.[83] These goals conflict because successful collecting requires catering to market ideas and values even if they promote invidious racial stereotypes and white supremacy. Consequently, museum collections are unavoidably marked by the potential conflict between public service and private ownership. Most institutions resolve this potential conflict by serving the public as long as it generally promotes their collections' market and cultural value. Through their organizational and taxonomic methods, museums promote their private interest by downplaying the ambiguity and irony in their galleries. Wilson observes that "with curating, the whole notion of irony is not involved, often for good reason—because the public in the museum space expects some form of universal truth or knowledge."[84] What Wilson identifies as the curatorial goal of universal truth, I would characterize perhaps more cynically as mere satisfaction of market demand, or giving audiences what they claim to want. Due to persistent economic inequalities and the ongoing cultural hierarchy maintained by many institutions, meeting market demands frequently means repeating dominant (i.e., white) historical perspectives.

In the exhibition catalog accompanying Wilson's retrospective show, Maurice Berger defines Wilson's narrative form as allegory. For Berger, allegory involves "the appropriation of preexisting or familiar narratives in order to generate a secondary narrative of extended metaphors or association."[85] What distinguishes allegory from other appropriative genres, according to Berger, is that it "isolates what is culturally significant from the past and then interprets it in ways that give it relevance to the present."[86] For Berger, Wilson's work is not ambiguous but generative because it demonstrates that past curatorial practices and exclusions continue to shape public memory. Berger argues that Wilson's museum installations, in effect, claim ownership over public memory by reorienting the past and making its influence on the present visible. Berger concludes that this turn to allegory enables Wilson "to make cultural experiences 'mine' by participating in the process of writing and presenting history."[87] For Corrin, Wilson's art provokes an endless litany of questions, interrogating how museums represent historically marginalized people. Reading his work through hip-hop aesthetics, I would argue that Wilson's installations offer a more ambiguous account of museums and curatorial practices, which does not provide a clear thesis or climax. Rather, Wilson finds hope and possibility within the various fractures and breaks unearthed.

Although he produces ambiguous or ironic renderings of American cultural history, Wilson differentiates his use of racialized imagery from that of Michael Ray Charles, Kara Walker, and David Levinthal.[88] While these and other artists have attempted to make art out of the most racist imagery imaginable, Wilson goes beyond copying or mimicking such imagery and interrogates the very discursive structures that maintain an unconscious, yet all too real, racial hierarchy. Rather, he questions the popularity among African Americans of acquiring racist collectibles as an antiracist strategy: "In my experience ownership [of racist collectibles] gives you less understanding. It numbs and anesthetizes you. Living with these objects in my studio for a period of time has diminished my anger. They're insidious."[89] For Wilson, mere copying or mimicry cannot transform racist imagery because neither challenges the viewer's stereotypes or assumptions enough. Using or possessing a racist image, as a result, offers a limited form of ownership because at its best it only deconstructs without offering an alternative vision or view.

Going beyond fair/unfair uses, Wilson deploys pronouns, such as *I* and *me*, to directly engage viewers and have them question the very "forms of ideological interpellation" or ways their own subjectivity is implicated in racial myths.[90] In pieces such as *Mine/Yours* (1995) and *Me & It* (1995), Wilson specifically contrasts racist collectibles with himself and other real African Americans through video installations, family photographs, and ceramic figures. Not simply criticizing or deconstructing racist imagery, Wilson represents the symbolic and metaphorical impasse between people, as raced or ethnically marked bodies, and popular stereotypes. Such imagery offers an ironic representation of black life because it captures the ambiguous position in which many similarly raced people find themselves, caught somewhere in between reality and fantasy. Wilson's museum installations assert the lived experience of African Americans against commonly held assumptions in order to transform the viewer's perceptions and attitudes.

Wilson's commitment to ironic representations is perhaps most fully realized in the concluding sections of the *Mining the Museum* show catalog, which includes interviews with docents and copies of questionnaires completed by museum visitors.[91] These materials democratize Wilson's art by allowing the viewer, not just the artist and the critic, to shape the public meaning of the work. These extra materials undermine any attempt at providing a central or unifying theme or narrative to the exhibit. Instead, they provide substantial evidence about the ambiguity of Wilson's project because a considerable number of docents and visitors offered critical commentary about his installations. Precisely because they articulate critical reviews, these materials demonstrate Wilson's commitment, and that of hip-hop aesthetics, to ongoing democratic dialogue. By providing space for this commentary, *Mining the Museum* allows the public, not just experts and artists, to claim ownership over visual culture and the repositories of public memory. Such gestures potentially undermine the coherence of the show because critics and artists no longer can assume that a visual image means the same thing for all viewers. The benefit of Wilson's emphasis on ambiguity and irony, however, is that it invites conversation about the role of the visual arts in a democratic culture. Social transformation can occur precisely to the extent that multiple viewpoints participate and are socially recognized. The time for racial or cultural monologues is over, and hip-hop aesthetics has offered one strategy for asserting cultural identities and engaging in public conversations about controversial topics.

Unlike Alice Randall, Fred Wilson has not needed to defend himself or his art in trademark or copyright litigation. Because he specifically receives the permission of museums before reworking their collections, his use and critique of racist or racialized imagery have not proven as legally problematic or controversial. This, however, does not suggest that current intellectual property doctrines operate in a racially neutral way or that his work has not been hindered by legal discourse. Less savvy artists or writers might have found themselves in legal trouble. Rather, Wilson's legal maneuvering reinforced the regulative force intellectual property law possesses. Despite his claims about revealing racialized aspects of American cultural memory, Wilson himself is limited to criticizing those institutions that agree to be criticized. His decision to find museums to serve as willing antagonists echoes or mirrors some early Civil Rights cases in which the defendants shared the plaintiffs' concern with the racial injustice produced by then-current legal doctrine. This approach relies on what Lawrence Lessig has termed this "permission culture," in which the only right a creator possesses is the right to "call your lawyer."[92] For Lessig, this produces inefficacy and stifles innovation. For African Americans and hip-hop aesthetes, current intellectual property law doctrines specifically limit their ability to produce texts and reconstruct American culture. Such doctrines extend ownership interests in whiteness into intellectual property law and maintain a form of white supremacy within the American cultural imagination.

Although both Randall and Wilson undermine specific ownership claims, neither questions the underlying logic behind property itself. Their efforts, as hip-hop aesthetes, question the current operation of property rights but do not lend themselves to being easily transformed into a full-blown critique of ownership, along the lines of Marxism or socialism. Rather, they seem to argue for a transformation of the cultural imagination based on existing principles and theories. In her settlement with the Mitchell estate, Randall negotiated the derivative rights to *The Wind Done Gone*.[93] Like many hip-hop aesthetes, she sought marketplace success and the ability to reap the financial rewards of that success. Similarly, Wilson's provocative juxtaposition of museum pieces ultimately does not transfer their ownership to him. Rather the museum continues to retain property rights over the potentially offensive items and could return the collections to their prior condition before Wilson's interventions. The only rights Wilson possesses are those over his photographs of the exhibits.[94] Wilson's work has brought him considerable fame and fortune, especially as he won a MacArthur "genius" grant in 1999, primarily for his museum work, and represented the United States in the 2003 Vienna Biennale. Their efforts for social change involve the redistribution and reallocation of property rights, but not a revisioning of the underlying logic of property. Hip-hop aesthetes such as Wilson and Randall deploy the rhetoric of transformative use and suggest an alternative trajectory for "property talk" from that offered by legal discourse. Transformative use enables-hip hop-inspired creators to articulate perspectives not readily available to dominant culture. The transformation contemplated by hip-hop aesthetics, much like the approaches offered by CRT, does not offer a revolutionary critique of cultural relations designed to rethink our founding principles. Rather, the goal of both hip-hop's materialism and CRT's manifold criticism of legal scholarship involves developing strategies to apply foundational legal principles more fully and to a wider range of people.

This chapter opens by situating hip-hop aesthetics' approach to social transformation within postcolonial theory, feminist theory, and CRT. Their work explores the possibilities for creating moments and spaces that enable the subaltern to speak. In a justly famous essay, Gayatri Spivak asks whether Western discourses allow the historically disenfranchised opportunities to speak. Spivak offers an ambiguous answer to her own question, suggesting that the subaltern cannot speak if no one hears her and that once she begins to be heard, she is no longer subaltern because her words become part of ongoing cultural dialogues.[95] Both Randall and Wilson provide literary and artistic spaces for audiences to begin to hear what has been silenced. Obviously, African Americans have been painting, writing, and engaging in other creative acts for hundreds of years. However, Wilson, Randall, and many others have developed an aesthetic form that not only allows African Americans to articulate social, political, and cultural concerns but reveals the absence of those same voices from the dominant narrative of American cultural history.

Implicit to their ironic narratives, transformation requires a certain amount of mimicry in order to be perceived and heard as discontent and critique. Thus, transformative use must operate through copying even as it seeks to create the space for a new *subject in law*. For much of American history, African Americans have been subject to law, as legal discourse frequently determined their fate even though they had few opportunities to make legal claims as subjects in their own right.[96] Legal discourse, whether slave or segregation law, regulated what African Americans could do without offering the corresponding right to utilize legal discourse for their own ends. The Civil Rights Movement resulted in numerous legislative acts that permitted African Americans formal equality and the right to vote, an education, housing, employment, and other basic rights. While Congress and the courts provided legal avenues to transform social structures and institutions, the Civil Rights Movement stopped short of developing mechanisms to confront cultural hierarchy and racialization. Hip-hop aesthetics, building on jazz and blues paradigms, offers contemporary African American cultural workers a form to foster intercultural dialogue and make ownership claims over the American cultural imagination. The transformative impulse of these claims coheres not in basic assumptions about property rights, but in their assertion that property rights are thoroughly intertwined with racial subjectivity and that ownership over intellectual properties, especially copyright and trademark, has unconsciously privileged white perspectives, aesthetics, and cultural forms. Intellectual property law has historically ignored the subjectivities of historically marginalized people and relegated their creations to the public domain. By construing those works as mere folk tales, intellectual property law has allowed dominant culture to plunder the traditions and forms of African Americans and other minority groups. In response, hip-hop aesthetics offers a strategy to copy property rights rhetoric so that these artists, writers, and musicians can be heard even if the desired recognition is rooted more in cultural capital and cultural worth than anything else.

Transformative use confers not ownership in itself, but a parody of ownership. While repeating or mimicking property rights claims, hip-hop aesthetes generally deploy materialism, commodification, and private interest as metaphors for ongoing cultural struggles. It is this play between the presence and absence of ownership rights that produces the ruptures and ambiguity of hip-hop aesthetics. While both claim ownership over cultural icons and aspects of American cultural history, Randall and Wilson also undermine these very claims by producing ironic texts that refuse to provide easy answers. Rather, they offer a series of ruptures that make visible the silencing and elision of African Americans. Randall's reader or a visitor to a Wilson exhibition comes to learn the injustice of past distributions of property, the challenge facing current ownership patterns, and the possibility the future holds. Inherited images and disciplinary practices cannot be transformed by any single attempt to claim ownership. Neither can a text or an artist complete this work alone. As their work suggests, claiming ownership over American cultural history requires a complex restructuring and redistribution of ownership rights. Acknowledging the reality that intellectual property law regulates the use and flow of copyrighted and trademarked images, texts, and characters and unconsciously sustains racial hierarchy, Randall and Wilson must negotiate this imperfect but governing legal terrain as they imagine possible alternatives that will give voice to African American culture and hip-hop aesthetics. This raced allocation of property rights cannot be easily resolved as legal discourse, and hip-hop aesthetics offers overlapping and diverging judgments. Failure to negotiate their competing demands ultimately means being doomed to silence, like Spivak's subaltern. In the post–Civil Rights era context, any claim to ownership necessarily must be an ironic one because the strategy to mimic property rhetoric falls back upon itself. The conditions by which speech is possible, for Randall as "fair-use" parody and with institutional permission for Wilson, structure and undermine the very ownership claims their art purportedly makes. But this may be the only avenue to be heard.

## CHAPTER 7

# From Invisibility to Erasure?
# The Consequences of Hip-Hop Aesthetics

In *Invisible Man* (1952), Ralph Ellison depicted the existential angst of his nameless protagonist who slowly comes to realize that he is invisible to whites. Through this novel, Ellison criticized existing social, cultural, political, legal, and economic discourses for failing to recognize African American subjectivity. In the novel's conclusion, the hero contemplates the actions necessary to cast off this invisibility and demand social recognition.[1] For Ellison, a series of masks have displaced authentic African American experience. Jon-Christian Suggs has argued that *Invisible Man* "brings the classical [African American literary] impulse as far as it can go" and constitutes a harbinger of the burgeoning Civil Rights Movement because it successfully illuminated the inner struggle faced by African Americans in a white supremacist culture.[2] Despite the novel's recognition and the many victories of the Civil Rights Movement, the visibility/invisibility binary has not steadily disappeared from African American literature, art, music, and cultural criticism. The quest for authenticity experienced and described by Ellison's narrator has become even more desperate in the post–Civil Rights era, albeit with an ironic twist.

African American cultural workers have increasingly found commercial and critical success precisely to the extent to which they produce images, lyrics, and texts that revel in presenting the sordid "reality" of the African American experience. During the 1990s, gangsta rappers created violent (and increasingly fictional or metaphorical) descriptions of urban life. Other rappers "kept it real" by demonstrating their street credentials through their clothes, use of slang, and adoption of Black Nationalist themes. In art and literature, neoslave novels and conceptual art deployed racist imagery and slave or folk stories to subvert dominant assumptions even as they experimented with strategies to recuperate and claim ownership over such stereotyped texts. Like Ellison's invisible man, hip-hop aesthetes express considerable doubt that authentic social recognition or cultural ownership can be achieved. They produce an ironic rendering of African American identity in which authenticity and experience are just another set of masks, concealing as much as they reveal. This dynamic also revealed itself during the 2008 presidential campaign in which Barack Obama was accused as being all style but no substance or all rhetoric and no action.

Due to hip-hop's reliance on layered samples, rhythmic asymmetries, and irony, hip-hop aesthetics consistently undermines its promise of liberation and self-ownership because it, too, only offers masks. Despite its identification of intellectual property law's racialized foundations, hip-hop aesthetics displaces and delegitimizes the very racial subjectivity it purportedly articulates, limiting its ability to redistribute ownership rights. This critique of copyright and trademark principles encounters its limit in hip-hop aesthetics' ambiguous attitude toward property rights rhetoric. Such skepticism exists because property law seems either too individualistic or too interwoven with white supremacy. Any attempt to reconstruct intellectual property law would likely rely on an essential, authentic, or romantic subject, which hip-hop aesthetics constantly distrusts and defers. The net result is a series of artistic, musical, and literary works that struggle against intellectual property law's complicity with racial hierarchy without suggesting a clear reform agenda. Exemplifying the conceptual uncertainty of the post–Civil Rights era, hip-hop aesthetics identifies the ongoing problem of an unjust distribution of resources and income without providing a ready solution. The irony that defines hip-hop aesthetics offers only a partial solution to racial hierarchy. This impasse presents distinct challenges to the various disciplines and theories discussed in this book. Although interdisciplinary inquiry has proved exceptionally useful for identifying a shared aesthetic and critique of American culture, the consequences of hip-hop aesthetics' relation to intellectual property law reveal the limits of current disciplinary debates. As a result, this book offers five related yet distinct conclusions.

## African American Literature

Hip-hop aesthetics has challenged romantic and tragic modes of African American literary representation. It has been wildly successful and productive. Precisely because it has rarely been the subject of litigation (the notable exception here is Alice Randall's *The Wind Done Gone*), contemporary texts that rely on hip-hop aesthetics have been able to sample more ambitiously and make bolder ownership claims over the American cultural imagination than hip-hop music. By the mid-1990s, litigation and changes in legal discourse caused producers to limit their use of sampling within music, and politically conscious or message rap had already peaked in popularity.[3] Ironically, this historical moment coincides with the point when younger African American writers began experimenting with sampling to contest the racialization of intellectual properties. Although it has been commonplace within literary and cultural studies to construct African American culture across generic boundaries, copyright law's disparate impact on music, literature, and film serves as an important reminder that such disciplinary boundaries matter, especially in terms of how legal discourse applies to different artistic forms. In this study, it is clear that contemporary African American writers and painters have had significantly fewer intellectual property hurdles than musicians.

By the late 1990s, the turn to layered samples and voices, rhythmic and temporal asymmetry, and irony, however, had begun to seem cliché and potentially ineffective as an approach to sophisticated renderings of the contemporary African American experience. While writers continue to challenge stereotypical depictions of black life and the effect of raced intellectual properties, the multiplicity of voices, images, symbols, and icons in these texts nonetheless fails to produce a complete or satisfying picture. Toni Morrison's multivocal texts with their communal subjects and Colson Whitehead's tales of young black professionals struggling for professional success in the post–Civil Rights era do not provide complete access to their characters' interior lives. It is absence, not complete or robust representation, that defines hip-hop aesthetics. If earlier artists offered masks as propaganda in the struggle for social justice, hip-hop aesthetes stress the partial and constructed nature of those masks. This "new" approach has failed to capture the rich and potentially contradictory subjectivity of their characters. *Beloved*, *John Henry Days*, and *The Wind Done Gone* rely on hip-hop aesthetics to make their ownership claims over the American cultural imagination, but they ultimately fall short of realizing their artistic ambitions. Morrison and Randall offer potentially romantic conclusions to otherwise ambiguous narratives, while Whitehead's protagonists simply disappear.

In *Erasure* (2001), Percival Everett brilliantly comments and signifies upon hip-hop aesthetics. Everett suggests that contemporary literature, with the aid of American popular culture, erases the complexity of African American identity and culture. For Everett, the challenge is not the social and political invisibility described by Ellison but the absence of ordinary African Americans from the American cultural imagination. *Erasure* tells the story of Thelonious Ellison (also known as "Monk"), a middle-aged African American writer whose books experiment with post-structuralist theory and rework classic texts from Western culture. When the novel opens, Monk has returned to Washington, D.C., his boyhood home, for an academic conference. The trip, however, quickly becomes a more permanent return as a number of family crises necessitate that he remain longer. Over the course of the novel, Monk must deal with his sister's murder by antiabortionists, his mother's emerging Alzheimer's, his brother's disclosure that he is gay, the revelation of his father's illegitimate daughter, and the dismissal of the family's longtime maid. To respond to these crises, Monk decides to stay in D.C. and take a leave from his academic position in California.

In the midst of sifting through his deteriorating family life, Monk reads a popular novel entitled *We's Lives in Da Ghetto* by Juanita Mae Jenkins and is disgusted by its stereotypical depiction of black life. Jenkins's novel provides a putatively realistic (and monolithic) account of black life, but it completely omits Monk, his family, and his favorite pursuits (fly-fishing, woodworking, and postmodern writing) in favor of stereotypes about black, urban poverty. Angered by Jenkins's book, Monk writes a parody of it. He writes it under the pen name Stagg R. Leigh[4] and initially titles the book *My Pafology*, only to demand that it be changed to *Fuck* once publishers demonstrate an interest in it. His book includes a retelling of Richard Wright's *Native Son*, but in the vein of 1980s-style autobiographies, which claim to speak the truth about multicultural America. Of course, the greatest irony is that this parody is mistaken for realism and wins (over his protestations as he sits on the award jury as Monk) the National Book Award. The novel concludes with Monk accepting the book award as Stagg R. Leigh. In the ultimate act of irony, Monk becomes Leigh and erases his "real" experiences from the publishing industry and the study of literature.

Everett's *Erasure* mimics hip-hop aesthetics, deploying layered samples, rhythmic asymmetry, and irony. Rather than exemplifying hip-hop aesthetics, the novel suggests that such artistic strategies constitute a failed response to the post–Civil Rights era because artists cannot control their reception and because audience perspectives increasingly determine decisions on whether to publish books or mount art exhibitions. For Monk, commercial success in the post–Civil Rights era means compromising his identity. Everett sides with the critics of Kara Walker and Michael Ray Charles against this commercialization of African American cultural production. For Everett, hip-hop aesthetics becomes a straitjacket, limiting expressive and representational possibilities. It relies on stereotypes, as either model or foil, and it requires its practitioners to adopt a series of masks or poses. Although Everett's narrator has ostensibly lived an African American life outside of racial stereotypes, the publishing and film industry forces him to become a parody of himself in order to receive cultural recognition and material wealth. Even before his foray into mass-market publishing, Monk's interest in fly-fishing, woodworking, and postmodern theory, according to the novel, confused both fellow African Americans and non–African Americans. In the post–Civil Rights era, writers, painters, and musicians willingly contribute to their cultural invisibility and misrecognition because hip-hop aesthetics offers a parody of ownership, not ownership itself, due to its overreliance on samples, layering, asymmetries, and irony. As components of an aesthetic system, each provides partial or ambiguous views, which erase as much African American subjectivity as they reveal. Ellison's nameless narrator engages in an existential struggle against invisibility, created and maintained by educational, social, legal, and political institutions. Everett's Monk struggles not against institutional limitations, but cultural ones. Academic discourse, the cultural industries, and the unspoken cultural assumptions of legal discourse continue to promote a reified version of black life, whether categorized as signifyin' or something else. The overreliance on signifyin' as a central principle for African American literature places textual revision, a potentially problematic strategy due to the expansion of intellectual property law, at the center of contemporary African American writing.

Although critics have criticized hip-hop for the limited or partial views of African American life it offers, Everett's novel attempts to simultaneously criticize and transcend hip-hop aesthetics on its own terms. Like *Invisible Man* before it, *Erasure* seeks to demonstrate Everett's mastery over hip-hop aesthetics and transform them from within the tradition. Everett argues that this form has not resolved African Americans' struggle with and against literary discourse but merely translated it. The transition from metaphors of invisibility to those of erasure suggests that the post–Civil Rights era presents a similar yet distinct challenge for African American writers. Both invisibility and erasure result in the disappearance of African American humanity from public discourse. The metaphor of erasure, however, emphasizes the agency of those who elide the complexity of African American culture. Everett's main critical target is not simply hip-hop aesthetes, such as Toni Morrison, Colson Whitehead, and Alice Randall, who have relied on these literary strategies, but the market forces that demand publishers produce books with recognizable figures and tropes and the audiences who gravitate to such books precisely because they trade on such stereotyped imagery. Everett implicitly argues that publishing and literary discourses have consistently promoted such works, even though the underlying aesthetic continues to emphasize a faux racial authenticity. *Erasure* thus questions the entire enterprise of African American literature in the post–Civil Rights era because its growth and expansion as both a market and an academic discipline appear complicit in the ongoing marginalization and alienation of African American identity and culture. Hip-hop aesthetics and its effort to claim cultural ownership by engaging in revisionist histories and voicing the unspoken narratives hidden by extant intellectual properties has reinforced the history of slavery and American popular culture as the central forces shaping African American identity and culture. *Erasure's* Monk is rendered invisible precisely because he and other characters like him are conspicuous in their absence from African American literature. And if writers attempt to represent them, they are quickly transformed into more easily recognized stereotypes.

Some recent novels, such as Lalita Tademy's *Cane River* (2002), Martha Southgate's *Fall of Rome* (2002), and Bernice McFadden's *Sugar* (2000), have retreated from hip-hop culture and hip-hop aesthetics as primary influences. They suggest a movement away from layered samples, rhythmic asymmetries, and irony. To some, this work might reflect a return to more romantic or tragic narrative modes, which possess more confidence in literary representation to produce positive imagery. Unlike Everett's *Erasure*, these novels deemphasize fragmentation and the power of popular culture in shaping African American identity and culture. It could also be argued that these works seem less explicitly invested in claiming ownership over the American cultural imagination or redistributing property rights. Rather, they offer smaller narratives that chart the complexity of African American life and seek to represent the trauma of history. They do not conclude with a reconstructed imaginary domain that leaves the future open to limitless possibility. In a subtle but effective way, they suggest that hip-hop aesthetics may constitute merely one moment rather than a transcendental feature in the development of African American literature. They may also portend a shift from cultural politics to other potentially more successful venues for reform and transformation. In the late 1980s, Trey Ellis announced that the New Black Aesthetic (NBA), which Nelson George and Mark Anthony Neal have named Post-Soul Aesthetics, was in the process of transforming the aesthetic strategies inherited from the Black Arts Movement. Recent responses to these hip-hop-based movements and their relative shortcomings invite the conclusion that post–Civil Rights era literary and artistic movements fit more neatly within the ebb and flow of African American cultural history than previously thought. Perhaps the development of hip-hop aesthetics shares its strengths and weaknesses with the very movements, the Harlem Renaissance and the Black Arts Movement, it had apparently transcended.

## African American Art

Hip-hop aesthetics has also caused artists to explore new subject matter and deploy new methods. Adrian Piper, Michael Ray Charles, and Fred Wilson have each developed conceptual approaches that undermine the supposed stability and authority of American popular, mass, and public culture. They deconstruct the effects of newspapers, advertising, and museums in shaping public knowledge and opinion, especially by illustrating the racialization of visual culture. Their art has turned away from depicting African Americans to explore the relationship between dominant culture and African American culture. Burgeoning during the 1980s and 1990s, their work echoes the concerns about cultural ownership articulated in hip-hop music. It also focuses on the cultural life of stereotyped imagery. Like their literary counterparts, Piper, Charles, Wilson, and others deploy sampling, layering, asymmetry, and irony in ways that frequently exceed music's experimentation. Generally, visual artists have found greater freedom to sample copyrighted and trademarked imagery than their musical counterparts, in part because they have sold fewer copies of their work and because their critical commentary may seem more explicit.

This work, based on layered samples, asymmetry, and irony, has found considerable notoriety, winning Guggenheim fellowships for Fred Wilson and Kara Walker. Walker and Michael Ray Charles also became the focus of a generational dispute about the politics of post–Civil Rights era art during the mid-1990s. Perhaps even more so than African American writers, hip-hop generation artists find themselves writing a new chapter in the Harlem Renaissance debates among W. E. B. Du Bois, Alain Locke, and Langston Hughes.[5] Should art constitute propaganda; reflect cultural development; or express the beauty, romance, and tragedy of being a human being with a particular racial/ethnic history? For their critics, the danger implicit in the art of Walker, Charles, and Wilson is that they have lost connection or "empathy based on a rootedness within the center of African American cultural sensibilities and ancestral connections."[6] Their work, rooted in commodified identities, asymmetrical fissures, and irony, does not fit neatly within the paradigms articulated by the founding figures of African American cultural studies. Although hip-hop aesthetics attempts to reclaim ownership of raced texts, it fails as Du Boisian propaganda because the form performs the critique rather than the subject matter presenting one. Hip-hop aesthetics also fails to embody Lockean principles of cultural development, because of its reliance on dominant imagery. It could be argued that such work, due to its reliance on popular culture and its attempt to represent a particularly raced perspective way of viewing the world, could fit within Langston Hughes's paradigm for creating art that flows from the experiences of ordinary African Americans. However, too often this work mines the cultural landscape for symbols whose origin and flow extend far beyond the borders of the African American community. Rather, it was their popularity with non–African American audiences that produced or initiated the controversy. Contemporary African American art has challenged tradition precisely because it fails to conform to expectations about subject matter and its social purpose. For these reasons, Glenn Ligon and Thelma Golden have coined the term *post-black* art to capture this new situation.[7]

Few art critics or historians, however, have explicitly linked these new artistic paradigms to the emergence of hip-hop as a dominant musical force. Only recently, in a 2005 cover article, did the *International Review of African American Art* address "'Post-Black,' "Post-Soul,' or Hip Hop Iconography? Defining the New Aesthetics." The cover featured a Kehinde Wiley painting, depicting a young man clad in an Adidas warm-up suit and holding a flower adorned with a baroque arrangement of leaves and berries. In this issue, the editors and writers explore the work of young and/or new African American artists. Despite the inclusion of "aesthetics" in the subtitle, Soraya Murray and Derek Murray's cover article emphasizes primarily the range of imagery being deployed rather than shared methodologies or approaches to the production of art.[8] While Murray and Murray are quite correct in observing that Kehinde Wiley, Lisa Beane, Erick Mack, Wangechi Mutu, and Kori Newkirk, their article's subjects, have chosen a wide range of subject matter, they ignore or elide the shared deployment of layers, samples, rhythmic flows/asymmetries, and irony. The example of Wiley is particularly revealing on this point. It is not simply his choice of young, urban African Americans as models that invokes hip-hop, but the interaction of these models with Renaissance poses, religious imagery, and trademarked objects from popular culture. Together, these elements represent and criticize hip-hop aesthetics' ambiguous relationship with racialized commodities and the dominant culture it supports more generally. Subject matter analysis has dominated African American art criticism—especially for critics following Du Bois's or Hughes's approach to art—for so long that it will prove difficult to focus on the politics of form, which has become a hallmark of contemporary African American art.

Analogous to Percival Everett's criticism of contemporary African American literature, Lorna Simpson has consistently offered a counternarrative to the one offered by hip-hop aesthetics even as she relies on many of the same artistic devices and strategies. Simpson's photographs blend text and image. The photographs typically offer only a partial portrait of their subject, which is then given meaning in relation to the accompanying text or title. Focusing on particular clothing items or body parts, the images, especially those from the early 1990s, often dismember her subjects, who adopt dramatic but enigmatic poses. Alternatively, Simpson simply photographs the person from the back. Whereas hip-hop aesthetics typically revels in the ambiguity produced by sampling, layers, and rhythmic breaks, Simpson's photographs consistently mourn the loss of the subject ostensibly represented, frequently because racist and/or sexist narratives imprison them. Sampling and layers do not offer freedom for Simpson's subjects, only stale poses that frustrate the putative object of photographic representation.

Huey Copeland argues that the black body has slowly "retreated" from Lorna Simpson's work. While some critics have lauded this move because they perceive that this has made her work more universal, Copeland disagrees and argues that Simpson's work more forcefully than ever "assert[s] the presence of one black woman . . . even as her figure is ghosted away."[9] Copeland's brilliant reading of Simpson's oeuvre implicates hip-hop aesthetics in the erasure or continued cultural invisibility of African Americans. Simpson's work does not seek to destroy hip-hop aesthetics as an illusion, following Everett. Rather, Simpson has remained a steadfast residual or emergent voice remarking on the limits of hip-hop aesthetics as a mode of cultural representation. Against the playfulness of hip-hop aesthetics, with its carnivalesque upheaval of discourses and symbols, Simpson's work consistently evokes the violence hiding just beneath the surface of her images. For example, her well-known piece *Guarded Collections* (1989) consists of six identical African American women figures with their hands crossed behind them. Underneath the women, Simpson arranges twenty-one plaques that alternate between "Skin Attacks" and "Sex Attacks." By blending text and image, Simpson depicts the typically hidden violence that African American women must endure. Similarly, her installation *Wigs* (1994), which includes images of many wigs, invites viewers to wonder about how the hair was obtained and the effects of white standards of beauty that continue to damage the self-esteem of African American women. In this piece and others, the parts' detachment from actual bodies is so efficient, complete, and clinical that Simpson suggests the violence of severing the hair from the body without actually depicting it.

Drawing on and criticizing the logic of the sample, Simpson forces viewers to grapple with the violence of removing or creating such objects and texts. Simpson, especially in this early work, implicitly criticizes hip-hop's reliance on layers and sampling to produce irony and ambiguity. For Simpson, this constitutes a failed response to post–Civil Rights America because African American culture suffers from the effects of such partial views, due to the influence of newspapers, advertising, and other forms of popular culture. While she shares hip-hop aesthetes' concern with the effects of such intellectual properties, Simpson's work implicitly argues that these racialized images and texts cannot be reconstructed by simply deploying them as samples. Nor can African American artists gain ownership over them by clever or ironic layered samples. She suggests that they promote racism and sexism precisely because they are partial and incomplete. Further partial views, Simpson implies, cannot lead to complete and complex images and narratives. Simpson's work provides an exemplary reminder that hip-hop aesthetics has only constituted one strategy to claim cultural ownership over the persistence of racial stereotypes, especially those frequently associated with intellectual properties and popular culture. Pieces such as *Guarded Collections* and *Wigs* haunt contemporary African American art precisely because they require us to encounter the ongoing difficulty of representing black bodies. Layered samples, rhythmic flows/asymmetry, and irony may only defer this foundational problem without resolving it. Clarifying the relationships among art, literature, and music will allow scholars to better understand the central tensions, conflicts, challenges, successes, and failures of post–Civil Rights era cultural production.

## Intellectual Property Law

Many developments in digital culture, from Google's project to create a virtual library to the birth of YouTube.com, have eclipsed sampling as a cutting-edge issue within intellectual property law. These issues are important ones that need to be considered. However, the creation of new technologies and the resulting challenges for intellectual property lawyers cannot mask how "settled" case law and legislation never quite resolved the questions of property and cultural ownership that hip-hop aesthetes have put forward over the past two decades. For critical race theorists and other students of African American culture, the construction and allocation of intellectual property rights remain crucial issues because race has affected and continues to affect the distribution of wealth, especially as images of blackness remain key components of how American-style capitalism operates.

In his essay "A Portrait of the Trademark as a Black Man," David Dante Troutt creates an extended hypothetical about an African American named MarCus (or "Mark Us"), who owns an advertising company and decides to trademark himself as the symbol of his company. This hypothetical situation functions as an allegory about the perils of intellectual property law for contemporary African Americans. In his trademark application, MarCus imitates the language of legal discourse and describes himself and what makes him trademark worthy in color-blind terms.[10] Despite the potential difficulties with becoming a trademarked property, MarCus reasons that "being a registered trademark allows me both to name myself and to interpret the meaning of that name.[11] Taking seriously the commodification of identity, Troutt wants to examine hip-hop's apparent complicity in the propertization of African American identity and culture. He wonders how intellectual property law would understand this situation and explores the cultural consequences of MarCus's decision. Ultimately, Troutt concludes that law continues to perpetuate a de facto racist and racialized distribution of intellectual property law rights.[12]

Both Troutt and I suggest the difficulty of simply applying putatively color-blind doctrines to African Americans and their creative products. Throughout this book, I have examined how African American intellectuals and artists are continuing to struggle to deracialize the concepts of ownership, property, and intellectual property. As part of this effort, my account of hip-hop aesthetics challenges three assumptions that seem to structure the ongoing dialogue about intellectual property: (1) that copyright and trademark law prior to the 1990s balanced appropriately the rights of copyright owners and the public, without negatively impacting particular social and cultural groups; (2) that national and cultural boundaries pretty much overlap and that a text's meaning does not depend on cultural boundaries;[13] and (3) that the distinctions among copyright, trademark, patent, and increasingly publicity rights possess a quasi-transcendental character and that most cultural groups recognize them as valid. The growing concern about intellectual property law's expansion has been premised upon the basic assumption that, until recently, legal discourse appropriately balanced the rights of intellectual property owners and the public.[14] While the founding figures of critical intellectual property studies, such as Rosemary Coombe, Jane Gaines, Lawrence Lessig, Kembrew McLeod, and Siva Vaidhyanathan, have gestured to the historical inequalities resulting from intellectual property law, they have frequently opted for "color-blind" solutions, emphasizing free culture, freedom of speech, democratic dialogue, and creativity.[15] Even though I appreciate their attempts to speak in a language that courts understand, one of the central lessons to be drawn from CRT and hip-hop aesthetics is that such color-blind rhetoric has rarely realized African American dreams for freedom and equality.

The scholarship of Olufunmilayo Arewa, Stephen Best, K. J. Greene, Norman E. Kelley, and Frank Kofsky documents how property and contract discourses, along with discriminatory business practices, have systematically transferred the ownership rights over African American creativity to whites. The history of blues and jazz music also provides abundant evidence that African American artists, musicians, and storytellers have rarely received the ownership rights supposedly offered by intellectual property law. The current battle over the hip-hop aesthetic's reliance on sampling does not offer a novel instance of intellectual property law's racialized operation and effects. Rather, it provides another instance of legal discourse's marginalization and delegitimization of African American culture. By focusing on historic inequalities and their relation to contemporary intellectual property law issues, I would argue that today's copyright and trademark activists are participating in a civil rights effort whose origins can be traced back to when the first slaves and indentured servants stepped onto American soil.

On a deeper level, the putative goals behind many criticisms of recent intellectual property law—of promoting innovation, creativity, and democracy—distort the very voices such critics seemingly support. Hip-hop culture is a materialist discourse, and participants do want to get paid. While it certainly fosters innovation and offers an alternative public sphere for some disenfranchised African American youth, hip-hop aesthetics is fundamentally concerned with the fair distribution of ownership rights and claiming control over the American cultural imagination. To ignore or downplay these aspects of hip-hop aesthetics engages in epistemological violence against the very creators to whom these critics offer support. At stake in hip-hop's use of sampling is not simply some theoretical point about abstract principles or the public good. Rather, at stake is a battle over capital and capital formation in cash-starved urban communities and middle-class communities that have too often encountered the glass ceilings in American corporate life. Despite the partial view it offers of African American life, hip-hop aesthetics may constitute one of the few avenues to social, cultural, and economic capital for some African American cultural workers. While few musicians, artists, or writers will likely earn a big payday from their work, hip-hop culture and its accompanying aesthetics constitute one of the few "natural" resources possessed by many young African Americans. A cynical reader, following Derrick Bell, might conclude that copyright's and trademark's critics only discuss hip-hop or African American cultural history when it coincides with white and/or middle-class interests. While this reading may have some merit, this book is more concerned with encouraging legal critics to gain a deeper understanding of African American culture as a whole and how the marginalization of African Americans has been affected through seemingly innocuous and color-blind rules and doctrines.

One instance in which African American studies can help improve legal scholarship is through its attention to the shifting nature of cultural boundaries. Because federal law regulates copyright and trademark (although there is some state trademark legislation), courts and commentators tend to assume that cultural borders follow legal ones. While legal discourse distinguishes between genres in applying copyright law, it does not recognize how African American culture differs from dominant culture. As this book argues, African American culture possesses a distinct perspective about the definition of a text and the rules that govern ownership over a text. Through hip-hop aesthetics, African American culture has engaged in a vigorous discussion about the right to copy (i.e., sampling versus biting) and creating trademarked identities out of neologisms and commodities. Because copyright and trademark have adopted the color-blind rhetoric of most legal discourse, such cultural distinctions have not been judicially sanctioned even if they structure how audiences understand hip hop texts. Rather, courts have attempted to ignore cultural formations and racial identity even as key cases, such *Acuff-Rose v. Campbell* and *SunTrust v. Houghton Mifflin*, appear to hinge on racial and cultural distinctions. Following the cues of courts, many intellectual property law critics invoke de-raced and degendered "universal" creators, users, and subjects as if people do not create, use, and understand texts and objects through a particular cultural lens.

Perhaps most illustrative of hip-hop aesthetics' challenge to intellectual property law is its deconstruction of the idea/expression dichotomy. As discussed throughout this book, copyright and trademark assume that ideas can be articulated in many ways, but each expression possesses a singular meaning. Hip-hop aesthetics, rooted in signifyin', sampling, rhythmic asymmetry, and irony, challenges this foundational assumption of intellectual property law. Hip-hop aesthetics sees textual complexity where legal discourse assumes simple or surface meaning. Because many critics elevate the broad, general legal assumptions over the more nuanced and specific categories deployed by cultural studies, some analyses of intellectual property resolve prematurely the very cultural and economic conflicts between African Americans and white Americans that have found legal expression within intellectual property law. Attempting to remedy the inefficiencies or absurdities of intellectual property law without referencing its complicity in the de facto and probably de jure transfer of wealth from African Americans to white Americans is unlikely to prove successful. Resolving other cultural/economic conflicts, whether they involve fan fiction or unauthorized music trading, probably requires engaging with histories of discrimination and power inequalities, not simply a slight tweaking of abstract legal formulas.

Last, this cross-genre study of hip-hop aesthetics challenges the established distinctions among intellectual property law's subfields. Although doctrinal distinctions differentiate copyright, trademark, patent, and increasingly publicity rights, it is increasingly common for individuals and corporations, no matter their racial identity, to claim multiple forms of ownership over identical or similar materials. For this reason, judicial, intellectual, and scholarly attempts to divide discussions about intellectual property have proven unrealistic and unduly abstracted from the actual functioning of intellectual property law in everyday life. From the perspective of a particular cultural formation, in this case hip-hop culture, the doctrinal differences appear merely as roadblocks in the quest for freedom and equality. Nonlawyers, I found, in the course of working on this book, respond with bemusement to learn that trademark law applies to Michael Ray Charles's use of Aunt Jemima, but copyright regulates Alice Randall's parody of Scarlett O'Hara and *Gone With the Wind*. It has also proven difficult to explain to nonlawyers why John Henry is public domain but Uncle Ben is not, even though both figures originate from, more or less, the same time period and arguably embody similar racial stereotypes.

These legal distinctions do not immediately affect how African Americans deploy and rework such images, texts, and stereotypes. Rather, it appears as if genre, along with any racial stereotypes associated with it and the author's/artist's racial identity, can shape how courts analyze fair or transformative use, more than the formal elements contained within the work. Although much criticism focuses on the universal or cross-cultural effects of individual doctrines, hip-hop aesthetics suggests that copyright, trademark, and even publicity rights increasingly are asked to provide the procedural and substantive rules to negotiate among conflicting cultural groups. Perhaps efforts to persuade Congress to revise its copyright maximalist approach have failed because proponents have not been sensitive enough to cultural differences. I think the lessons from the Civil Rights Movement are illustrative. Although general principles about voting, housing, and employment discrimination grounded the efforts of activists, it was the specific instances of race-based discrimination that moved Congress to enact legislation. Today, most people accept race or cultural arguments as necessary elements of employment or voting law. It seems that a similar revolution is needed for intellectual property law if we aim to create a vibrant intercultural discussion about American culture.

## Critical Race Theory

Although the two movements responded to the same events and developed concurrently, few scholars have examined the relationship between hip-hop and CRT. This book frequently juxtaposes seminal critical race theorists with hip-hop aesthetes because each provides important contextual clues to understand the other. I have not claimed or even suggested that critical race theorists are hip-hop artists or vice versa. Rather, this book provides some evidence that the aesthetic strategies adopted by both enable them to make similar criticisms about how white perspectives dominate American culture and have largely shaped the distribution of property rights. A more thorough study might reveal that hip-hop aesthetics—sampling, layering, rhythmic asymmetry, and irony—provided the form through which CRT articulated its alternative vision for legal discourse. Similarly, further study might conclude that hip-hop and CRT constitute complementary social justice strategies.

In late 2003 and early 2004, Richard Delgado and Kevin Johnson engaged in a spirited debate about CRT's future. In a review essay that contrasted a collection of recent CRT writings[16] and Derrick Bell's autobiography *Ethical Ambitions* (2002), Delgado expressed concern that CRT lost its focus during the 1990s and has become splintered into various factions, especially as Latino/a Critical scholarship (Lat Crit) and its annual conference have become more active.[17] He argued that the conceptual framework underlying this new scholarship has shifted from a materialist outlook to a more idealistic one, favoring textual analysis over interrogations of the specific interrelationships among race, racism, and American law.[18] Foundational CRT themes and arguments, such as the interest convergence thesis, voice scholarship, intersectionality, law school hiring and promotion policies, and racialized scholarly networks, have disappeared, according to Delgado, and abstract analyses that seem far removed from the lived experiences of African Americans and other racial minorities have become the norm in CRT and Lat Crit scholarship. Supporting his claim, Devon Carbado and Mitu Gulati have noted that CRT has increasingly viewed race as macrolevel phenomena rather than as the result of concrete actions and decisions.[19] They, like Delgado, suggest that CRT needs to adopt a more pragmatic and materialist outlook and examine how specific policies and doctrines contribute to the persistence of racial inequality.

Within a few months of the review, Kevin Johnson defended recent trends in CRT against Delgado's attack. Johnson made an effort to show how Lat Crit had developed, in part, because CRT, de facto, had ceased to exist, no longer holding regular meetings, and because CRT needs to transcend the black-white binary, which it may have strengthened inadvertently.[20] In addition, he attempted to show that "Delgado overstates the distinction between ideal and material forms of discourse."[21] For Johnson, the recent focus on discourse analysis helps explain how social, political, and economic forces have impeded legal efforts to address the ongoing effects of race, racialization, and racism in American culture. He argues that Delgado's claim that contemporary iterations of CRT do not offer strategies to reduce poverty, housing discrimination, and economic underdevelopment in minority communities neglects the relationship between material and discursive realms. Using the example of immigration, Johnson attempts to show how Lat Crit has tackled a practical issue facing minority communities. The cultural politics around immigration also offers an exemplary instance of how the racialization of American culture gets translated into both international and domestic policies.[22] Through their engagement with immigration, Lat Crits have mapped out the forces that have been used to divide communities of color, splitting the Latino/a community and pitting African American and Latino/a leaders against one another. Johnson concludes his response to Delgado by suggesting that Lat Crit has staked out new territory that complements the arguments offered by CRT's founding figures.

Hip-hop aesthetics, in many ways, provides a ready analogy for the dispute between Delgado and Johnson about recent developments in CRT and Lat Crit. Like CRT, hip-hop has exceeded its original boundaries and come to dominate contemporary African American art, music, and literature. As it has grown and developed, hip-hop is no longer the exclusive property of urban youth of color, adopting multiple forms and being adapted to many audiences. The original innovators have generally receded from the scene, and a new generation, for whom hip-hop has always existed, now dominates contemporary African American music, art, and literature. By identifying 1991 as the baseline year, this book recognizes the shifting nature of cultural movements and thus maps hip-hop's effects on multiple genres and traditions.

Like hip-hop culture, CRT has also changed since its inception. The debate between Delgado and Johnson, however, need not harden into two competing camps: materialism and idealism. As both Delgado and Johnson suggest, CRT need not choose one over the other, because the ideological and the material are linked domains. Hip-hop offers a ready example of one strategy for crossing this apparent divide. Hip-hop aesthetes question the definition and distribution of property rights even as they create texts that make ownership claims. This seemingly contradictory attitude reflects both law's historic complicity in racial hierarchy and its unrealized potential for creating racial justice. More surprising than its turn to ideological criticism has been hip-hop's absence in the writing of CRT and Lat Crit. Although hip-hop began in the mid-1970s, only recently has CRT or Lat Crit seriously engaged with law's regulation of the hip-hop generation and hip-hop culture. As the dominant aesthetic structure in the post–Civil Rights era, hip-hop has increasingly served as the voice for and representation of urban youth of color, even if many judges, legislators, and legal scholars may lack the skills or cultural competence to decode its meaning.

CRT and now Lat Crit articulate the need for outsider voices in policy making and legal analysis. Most frequently, they have turned to autobiography, dialogue, and other realistic modes of representation as their principle means. Questions of genre, aesthetic structure, and narrative mode have rarely been engaged, resulting in a fairly uncritical reliance on romantic notions underlying authorship—assumptions these theorists share with intellectual property law.[23] CRT's literary turn during the 1980s and early 1990s coincided with growing suspicion about the stability of textual meaning, especially as texts move across cultural and historical boundaries. Lat Crits' more recent focus on discourse analysis reflects contemporary intellectual debates. Lat Crit has attempted to explain the relative marginalization of CRT doctrines within legal discourse even as CRT has been moderately successful in publishing books and creating a network of scholars across the country. Bill Clinton's failed nomination of Lani Guinier reflects the relative failure of CRT's influence on legal doctrine. Guinier's critics easily distorted her ideas about reforming elections law by characterizing her as a "quota queen," out of touch with mainstream values. Guinier's example suggests that knowledge of material inequality does not necessarily provide a corresponding politically viable solution to that problem. Part of this challenge results from the malleability of language, image, and sound. Content alone does not determine a text's meaning. As a reterritorializing method for creating art, music, and literature, hip-hop aesthetics challenges CRT's trust in alternative narratives and reconstructed doctrines for remedying inequality because hip-hop struggles to "keep it real" in the endless cycle of textual and symbolic appropriation and reappropriation.

Hip-hop and intellectual property law have become significant prisms through which politicians, cultural critics, activists, and artists of all races, ethnicities, and classes discuss the nature of creativity and the optimal way to distribute the ownership rights of creative properties. By and large, CRT and Lat Crit have not participated in this conversation, nor have critics and lawyers engaged in an exhaustive analysis of how the doctrines of intellectual property law further the racialization of American cultural life and distribute the ownership rights of those racialized properties. This book has attempted to bridge the materialist-idealist divide within CRT and Lat Crit by exploring how hip-hop aesthetics constitutes a literary-artistic-musical style where material and ideological concerns exist together. To participate in this debate most productively, CRT and Lat Crit will need to find ways to blend methods and theories with the approaches of those trained in fields of law that have typically be absent from their conversations. While Delgado is quite correct that poverty, housing, education, immigration, and the prison-industrial complex continue to affect the lives of people of color disproportionately, CRT and Lat Crit cannot ignore how current intellectual property doctrines commodify cultural products in a manner that tends to distribute ownership rights over African American creativity to predominately white corporate interests. Activism efforts should not only ameliorate poverty and social inequality but promote the structural conditions whereby African American communities can capitalize on existing cultural wealth. Perhaps even more importantly, CRT and Lat Crit need to maintain open dialogues with the communities they purport to represent. Hip-hop's materialism, its development of an aesthetic form as the basis of its ownership claim over American culture, and its attempt to distinguish itself from previous generations all require careful attention as CRT and Lat Crit develop the next generation of legal-cultural criticism. The relative absence of hip-hop and the hip-hop generation as specific CRT and Lat Crit themes constitutes a major oversight, but one that can be remedied fairly easily, especially given the large number of hip-hop texts.

## Hip-Hop Studies

Mark Anthony Neal, one of the founders of hip-hop studies, recently observed that hip-hop culture has consistently defined itself not only as a racial or ethnic movement but as the product of working- or lower-class norms, values, and experiences. According to Neal, "the concept of 'ghetto fabulous' . . . celebrates certain notions of a normative 'ghetto' experience" as central to hip-hop culture.[24] Even though many of hip-hop's stars, including Chuck D, Run DMC, Russell Simmons, and Sean "Diddy" Combs, possess middle-class roots, hip-hop culture has largely identified itself in opposition to middle-class values and behaviors. Hip-hop studies has reinforced this distinction by, all too frequently, isolating hip hop-music and street culture from contemporary art, literature, and cultural criticism. The unsurprising result is that much, but not all, hip-hop scholarship has severed hip-hop from its relationship to African American culture, writ large. Hip-hop culture thus appears to transcend the traditional debates of African American cultural studies as articulated by Du Bois, Locke, Hughes, Hurston, and Gates and articulate the pure perspective or experience of disenfranchised and marginalized African Americans.

Although generally separated by academic scholarship and the public, the forces that shape hip-hop culture also influence contemporary African American art and literature. Increasingly, African American artists and writers make explicit references to hip-hop culture within their work and, like Kehinde Wiley, use hip-hop music to create the context for showing their work. Hip-hop music does not speak simply to the urban working class, but to a broad range of African Americans who are still waiting for legal discourse to deliver on its promises of freedom and equality. Like blues and jazz before it, hip-hop has become a central artistic paradigm for cultural production that cuts across disciplinary boundaries. Contemporary artists and writers rely on sampling, layering, rhythmic asymmetry, and irony in their work. These writers and artists have also become the focus of public controversies and lawsuits regarding their use of racist imagery. In order for scholars to capture the full impact of hip-hop aesthetics, we will need to get beyond the romantic view of working-class culture that underwrites much hip-hop scholarship.[25] The debate inaugurated by hip-hop aesthetics involves a broader range of African Americans than typically considered, and it may demand a profound reworking of our understanding of African American culture. Hip-hop's criticism of property law cannot be characterized as a "pure" or "authentic" working-class perspective. Isolating hip-hop as the music of poor urban youth in effect marginalizes its critique and encourages class and generational conflict. It also decontextualizes the many African American writers and artists who have engaged with similar questions, albeit from different cultural and professional locations. By linking generations and art forms, scholars and intellectuals can foster community building around shared political, economic, and cultural concerns.

Although Chuck D described rap as "Black America's CNN," hip-hop studies should not mistake the music, art, and literature of the post–Civil Rights era for unmediated realism.[26] Grandmaster Flash and the Furious

Five, Kurtis Blow, and countless others have insisted on "keepin' it real." This rhetorical realism, however, does not mean that these artists simply describe everything they see or experience. Such an understanding would neglect the many stylistic and aesthetic choices they make. From Run DMC's "Peter Piper" to Jay Z's "Hard Knock Life" and Kanye West's "Gold Digger," rappers and deejays display conscious efforts to transform familiar imagery and sounds. These songs display aesthetic traits similar to those found in texts and images produced by post–Civil Rights era African American artists and writers. Rather than separating their work, this book suggests that scholars must engage in greater efforts to examine how hip-hop aesthetics shapes multiple genres. Perhaps we will learn that KRS One, of Boogie Down Productions, and CRT share an understanding about how best to transform American culture. We might also learn to hear the feminism of Lauryn Hill in the writing of Alice Walker, and vice versa. The wordplay and humor of De La Soul might have analogs in the writing of Paul Beatty and the art of Ellen Gallagher. This book challenges the assumption that music is the best or most authentic source for learning about African American criticism of cultural, social, political, economic, and legal structures. Rather, it argues that African American music, literature, art, theater, and film frequently work together to develop such criticisms of American culture.

Most analyses of hip-hop, especially those that consider lyrics, eventually grapple with their putative violence and misogyny. Such examinations rarely connect rappers with visual or literary artists. While Dr. Dre, Snoop Dogg, and many others have been roundly criticized for writing lyrics that degrade women and/or rely on invidious stereotypes, scholars rarely examine how their imagery compares to that of Kara Walker, Robert Colsecott, Ishmael Reed, Darius James, Dave Chappelle, or Spike Lee. Perhaps the existence of similar imagery in other genres can help provide a fuller account of this cultural dynamic. Similarly, the tales of violence found in the music of N.W.A., Ice T, and Jay-Z may have a greater relation to the violence depicted and referenced by Alice Walker, Toni Morrison, Fred Wilson, and Allison Saar than previously thought, even if the nature of the violence is quite different. Of course, scholars should try to understand hip-hop music on its own terms, but that effort should not cause them to forgo examining the overlap with other artistic forms. Why is it that African American musicians, artists, and writers—no matter their connection to hip-hop—continued to offer such violent narratives even after the victories of the Civil Rights Movement? The answer to this question, I believe, is more linked to ongoing race relations than to the nature or essence of hip-hop music. I hope that this study convinces many hip-hop studies scholars to look beyond music, graffiti, and dance to engage with a fuller range of post–Civil Rights era cultural productions in answering questions like these. Hip-hop exemplifies contemporary tensions, but it is not the sole repository of those tensions within the post–Civil Rights era.

The conflict between hip-hop aesthetics and intellectual property law reflects the broader and continuing gap between law's promise and the reality many African Americans face. Hip-hop aesthetics has offered many African American artists, writers, and musicians a form to articulate this social frustration and offer cultural criticism. Because of its increasing importance in defining and distributing property, intellectual property law has regulated how these cultural workers create texts and has become the subject of considerable discussion within contemporary African American culture. By viewing each through the lens offered by the other, it is clear that the turn to intellectual property does not provide a ready solution to the maldistribution of property rights African Americans have inherited, nor has legal discourse developed a coherent strategy for applying legal principles to contemporary African American cultural production that respects its creativity and originality. Like cultural studies scholars who view hip-hop as realism, legal discourse tends to view hip-hop aesthetics in simple terms and underestimates and misinterprets the resulting texts. While African American writers, artists, and musicians clearly rely on property rhetoric and demand ownership over their work and African American culture, they also see property law's limitations and express doubt that such property claims will produce the results they seek. At this time, intellectual property law has apparently settled on its method for resolving sampling cases without fully addressing the cultural conflict that underlies the tension between hip-hop aesthetics and legal discourse. It is my hope that one day lawyers, judges, and scholars can create an intellectual property law regime that recognizes the creativity of hip-hop and other African American cultural forms and allocates the ownership rights over these songs, images, and stories to their African American producers.

# Notes

1. For a fuller overview of hip-hop photography, see Adler 2006.
2. Cooper 2004, 7–24, 57–63.
3. Cooper 2004, 72–109.
4. Marshall 1993, 16. For a literary version of this satirical use of copyright symbols and discourse, see Ellis 2003, 19, 109.
5. The scholarship of Funmi Arewa, Stephen Best, Michael Brown, Julie Cohen, Rosemary Coombe, Jane Gaines, K. J. Greene, Henry Jenkins, Lawrence Lessig, Kembrew McLeod, Richard Posner, Carol Rose, Susan Scafidi, Patricia Sluby, Siva Vaidhyanathan, and many others has created the intellectual space for this project.
6. The research of H. Sami Alim, Derrick Alridge, Todd Boyd, Yvonne Bynoe, Jeff Chang, William Jelani Cobb, Murray Forman, Bakari Kitwana, Joan Morgan, Mark Anthony Neal, Patrick Neal, William Eric Perkins, Gwendolyn Pough, Tricia Rose, Joseph Schloss, Craig Watkins, and many others has provided the foundation for my discussion of hip-hop culture.
7. The writings of Derrick Bell, Devon Carbado, Kimberlé Crenshaw, Richard Delgado, Lani Guinier, Charles Lawrence, Mari Matsuda, Patricia Williams, and many others have shaped my understanding of critical race theory.
8. Because this book is illustrative, not exhaustive, in its approach, I have been forced to omit many important writers and painters. Significant omissions include Paul Beatty, Trey Ellis, Percival Everett, Ellen Gallagher, Darius James, Jake Lamar, Glenn Ligon, Kerry James Marshall, Allison Saar, Danzy Senna, Clarissa Sligh, Touré, Kara Walker, Kehinde Wiley, and George C. Wolfe. In their works, the elements of the hip-hop aesthetic are clearly present, but the critique of intellectual property law is not always as pronounced, even if as these texts clearly stake ownership claims and analyze the relationships among property, propriety, and self-ownership.

9. Fouché 2006, 641. See also Sluby 2004; Weheliye 2005; Fouché 2003.
10. See generally Alridge 2005.

CHAPTER I

1. Pough argues that *Barbershop* offers a criticism of the bourgeois orientation of the Civil Rights Movement (2004, 229 n39).
2. Boyd 2002, xxi–xxii. See also Boyd 2004. Therein Yusuf Nuruddin questions Boyd about his 2002 book and his view of the divide between the Civil Rights and hip-hop generations.
3. Blackburn 2004, 81–87.
4. Best 2004, 30–41.
5. For an interesting account of how some slaves understood their status as property, see Penningroth 2003, 137–144.
6. I have intentionally omitted discussion of the reparations debate here, although I would argue that the majority of reparations proponents have developed arguments that hinge on the symbolic properties of any potential economic redistribution. It appears as if reparations would recognize and repay the contributions (both physical and cultural) of African Americans to the building of America's wealth. See generally Robinson 2000.
7. Related to my focus on property, Derrick Alridge argues that the Civil Rights and hip-hop generations share the rhetoric of self-determination and Black Nationalism (2005, 233–245).
8. Stepto 1991, 3 (italics in original).
9. Stepto 1991, 26.
10. Carby 1987, 36.
11. Gates 1987, xi.
12. See Washington 1959.
13. Lamar 1996, 342.
14. Dixon 2002, 47.
15. Dixon 2002, 20.
16. Equiano 1995, 187–196.
17. Jacobs 1988, 290.
18. Jacobs 1988, 302–303.
19. Houston Baker argues that the slave narratives, including those of Frederick Douglass, endorse commercial exchange because the "nineteenth-century slave, in effect, *publicly* sells his voice in order to secure *private* ownership of his voice-person" (1984, 50).
20. Douglass 1997b, 126.
21. Douglass 1969, 375 (italics mine).
22. C. Harris 1993, 1791.
23. Antebellum legal discourse specifically recognized the potential links or conflicts between slavery and patent law. See Lubar 1991, 954; Forness 1980, 25; Sluby 2004, 31–32.
24. Washington 1959, 154.

25. Washington 1959, 155.

26. Washington presented his famous speech at the 1895 Atlanta Exposition, which, among other things, showcased African American innovation and ingenuity (Sluby 2004, 51–55). Questioning Washington's implicit linkage of patented inventions and wealth, Fouché argues that patents rarely translated into wealth because of racism (2003, 5–8).

27. Washington 1959, 156.

28. Washington 1959, 158.

29. Washington 1959, 3. For a genealogical account of the black thief from the slave narrative to Hurricane Katrina, see L. King 2007, 255.

30. See generally Neal 2004.

31. Du Bois 1969, 87.

32. Du Bois 1969, 45.

33. See Allen 2002.

34. See Lewis and Willis 2003.

35. Du Bois 1969, 88.

36. "It is a peculiar sensation, this double-consciousness, *this sense of always looking at one's self through the eyes of others*" (Du Bois 1969, 45 [italics mine]).

37. A. Locke 1997, 19 (italics mine).

38. See *Ancient Egyptian Order of Nobles of the Mystic Shrine v. Michaux* 1929; *Creswill v. Grand Lodge Knights of Pythias of Georgia* 1912.

39. Schmidt and Babchuk 1973, 277.

40. Liazos and Ganz 2004, 488–489.

41. K. Greene 1999, 356–357. See also Kofsky 1998, 15–24.

42. Sanjek and Sanjek 1996, 351.

43. Kofsky 1998, 21–22, 29–34.

44. Garofalo 2002, 114.

45. T. Rose 1996, 243–244; Perry 2004, 49.

46. Hansberry borrowed the situation from her parents' struggle fighting restrictive covenants in 1930s Chicago. *Hansberry v. Lee* was one of many cases developed by the NAACP to challenge residential discrimination and the way whites used property law doctrines to maintain racial hierarchy. The U.S. Supreme Court ultimately ruled in another case that such restrictive covenants were unconstitutional in 1948. See *Hansberry v. Lee* 1940; *Shelley v. Kraemer* 1948.

47. Cone 1991, 316.

48. M. King 1969, 65.

49. M. King 2001, 82.

50. M. King 2001. 82.

51. Malcolm X 1965b, 9–10.

52. Malcolm X 1965b, 11.

53. Malcolm X 1965a, 39.

54. 42 U.S. Code Sec. 2000a (2004).

55. Lani Guinier questions whether color-blindness makes sense as a policy or legal objective. She reminds us that "color blindness is a vision defect" or an "abnormal medical condition" (1998, 287).

56. D. King and Wiley 2003, 197–211.

57. Eakin 2002.
58. Alkalimat 2002a, 2002b.
59. Lee 2002.
60. See *Parks v. Laface Records* 2003.
61. Neal 2002, 22.
62. Boyd 2002, 11–12.
63. See *Seale v. Gramercy* 1997; *Ringgold v. Black Entertainment Television* 1997.
64. George 1998, 155.
65. A summary judgment motion asks the court to assume the truth of all the plaintiff's (in this case, Rosa Parks) allegations and determine whether a cause of action exists.
66. *Parks v. Laface Records* 2003, 449.
67. Schloss offers the Bearden analogy (2004, 152–153).
68. R. Kelley 1997, 37.
69. *Parks v. Laface Records* 2003, 458.

CHAPTER 2

1. See *Arlington Heights v. Metropolitan Housing Development Corp.* 1977.
2. Kelman 1987, 3.
3. Unger 1986, 8.
4. See Minda 1995, 117–122; P. Williams 1991, 7.
5. Goodrich 1998, 237.
6. For an example, see Kelman 1984.
7. P. Williams 1991, 146–165.
8. See Crenshaw 2002, 1354–1365.
9. Crenshaw et al. 1995, xi.
10. Kitwana 2002, 9–22.
11. See also Haney Lopez 1998.
12. See D. Bell 1987, 1992, 1996; Delgado 1995.
13. P. Williams 1991, 6–8.
14. See Farber and Sherry 1997, 13.
15. Delgado 1993, 110.
16. Gutièrrez-Jones 2001, 21–47.
17. Neal 2002, 116.
18. Gates 1988, xix.
19. Gates 1988, 88.
20. Gates 1988, 78 (italics in original).
21. Gates 1988, 86.
22. Gates 1988, 68, 78.
23. Gates 1988, 77.
24. R. Kelley 1997, 1.
25. Mitchell-Kernan 1999, 311.
26. Gates 1988, 79.
27. McGruder 2003, 79.

28. McGruder is not the first to parody the whiteness of comic strips. See Stromberg 2003, 141.

29. Gates 1988, 104.

30. McGruder 2003, 179–180.

31. Gates 1988, 94, 107, 124.

32. Tate 1992, 158.

33. Gates 1988, 124.

34. Perry 2004, 61–63; T. Rose 1994, 123.

35. See Krims 2000, 95; Vaidhyanathan 2003, 312; Schloss 2004, 161–163; Tate et al. 2006, 45.

36. Gates 1988, 66.

37. Douglass 1997a, 78–80. Not all reprints of Douglass's narrative include the appendix, where this song appears.

38. A Tribe Called Quest 1990.

39. Demers 2006, 81.

40. This description owes much to Jon-Christian Suggs's argument that "another metaphor for the relationship between American law and African American narrative is that of the palimpsest, in which one text is written over another" (2000, 11).

41. Aoki 2007, 760. Other intellectual property law scholars have argued that copyright should be rewritten from the perspective of the ordinary people who use copyrighted materials by taking account of practices like signifyin' (Litman 2002, 134; J. Cohen 2005, 348).

42. See Neal 2002, 116.

43. Penalver and Katyal 2007, 1098–1101.

44. Katyal 2006, 493.

45. See T. Rose 1994, 100–101; Perry 2004, 102–112; Demers 2006, 91; Schumacher 2004, 451–454. Ironically, hip-hop generation artists do want to "get paid" even if they are also engaging in semiotic disobedience. For examples, see Adler 2006, 116; Peterson 2006, 896–897.

46. Many posit the hip-hop nation as a key force in shaping the culture. Heath finds this framing problematic but nonetheless argues that hip-hop "demands its own degree of *cultural* literacy (2006, 848–849 [italics in original]). Heath later suggests that in addition to the traditional four elements of hip-hop culture (deejaying, graffiti, breaking, and emceeing), we might add the hip-hop nation (862–863). See also Schloss 2004, 176.

47. Gaines (1998, 1991), Coombe (1998), McLeod (2001, 2007), and Vaidhyanathan (2003, 2004) have helped intellectual property lawyers understand the cultural processes that shape the texts that become the subject of copyright disputes. Gaines initiated the field with her *Contested Cultures* (1991), and Coombe demonstrated the essential role copyrighted and trademarked texts play in our cultural and political lives. Following in their footsteps, Kembrew McLeod has offered a wonderful description of how hip-hop artists have responded to legal intrusions into sampling (2001, 77–99). His account includes some discussion of how producers rely on samples for the purposes of parody and signifyin'. In his book *Freedom of Expression®*, McLeod shows how African American uses of sampling fit

within the greater conflict about fair use in the music industry. At times, there is some slippage as he equates African American instances of signifyin' with other forms of critical copying (2007, 63–113). Similarly, Siva Vaidhyanathan has argued, in the midst of his discussion of hip-hop and copyright, that "the tension in the law is not between urban lower class and corporate uberclass. It's not between black artists and white record executives. It's not always a result of conflicts between white songwriters and the black composers who sample them. It is in fact a struggle between the established entities in the music business and those trying to get established. It is a conflict between old and new" (2003, 133). From the vantage point of African American cultural history, the very construction of the music business and the battle between existing and emerging musical forms are deeply intertwined with racial politics and the history of racism that pervades all aspects of American life, including intellectual property law. Rather than seeking to resolve the debate, this book seeks to identify the conflicting assumptions between cultural studies and intellectual property law accounts of the law's regulation of hip-hop. The former tend to assume that hip-hop possesses a unique aesthetic vision based on a shared cultural tradition, whereas the latter view hip-hop as one aspect of shared contemporary conflict regarding the circulation of ideas, images, and texts. See Perry 2004, 114; Miller 2006, 154. Because I am relying on hip-hop aesthetics as the unifying element of my analysis, my assumptions about the nature of African American culture diverge at times with those of McLeod and Vaidhyanathan. My emphasis here is on the *meaning* of cultural texts and how they perform a political critique (similar to Coombe), not the *freedom* of their creators to engage in musical, literary, or artistic endeavors. Regardless of this relatively minor debate, McLeod, Vaidhyanathan, and I all are extending Rosemary Coombe's project of reorienting the conversation about intellectual property law as a way of fostering engaged democratic debate and keeping culture relatively safe from legal regulation. See Coombe 1998, 266.

48. See generally Fouché 2003.

49. From my initial question about copyright, it quickly became apparent that trademark law was also implicated in these questions. Because Gates is primarily concerned with copyrighted texts, my discussion here focuses on copyright. Later discussions, especially the section on Michael Ray Charles, engage trademark law. See K. Greene 1999; Schumacher 2004; McLeod 2001; Demers 2006; and Arewa 2006a, 2006b for insightful analyses of this question.

50. See Gaines 1991, 1998; Coombe 1998; McLeod 2001, 2007; Vaidhyanathan 2003, 2004.

51. 17 U.S.C. sec 106.

52. See Arewa 2006a, 2006b; Aoki 2007.

53. See Gaines 1991, 1998; Coombe 1998; Vaidhyanathan 2003, 2004; McLeod 2001, 2007; J. Cohen 2005; Lessig 2002, 2004; Jenkins 2006; Gillespie 2007.

54. During the late 1970s and early 1980s, Colescott re-visioned a number of classic images from European art and American popular culture.

55. See Demers 2006 and McLeod 2007 for a nice overview of how courts answer these questions.

56. For an excellent discussion examining whether intellectual property rights are human rights, see Yu 2007.

57. For a discussion of other legal cases during the early days of hip-hop, see McLeod 2001, 87–96.

58. *Grand Upright Music v. Warner Brothers* 1991, 183.

59. *Grand Upright Music v. Warner Brothers* 1991, 185.

60. Walter McDonough, a copyright lawyer with experience clearing samples, reports that Gilbert O'Sullivan refused to license the samples because the sampled material came from a song describing his parents' death. This exemplifies why many copyright activists argue the need for a compulsory licensing system. See McLeod 2007, 112–113.

61. See P. Williams 1991; C. Harris 1993; Ross 1996; Headley 2006.

62. *Grand Upright Music v. Warner Brothers* 1991, 185.

63. See Baldwin 1985; Lawrence 1987; Austin 1989; P. Williams 1991; Morrison 1992b; Lubiano 1996; Omi 1996; R. Kelley 1997.

64. *Jarvis v. A&M Music* 1992.

65. *Tuff 'N' Rumble Management v. Profile Records* 1997.

66. *Newton v. Diamond* 2003.

67. *Bridgeport Music v. Dimension Films* 2005.

68. *Ty v. Publications International Limited* 2002. This case did not involve hip-hop sampling, but courts and commentators saw it as being particularly relevant to sampling disputes.

69. *Campbell v. Acuff-Rose* 1994, 579.

70. *Campbell v. Acuff-Rose* 1994, 581. In *Ty v. Publications International Limited* (2002), the Seventh Circuit apparently endorsed this distinction and suggested that much hip-hop sampling and ironic copying might be permissible under fair use.

71. *Campbell v. Acuff-Rose* 1994, 593.

72. *Campbell v. Acuff-Rose* 1994, 572.

73. *Rogers v. Koons* 1992.

74. Gates 1990.

75. Schumacher 2004, 451–454.

## CHAPTER 3

1. See generally L. Jones 1963.

2. Walker 1982; G. Jones 1975.

3. See Powell 1998.

4. I have developed my definition of hip-hop aesthetics by synthesizing the work of numerous hip-hop studies scholars, including H. Sami Alim, Jeff Chang, William Jelani Cobb, Nelson George, Mark Anthony Neal, William Eric Perkins, Tricia Rose, Joseph Schloss, Greg Tate, and Craig Watkins.

5. Originally, I included orality as a fifth characteristic of hip-hop. After reviewing Aldon Nielsen's *Black Chant* (1997), exploring hip-hop's connection to the Black Arts Movement, I found that Neilsen's observation that "African American traditions of orality and textuality were not opposed to one another and did not ex-

ist in any simple or simplistic opposition to modernity and postmodernity" suggested that any attempt to label hip-hop as either oral or textual was too simplistic (Neilsen 1997, 34). Thus, I reframed my analysis and have been better able to view the play between orality and textuality within hip-hop aesthetics.

6. A. Murray 1976, 16–20.

7. See Chang 2005, 416; Sanjek and Sanjek 1996, 680. For numerous instances of how hip-hop was entering mainstream consciousness during the 1980s, from Run DMC's "Walk this Way" to the creation of *Yo! MTV Raps*, see George 2004.

8. For a fuller historical or chronological account of hip-hop music, see Chang 2005; George 1998; Toop 2000; Perkins 1996; Krims 2000.

9. Smith 1993, xxii.

10. C. West 1993, xix.

11. Thompson 2003, 137; Modleski 1997, 72–73.

12. Kennell Jackson uses the term *cultural traffic*, rather than *sampling*, to describe this process (2005, 11).

13. Schloss 2004, 152–153. See also George 2004, x.

14. See A. Murray 1976.

15. See Gates 1988.

16. Schloss 2004, 65–66.

17. Fricke and Ahearn 2002, 46–47.

18. Fricke and Ahearn 2002, 58.

19. Schloss 2004, 36–37.

20. Schloss 2004, 49.

21. See T. Rose 1994, 79.

22. J. Locke 1980, 19. For a recent effort at supplying a Lockean framework for intellectual property law, see Horowitz.

23. Borrowing from law and economics, I argue that sampling fosters innovation because it encourages artists to take symbols, texts, or objects that may have little contemporary value and gives them new meaning. See Landes and Posner 2003, 56–68. Within law and economics, the question is not whether intellectual property should be protected (it clearly should be), but what is the socially optimal and most efficient way to balance the competing goals of fostering innovation and providing a sufficient reward structure for creators. See Liebowitz 2002, 197.

24. Schloss 2004, 79.

25. Smith 1993, xxxi.

26. Martin 1993, 57.

27. Smith 1993, xxiii.

28. Smith 1993, xxv–xxvi.

29. Smith 1993, xxvii.

30. Smith 1993, xxviii.

31. T. Rose 1994, 41.

32. Vlach 1978, 55.

33. Kiracofe 1993, 202.

34. Modleski 1997, 69.

35. Smith 1993, 16.

36. Smith 1993, 17.

37. Smith 1993, 21–22 (errors and italics in original).

38. Smith 1993, 25.

39. Patricia Williams explains that Smith creates "constructed dialogues" where people appear to engage in conversations that contemporary society needs but that have been missing from our culture (2004, 16–17).

40. Smith 1993, xxxii.

41. T. Rose 1994, 64–65.

42. T. Rose 1994, 67.

43. See A. Murray 1997, 95; Ripani 2006, 44–45.

44. See also Miyakawa 2005, 75.

45. Radano 2003, 103.

46. T. Rose 1994, 38–39. See also Miyakawa 2005, 81.

47. Obviously, there are notable exceptions, such as Charles Mingus, Duke Ellington, the Chicago Art Ensemble, and Carla Bley, who have relied on numerous sounds and songs.

48. See Harvey 1989, 284–307.

49. Smith 1993, xl.

50. Smith 1993, xxxix.

51. Smith 1994, xxxiii–xxxiv.

52. A. Murray 1997, 94.

53. A. Murray 1997, 95.

54. Reinelt 1996, 614.

55. Smith 1994, xxiv (italics in original).

56. T. Rose 1994, 2.

57. A. Murray 1973, 25–33.

58. Frye 1957, 223.

59. Frye 1957, 40–41.

60. White 1973, 38–39.

61. Rorty 1989, 73–74.

62. Rorty 1989, 94–95.

63. Deleuze 1994, 7. See also Colebrook 2004, 140.

64. Deleuze 1994, 68.

65. Suggs relies on this approach to irony in showing that African American literature sought to rewrite American legal discourse via irony (2000, 100–110).

66. Hutcheon 1994, 19–21.

67. Hutcheon 1994, 94–95. See also Colebrook 2004, 169. Colebrook argues that postmodern irony reveals how "inhuman, machinic or errant forces" help define the meaning of language even as irony interrogates the instability of those social forces.

68. Dickson-Carr 2001, 17.

69. Dickson-Carr 2001, 164–207.

70. Perry 2004, 95.

71. Peterson 2006, 898, 904–905.

72. Peterson 2006, 903.

73. "Episode Thirteen," *Chappelle's Show: Season Two.*

74. See "Episode One," *Chappelle's Show: Season One.*
75. T. Rose 1994, 128–129; George 2004, 214; Chang 2005, 325–329.
76. N.W.A. 1988.
77. N.W.A. 1988.
78. T. Rose 1994, 100. See also Perry 2004, 50.
79. Hutcheon describes this as an essential characteristic of postmodern irony (1994, 94–95).
80. Smith 1993, xli.
81. Smith 1994, xxv.
82. Smith 1994, 243.
83. Smith 1993, xxxiii.
84. Smith 1993, xxviii.
85. DeLong 2002, 25.
86. 17 U.S.C. sec. 106.
87. *MGM Studios v. Grokster* 2005, 926.
88. See Best 2004, 98.
89. It is not my claim that this pure romantic conception of authorship has ever existed within U.S. legal doctrine. See Saint-Amour 2003, 6–7, 14; Chartier 2003, 28.
90. For an overview of the debate about how the romantic theory of ownership intersects with intellectual property law, see T. Rose 1993; Woodmansee and Janzi 1994; Vaidhyanathan 2003.
91. See George 1998, 154–175, 193–200.
92. Because intellectual property law is changing so quickly, it is quite possible that future readers will find that courts have abandoned the idea/expression dichotomy.

CHAPTER 4

1. See generally Chang 2005.
2. See generally Chang 2005.
3. See Croyden 1994, 220; Angelo 1994, 257; Fussell 1994, 289. For Morrison's recent decision to include rap as part of the show she curated for the Louvre, see Riding 2006.
4. See Fussell 1994, 285; Morrison and West 2004; Moses 1999; Rice 2000; Randle 2001; Eckstein 2006.
5. For an account of how Morrison's texts overlap essentialist and antiessentialist rhetorics, see McBride 1997.
6. Krumholz 1999, 109.
7. B. Bell 1998, 175.
8. Ellis 1989, 234–237.
9. See Perez-Torres 1997.
10. See chapter 3.
11. Middleton Harris 1974, 10.
12. Weisenburger 1998, 77–78.

13. Darling 1994, 248.
14. Morrison 1987a, 148.
15. Morrison 1987a, 151–152.
16. Morrison 1987a, 88.
17. For a vivid illustration, see Morrison 1994, 21.
18. Morrison 1987a, 164.
19. Morrison's sampling of multiple voices constitutes a literary response or articulation of Kimberlé Crenshaw's theory of "intersectionality," developed within critical race theory during this same historical period. For Crenshaw, intersectionality acknowledges that individuals do not hold simply one identity (race, gender, or class), but possess multiple identities simultaneously. See Crenshaw 1991.
20. Dubey 1999, 187.
21. L. King 1998, 272.
22. As with any piece of literature, scholars have noted *Beloved*'s links to other texts. Lori Askeland has observed that *Beloved* borrows from Harriet Beecher Stowe's *Uncle Tom's Cabin* and includes reconfigured "samples" from it (1999, 161). Similarly, Richard Moreland argues that Morrison sampled Amy, the girl who helps Sethe deliver Denver, from Twain's *Huckleberry Finn*, and Caroline Woidat finds borrowed characters from Hawthorne as well. *Beloved* also contains references and samples from the Old and New Testaments, with its use of the word *beloved*.
23. Although they do not connect *Beloved* to hip-hop or its underlying aesthetic, Nellie McKay, Barbara Christian, and Deborah McDowell share my conclusion that the novel relies on layers as key narrative tool (1999, 207–210).
24. Morrison 1987a, 190.
25. Morrison 1987a, 190.
26. Morrison 1987a, 216.
27. See Dussere 2003, 60.
28. Morrison 1987a, 199.
29. Morrison 1987a, 273.
30. Perez-Torres 1997, 92–93
31. Gilroy 2000, 222.
32. See Morrison 1992b, 1996.
33. Morrison 1992b, 13 (italics in original).
34. Rushdy 1999, 52–53.
35. Christian, McDowell, and McKay 1999, 219.
36. Suggs 2000, 290.
37. Crouch 1990, 205.
38. Crouch 1990, 206.
39. Morrison 1994, 21.
40. See also McBride 1997.
41. See Croyden 1994.
42. Morrison 1987a, 275.
43. Morrison 1987b, 110.
44. Morrison 1994, 11.
45. Morrison 1994, 12.
46. See Piper 1996, 1: 234. See also John Bowles 2006.

47. Mercer 1999, 48. See also Piper 1996, 1: 248.

48. See Morrison 1992b, xi.

49. Fisher 1999, 39–40.

50. Piper has not always explicitly linked her own work to hip-hop music or the rest of hip-hop culture. Rather, she has attempted to show solidarity with black working-class culture through her discussion and use of funk and R&B in her work. In *Funk Lesson*, she prepared a handout for participants that identified the five basic structures of funk (dissonance, multilayered melodies, polyrhythms, self-composition, and orality) and its three basic themes (self-transcendence, sexual love, and affirmation of self-respect or unity) (1996, 1: 213–214). During the 1980s and 1990s, Piper began to reference hip-hop.

51. Piper 1996, 1: 9.

52. See Schloss 2004.

53. Hayt-Atkins 1991, 49–50.

54. Piper 1996, 2: 183.

55. Piper 1996, 2: 268.

56. It is unclear whether she received permission to incorporate other artists' songs into her artwork. By contrast, Piper has explicitly recognized photographers and gotten their permission when incorporating their work.

57. Piper 1996, 2: 253

58. Piper 1996, 2: 241.

59. Piper 1996, 2: 266.

60. Piper 1996, 2: 158.

61. Wallace 2004, 243; Wallace 1994, 204–205.

62. Piper 1996, 1: 181.

63. Storr 1996, xxvi.

64. Piper 1996, 1: 267.

65. Lippard 1990, 241.

66. K. Greene 1999, 343.

67. See Arewa 2006a.

68. Best 2004, 15–16.

69. Best 2004, 94–98.

70. Best 2004, 274–275.

71. Best 2004, 275.

72. Gaines 1998, 546–547.

73. Piper 1996, 1: 273. For an explanation of why newspapers do not have the same interest in protecting their intellectual property as other copyright and trademark holders, see Benkler 2006, 40.

74. Best 2004, 276.

75. See Delgado and Stefancic 1994; Levine 1996; Schur 2003.

76. Delgado 1995, xviii.

77. P. Williams 1991, 17–19, 44–51, 156–157.

78. P. Williams 1991, 164–165.

79. P. Williams 1991, 152 (italics in original).

80. P. Williams 1991, 149.

81. P. Williams 1991, 233–234.

82. Morrison 1996, 21.
83. Gates 1992, xvi.

## CHAPTER 5

1. D. Bell 1985, 13.
2. D. Bell 1987, 24–25.
3. D. Bell 1987, 31.
4. D. Bell 1987, 43.
5. See D. Bell 1992, 20.
6. D. Bell 1992, 22.
7. D. Bell 1996, 145.
8. D. Bell 1996, 147–148.
9. D. Bell 1996, 150.
10. See generally D. Bell 1980.
11. D. Bell 1987, 28.
12. See *Campbell v. Acuff-Rose* 1994; *SunTrust Bank v. Houghton Mifflin* 2001.
13. See 17 U.S.C. sec 101–106.
14. 17 U.S.C. sec 107.
15. Nimmer 2003, 282.
16. Nimmer 2003, 280.
17. J. Cohen 2005, 370.
18. See also Coombe 1998.
19. J. Cohen 2005, 372.
20. Bradford 2005, 760.
21. Bradford 2005, 761–767.
22. Bradford appears to have directed her proposed doctrine at primarily commercial, as opposed to critical or academic, uses. See also Litman 2002, 134–139.
23. Austin 1995, 157.
24. See Dinerstein 2003, 318–320.
25. In some respects, *John Henry Days* elaborates on and anticipates concerns articulated by scholars during the past twenty years. See Gaines 1991; Coombe 1998; Vaidhyanathan 2003; McLeod 2001, 2007.
26. See Aoki 2007; Arewa 2006a, 2006b; K. Greene 1999.
27. Whitehead 2001, 198–205, 250–261.
28. Whitehead 2001, 102.
29. Whitehead 2001, 88.
30. Whitehead 2001, 49.
31. Whitehead 2001, 35–38.
32. Whitehead 2001, 59.
33. Whitehead 2001, 265.
34. Whitehead 2001, 263.
35. Whitehead 2001, 265.
36. Whitehead 2001, 107.
37. Whitehead 2001, 108.

38. Whitehead 2001, 112–117.

39. 17 U.S.C. sec. 107(1).

40. UNESCO 2005, 4–5.

41. See *Grand Upright Music v. Warner Brothers* 1991; *Jarvis v. A&M Music* 1992; *Campbell v. Acuff-Rose* 1994; *SunTrust Bank v. Houghton Mifflin Company* 2001; *Newton v. Diamond* 2003; *Bridgeport Music v. Dimension Films* 2005.

42. *Campbell v. Acuff-Rose* 1994, 581.

43. D. Sanjek 2006, 279–280.

44. *Campbell v. Acuff-Rose* 1994, 589.

45. *SunTrust Bank v. Houghton Mifflin Company* 2001, 1271.

46. *SunTrust Bank v. Houghton Mifflin Company* 2001, 1270.

47. *SunTrust Bank v. Houghton Mifflin Company* 2001, 1273.

48. Whitehead 2001, 380–383.

49. See generally New n.d.

50. Whitehead 2001, 204.

51. Whitehead 2001, 101.

52. Whitehead 2001, 102–103.

53. Whitehead 2001, 205.

54. For an effort to revise copyright to permit hip-hop and African American ironic uses of existing texts, see Madison 2005, 413.

55. 17 U.S.C. sec. 107(3).

56. A confusing jurisprudence has developed around this factor and the threshold test for making a copyright infringement claim. In order for a copyright owner to demonstrate a prima facie case, they must show that the copying was substantial enough to rise to the level of infringement. The de minimis doctrine requires that the copying must go beyond "a technical violation of a right so trivial that the law will not impose legal consequences" (*Ringgold v. Black Entertainment Television* 1997, 74). In *Bridgeport*, the court held that *any* copying of recorded sound constitutes an infringement (*Bridgeport Music v. Dimension Films* 2005, 803). See also Beck 2005; Schietinger 2005.

57. Arewa 2006b, 626–627.

58. Jeremy Beck asks a provocative question about how courts ought to determine or observe similarity between musical compositions. Beck argues that books, paintings, and film stills constitute "fixed time" objects, whereas music offers a "real time" text. He asks: "How many times would a fact finder need to listen in real time to a pair of recordings in order to analyze them? Would such incessant repetition— and the resulting familiarity—present a greater risk of infringement?" (2005, 10–11).

59. Arewa 2006b, 627, 641–644.

60. Gilroy 2000, 337.

61. 17 U.S.C. sec. 107(4).

62. *A&M Records v. Napster* 2001, 1024–1029.

63. *A&M Records v. Napster* 2001, 1034.

64. *Field v. Google* 2006, 20.

65. *Ty v. Publications International Limited* 2002, 518.

66. *SunTrust Bank v. Houghton Mifflin Company* 2001, 1276.

67. *SunTrust Bank v. Houghton Mifflin Company* 2001, 1277.

68. Courts' willingness to enforce copyright against hip-hop has not necessarily or uniformly enriched the sampled artists, such as George Clinton and James Brown. Rather, it provides further illustration of the historical racism within the recording industry in which the major labels required even popular African American artists to sign contracts that did little to protect their interests.

69. Richards 2006, 10.

70. See generally New n.d..

71. Cadenhead 2006. See also N. Kelley 2003, 115–127; Kennedy 2002; Ayo 2005.

72. Kennedy 2002, 45. See also M. Watkins 1994, 131–132.

73. Kennedy 2002, 130–133.

74. In an ironic twist, Randall Kennedy recently testified on behalf of a white man accused of a hate crime because the man had shouted the N-word at his African American victim during the assault. Kennedy agreed to be an expert on the use and meaning of the N-word, sharing his insight that the N-word possesses many meanings, not just its function as a term of white supremacy. See Kilgannon 2006.

75. Moffat 2004, 1483.

76. Moffat 2004, 1488–1489.

77. 15 U.S.C sec 1127.

78. Halpern 2005, 241.

79. For a discussion of the complexity of the Black Arts Movement, see Smethurst 2005, 15.

80. Richards 2006, xxvii.

81. Judy 2004, 114.

82. Judy 2004, 115.

83. Sirmans 2005, 92.

84. Basquiat frequently relies on the copyright symbol in his work. The context of these symbols, however, suggests he ought to be invoking trademark. This mistaken use, because of its ubiquity within his oeuvre, calls attention to Modernism's privileging of mimesis and representation over authenticity. In other words, Basquiat situates copyright and trademark as opposing logics in which there is a sliding scale upon which viewers can rate the relative originality or derivative quality of a given work. Thus, Basquiat offers a subtle but ironic commentary on intellectual property's symbol of authenticity by replacing trademarks with copyright marks, which regulate who can possess the rights to copy a text or phrase.

85. Nielsen 1997, 34.

86. See R. Kelley 1998, 213.

87. See generally Tate 2003.

88. Anten 2006, 433.

89. Coombe 1998, 61.

90. 15 U.S.C. sec 1125 (c)(3)(A)(ii).

91. S. Greene 2006, 44.

92. S. Greene 2006, 77.

93. Halpern 2005, 238; Doellinger 2005, 404.

94. In a related development, a 2001 exhibition brought together patents, copyrighted texts, and trademarked items in one show. See *Pictures, Patents* 2001.

95. See also the artwork of Tania Hargest (*Freestyle* 2001, 40–41).

96. Michael Harris 2003, 107.

97. Reid 1998, 5.

98. Ellison 1995, 196–250.

99. For quotation, see Bacigalupi and Kern-Foxworth 1997, 21.

100. Michael Harris 2003, 202.

101. Urban legends identify the model for the logo as Jerry West.

102. Juliet Bowles 1997, 3.

103. Charles has commented that the painting also provides a commentary on Ice Cube's character from the movie *Boyz in the Hood*, whose name is Dough Boy. According to Charles, "serving" is "slang for selling drugs" (1998, 10).

104. Charles 1998, 2.

105. Bacigalupi and Kern-Foxworth 1997, 28.

106. R. Cohen 1997; Heller 1998.

107. Wallace 2004, 120–121.

108. Bacigalupi and Kern-Foxworth 1997, 28.

109. Bacigalupi and Kern-Foxworth 1997, 30.

110. Obviously, this analogy will inevitably break down because trademarks are alienable (i.e., the owner can disavow his trademark) and racial identity tends to be inalienable, although historical concerns about passing suggest that some people have alienated their racial identity.

111. A. Johnson 1996, 906.

112. A. Johnson 1996, 908–909.

113. A. Johnson 1996, 917.

114. A. Johnson 1996, 914.

115. A. Johnson 1996, 926.

116. A. Johnson 1996, 928.

117. A. Johnson 1996, 941–942.

118. A. Johnson 1996, 944–945.

119. Troutt 2005, 1205.

120. Troutt 2005, 1194.

121. Whitehead 2006, 211.

122. This is not to suggest that previous generations of activists did not engage with the racism of popular culture. Rather, it acknowledges that such interventions have increasingly become the central focus of civil rights activism. See N. Kelley 2004, 146–147; Bynoe 2004, 17–18.

123. See N. Kelley 2004; Kitwana 2002; Bynoe 2004; Boyd 2002, 2004.

124. See Michael Harris 2003, 101–124.

125. See Kern-Foxworth 1994, 61–113.

126. See also Public Enemy 1990.

127. Kern-Foxworth 1997, 14.

## CHAPTER 6

1. Cornell 1993, 1.
2. Bhabha 1994, 191.
3. hooks 2003, 28–29.
4. hooks 1995, 211.
5. P. Williams 1998, 73.
6. Guinier 1994, 132.
7. Guinier 1998, 256.
8. Guinier 1998, 287.
9. See also Overton 2002, 1574.
10. See Coombe 1998, 248–299; Scafidi 2005, 9.
11. See Leval 1990, 1111–1112.
12. Leval 1990, 1111.
13. See Arewa 2006b, 576–577; Tushnet 2004, 546.
14. See Arewa 2006b, 577; Demers 2006, 26.
15. *Campbell v. Acuff-Rose* 1994, 593.
16. Madison 2005, 414–415.
17. *SunTrust Bank v. Houghton Mifflin Company* 2001, 1269–1272.
18. *Campbell v. Acuff-Rose* 1994, 593.
19. *SunTrust Bank v. Houghton Mifflin Company* 2001, 1262.
20. See Vaidhyanathan 2004, 81–84; Lessig 2001, 19A.
21. Rubenfeld 2002, 2.
22. Rubenfeld 2002, 37.
23. For an application of this idea to DJ Danger Mouse's *Grey Album*, see Demers 2006, 138–142.
24. See C. Rose 2005, 993.
25. Posner 2002, 12.
26. See *Ty v. Publications International Limited* 2002, 518.
27. Landes and Posner 2003, 123.
28. Landes and Posner 2003, 70.
29. Landes and Posner 2003, 158–159.
30. See Randall 2001, copyright page, 210.
31. See generally Conde 1996.
32. See generally Crips 1983.
33. See Taylor 2001, 28–62.
34. Spears 2005, 225.
35. See Randall 2002. Randall's second novel further illustrates this point. Like *The Wind Done Gone*, which rewrites *Gone With the Wind,* her *Pushkin and the Queen of Spades* (2004) relies on Pushkin's short story "Queen of Spades" and offers an even more highly developed hip-hop aesthetic. See Randall 2004, 217, 222. Randall's choice to sample Pushkin suggests that she continues to engage in hip-hop aesthetics despite the copyright barriers.
36. Randall 2001, 36–37.
37. Randall 2001, 40.

38. Randall 2001, 54.
39. Randall 2001, 51–52.
40. Randall 2001, 55.
41. Randall 2001, 185.
42. Randall 2001, 164.
43. Randall 2001, 194.
44. Randall 2001, 191.
45. Randall 2001, 202.
46. Randall 2001, 162.
47. Randall 2001, 164.
48. See Gates n.d.
49. Morrison n.d., 2.
50. Morrison n.d., 3.
51. L. King 2007, 59.
52. Best 2004, 270.
53. See *Newton v. Diamond* 2003, 596–597.
54. Randall 2001, 111.
55. Morrison n.d., 183.
56. See U.S. House of Representatives 2006; N. Kelley 2002; Kofsky 1998.
57. See Chang 2005, 439–445; Folami n.d.
58. See Conroy n.d.
59. See Berger 2001b, 10; Berger 2001a, 34.
60. F. Wilson 2003, 22.
61. See Corrin 1994, 6–8.
62. Corrin 1994, 2; Berger 2001a, 34.
63. Gonzalez 2001, 24.
64. Corrin 1994, 6–7.
65. Corrin 1994, 7–8.
66. Berger 2001b, 12.
67. Corrin 1994, 18.
68. See King-Hammond 1994, 23, 34; Berger 2001a, 38.
69. See Wilson 1994, 47–76. To further muddy the conceptual waters, the New Press copyrighted the docent and visitor comments they published. Therefore, they own the written expressions of these people's responses. This creates the question of whether their impressions have become part of the text known as *Mining the Museum*.
70. King-Hammond 1994, 30.
71. Berger 2001a, 38.
72. Rarely, if at all, do critical examinations of Wilson's work place it into the context of hip-hop despite Wilson's upbringing in and around New York City during the 1970s. Wilson worked in Harlem as an arts educator at the very moment hip-hop was created and became extremely popular throughout the city (King-Hammond 1994, 28). Even if he had no knowledge of hip-hop, his upbringing, during which he moved between the city and the affluent, white suburbs, and the resulting dislocations reflect the struggle many hip-hop generation youth feel in the post–Civil Rights era.

73. Schloss 2004, 36.
74. See Wilson 1994, 62, 68.
75. Berger 2001a, 33.
76. For a related set of images, see Glenn Ligon's *Runaways* series (1993).
77. Winter 1996, 188.
78. Winter 1996, 189.
79. Buskirk 1994, 112; F. Wilson 2003, 22.
80. Gonzalez 2001, 25.
81. Gonzalez 2001, 25.
82. Berger 2001b, 9, 12; Berger 2001a, 36.
83. Stocking 1985, 11.
84. Buskirk 1994, 109.
85. Berger 2001b, 15.
86. Berger 2001b, 15.
87. Berger 2001b, 18.
88. David Levinthal, although a white photographer, has produced work that functions similarly to that of Charles and Walker and is frequently included within discussions of their work and contemporary African American art.
89. Michael Harris 2003, 208.
90. Gonzalez 2001, 28.
91. Wilson 1994, 147–176.
92. Lessig 2004, 192.
93. See Chakraborty 2002.
94. F. Wilson 2001b, 54–55.
95. See Spivak 1994.
96. See Suggs 2000; L. King 2007.

CHAPTER 7

1. Ellison 1995, 581.
2. Suggs 2000, 284.
3. Norfleet 2006, 368.
4. Stagg R. Leigh is an allusion to the blues figure Stagolee or Stagger Lee, known for his violent behavior.
5. Interestingly, literary analogs to Charles and Walker, such as Alice Randall, Paul Beatty, Colson Whitehead, and Darius James, found considerable support within African American literary circles. However, Spike Lee's film *Bamboozled* encountered similar resistance within the African American community. The film explores an African American television executive who proposes a modern-day minstrel show after his employer, a fictional television station manager, criticizes him for being insufficiently black. One effect of exploring hip-hop aesthetics through an interdisciplinary lens is that variations in audience response by genre or form can be contrasted and compared. On a slightly more optimistic note, Ellen Gallagher has covered massive canvases with hundreds, if not thousands, of exaggerated lips and eyes reminiscent of minstrelsy. She has also created massive collages

of advertising images whose eyes and hair have been altered. Unlike Charles's and Walker's, Gallagher's works have been more warmly received over the past decade.

6. Michael Harris 2003, 245.

7. Golden 2001, 14.

8. D. Murray and Murray 2005, 3.

9. Copeland 2005, 76.

10. Troutt 2005, 1150–1151.

11. Troutt 2005, 1155.

12. Troutt 2005, 1205–1206.

13. For discussions about why indigenous cultures require alternative legal structures to protect their cultural property, see generally Boateng 2005; Brown 2003; Scafidi 2005; Strathern 2005.

14. For examples, see Coombe 1998, 299; Vaidhyanation 2004, 188; Lessig 2004, xv.

15. For another recent example of reliance on color-blind solutions that tend to ignore how race and other cultural practices influence the flowing of social power, to copyright's limitations, see Netanel 2008.

16. See Valdes, Culp, and Harris 2002.

17. Delgado 2003, 127.

18. Delgado 2003, 130–131.

19. Carbado and Gulati 2003, 1760.

20. K. Johnson 2004, 729.

21. K. Johnson 2004, 718.

22. K. Johnson 2004, 728–729.

23. See Schur (forthcoming).

24. Neal 2006, 635.

25. John Jackson Jr. astutely observes that hip-hop culture tends to present a "paranoid style" and "is invested in 'appearances' even as it simultaneously denounces them for being misleading" (2008, 148). Jackson's observation about hip-hop's ambiguous relationship with and critique of representation ought to make scholars wary of relying too directly on lyrical analysis or the direct words of hip-hop artists as the *sole* authority on hip-hop culture, especially as hip-hop artists frequently speak in a guarded or veiled manner.

26. Chang 2005, 251.

# Bibiliography

*A&M Records v. Napster.* 2001. 239 F.3d 1004 (9th Cir.).

Adler, Bill. 2006. "Who Shot Ya: A History of Hip Hop Photography." *Total Chaos: The Art and Aesthetics of Hip Hop.* Ed. Jeff Chang. New York: Basic Books. 102–116.

Alim, Salim. 2006. *Roc the Mic Right: The Language of Hip Hop Culture.* New York: Routledge.

Alkalimat, Abdul. 2002a. Editor's Notes. "Archive of Malcolm X For Sale." By David Chang. February 20. www.h-net.org/~afro-am/. People can find the discussion loss there H-Afro-Am. August 9, 2004. http://h-net.msu.edu/cgi-bin/logbrowse.pl?trx=vx&list=H-Afro-Am&month=0202&week=c&msg=c PR4wypSByppLKU61e5Diw&user=&pw=.

Alkalimat, Abdul. 2002b. Editor's Notes. "Archive of Malcolm X For Sale." By Gerald Horne. February 20. H-Afro-Am. August 9, 2004. http://h-net.msu.edu/cgi-bin/logbrowse.pl?trx=vx&list=H-Afro-Am&month=0202&week=c&msg=JQnoJ7FS8tJmazqZ6J5S3Q&user=&pw=.

Allen, Ernest, Jr. 2002. "Du Boisian Double Consciousness: The Unsustainable Argument." *Massachusetts Review* 43.2: 215–253.

Alridge, Derrick. 2005. "From Civil Rights to Hip Hop: Toward a Nexus of Ideas." *Journal of African American History* 90.3: 226–252.

*Ancient Egyptian Order of Nobles of the Mystic Shrine v. Michaux.* 1929. 279 U.S. 737.

Angelo, Bonnie. 1994. "The Pain of Being Black: An Interview with Toni Morrison." *Conversations with Toni Morrison.* Ed. Danille Taylor-Guthrie. Jackson: University Press of Mississippi. 255–261.

Anten, Todd. 2006. "Self-Disparaging Trademarks and Social Change: Factoring the Reappropriation of Slurs in Section 2(A) of the Lanham Act." *Columbia Law Review* 106 (March): 388–433.

Aoki, Keith. 2007. "Distributive and Syncretic Motives in Intellectual Property

Law (with Special Reference to Coercion, Agency, and Development)." *University of California Davis Law Review* 40.3: 717–801.

Arewa, Olufunmilayo. 2006a. "Copyright on Catfish Row: Musical Borrowing, *Porgy and Bess*, and Unfair Use." *Rutgers Law Journal* 37.2: 277–353

Arewa, Olufunmilayo. 2006b. "From Bach to Hip Hop: Musical Borrowing, Copyright, and Cultural Context." *North Carolina Law Review* 84 (January): 547–645.

*Arlington Heights v. Metropolitan Housing Development*. 1977. 429 U.S. 252.

Askeland, Lori. 1999. "Remodeling the Model Home in *Uncle Tom's Cabin* and *Beloved*." *Toni Morrison's Beloved: A Casebook*. Ed. William Andrews and Nellie McKay. New York: Oxford University Press. 159–178.

Austin, Regina. 1989. "Sapphire Bound!" *Wisconsin Law Review* (May–June): 539–578.

Austin, Regina. 1995. "'The Black Community,' Its Lawbreakers, and a Politics of Identification." *After Identity: A Reader in Law and Culture*. Ed. Dan Danielsen and Karen Engle. New York: Routledge. 143–164.

Austin, Regina. 2005. "Kwanzaa and the Commodification of Black Culture." *Rethinking Commodification: Cases and Readings in Law and Culture*. Ed. Martha Ertman and Joan Williams. New York: New York University Press. 178–190.

Ayo, Damali. 2005. *How to Rent a Negro*. Chicago: Lawrence Hill.

Bacigalupi, Don, and Marilyn Kern-Foxworth. "An Interview with Michael Ray Charles." *Michael Ray Charles, 1989–1997, An American Artist's Work*. Houston: Baffler Gallery of the University of Houston, 19–33.

Baker, Houston. 1984. *Blues, Ideology, and African American Literature: A Vernacular Theory*. Chicago: University of Chicago Press.

Baker, Houston. 1993. *Black Studies, Rap, and the Academy*. Chicago: University of Chicago Press.

Baldwin, James. 1985. *The Evidence of Things Not Seen*. New York: Henry Holt.

*Barbershop*. 2002. Dir. Tim Story. Perf. Ice Cube, Cedric the Entertainer. MGM/UA.

Beatty, Paul. 1996. *The White Boy Shuffle*. New York: Houghton Mifflin.

Beck, Jeremy. 2005. "Music Composition, Sound Recordings and Digital Sampling in the 21st Century: A Legislative and Legal Framework to Balance Competing Interests." *UCLA Entertainment Law Review* 13 (Fall): 1–31.

Bell, Bernard. 1998. "*Beloved*: A Womanist Neo-Slave Narrative; or, Multivocal Remembrances of Things Past." *Critical Essays on Toni Morrison's Beloved*. Ed. Barbara Solomon. New York: G. K. Hall. 166–176.

Bell, Derrick. 1980. "*Brown v. Board of Education* and Interest-Convergence Dilemma." *Harvard Law Review* 93 (January): 518–533.

Bell, Derrick. 1985. "The Supreme Court, 1984 Term: Foreword: The Civil Rights Chronicles." *Harvard Law Review* 99 (November): 4–83.

Bell, Derrick. 1987. *And We Are Not Saved: The Elusive Quest for Racial Justice*. New York: Basic Books.

Bell, Derrick. 1992. *Faces at the Bottom of the Well: The Permanence of Racism*. New York: Basic Books.

Bell, Derrick. 1996. *Gospel Choirs: Psalms of Survival in an Alien Land Called Home*. New York: Basic Books.

Bell, Derrick. 2002. *Ethical Ambition: Living a Life of Meaning and Worth*. New York: Bloomsbury.

Benkler, Yochai. 2006. *The Wealth of Networks: How Social Production Transforms Markets and Freedom*. New Haven: Yale University Press.

Berger, Maurice. 2001a. "Collaborations, Museums, and the Politics of Display: A Conversation with Fred Wilson." *Fred Wilson: Objects and Installations: 1979–2000*. Baltimore: Center for Art and Visual Culture. 32–39.

Berger, Maurice. 2001b. "Viewing the Invisible: Fred Wilson's Allegories of Absence and Loss." *Fred Wilson: Objects and Installations: 1979–2000*. Baltimore: Center for Art and Visual Culture. 8–21.

Berlin, Ira. 1994. "Mining the Museum and the Rethinking of Maryland's History." *Mining the Museum*. By Fred Wilson. New York: New Press. 35–46.

Best, Stephen. 2004. *The Fugitive's Properties: Law and the Poetics of Possession*. Chicago: University of Chicago Press.

Bhabha, Homi. 1994. *The Location of Culture*. New York: Routledge.

Blackburn, Regina. 2004. "Binary Visions, Black Consciousness and Bling Bling." *Socialism and Democracy* 18.2: 79–105.

Bloom, Harold. 1973. *The Anxiety of Influence: A Theory of Poetry*. New York: Oxford University Press.

Boateng, Boatema. 2005. "Square Pegs in Round Holes? Cultural Production, Intellectual Property Frameworks, and Discourses of Power." *CODE: Collaborative Ownership and the Digital Economy*. Ed. Rishab Aiyer Ghosh. Cambridge: MIT Press. 61–73.

Bollier, David. 2005. *Brand Name Bullies: The Quest to Own and Control Cultures*. Hoboken: John Wiley.

Boogie Down Productions. 1987. "Dope Beat." *Criminally Minded*. BBoy Records.

Bowles, John. 2006. "Adrian Piper as an African American Artist." *American Art* 20.3: 108–117.

Bowles, Juliet. 1997. "Extreme Times Call for Extreme Heroes." *International Review of African American Art* 14.3: 3–16.

Boyd, Todd. 2002. *The New H.N.I.C.: The Death of Civil Rights and the Reign of Hip Hop*. New York: New York University Press.

Boyd, Todd. 2004. "Intergenerational Culture Wars: Civil Rights vs. Hip Hop: Interviewed by Yusuf Nuruddin." *Socialism and Democracy* 18.2: 51–69.

Bradford, Laura. 2005. "Parody and Perception: Using Cognitive Research to Expand Fair Use in Copyright." *Boston College Law Review* 46: 705–770.

*Bridgeport Music v. Dimension Films*. 2005. 410 F. 3d 792 (6th Cir.).

Brown, Michael. 2003. *Who Owns Native Culture?* Cambridge: Harvard University Press.

Buskirk, Martha. 1994. "Interviews with Sherrie Levine, Louise Lawler, and Fred Wilson." *October* 70 (Autumn): 98–112.

Bynoe, Yvonne. 2004. *Stand and Deliver: Political Activism, Leadership, and Hip Hop Culture*. Brooklyn: Soft Skull Press.

Cadenhead, Rogers. 2006. "Actor Tries to Trademark 'N' Word." *Wired News*. February 27. http://www.wired.com/news/technology/1,70259-0.html.

*Campbell v. Acuff-Rose*. 1994. 510 U.S. 569.

Carbado, Devon, and Mitu Gulati. 2003. "The Law and Economics of Critical Race Theory." *Yale Law Review* 112 (May): 1757–1827.

Carby, Hazel. 1987. *Reconstructing Womanhood: The Emergence of the Afro-American Woman Novelist.* New York: Oxford University Press.

Chakraborty, Barnini. 2002. "Settlement Reached in Lawsuit over *Wind Done Gone.*" *Associated Press State and Local Wire,* May 9.

Chang, Jeff. 2005. *Can't Stop, Won't Stop: A History of the Hip Hop Generation.* New York: St. Martin's Press.

Chang, Jeff, ed. 2006. *Total Chaos: The Art and Aesthetics of Hip-Hop.* New York: Basic Books.

Charles, Michael Ray. 1998. *Michael Ray Charles.* New York: Tony Shafrazi Gallery.

*Chappelle's Show.* 2004. Paramount.

Chartier, Roger. 2003. "Foucault's Chiasmus: Authorship between Science and Literature in the Seventeenth And Eighteenth Centuries." *Scientific Authorship: Credit and Intellectual Property in Science.* Ed. Mario Biagoli and Peter Galison. New York: Routledge. 13–32.

Christian, Barbara, Deborah McDowell, and Nellie McKay. 1999. "A Conversation on Toni Morrison's *Beloved.*" *Toni Morrison's* Beloved: *A Casebook.* Ed. William Andrews and Nellie McKay. New York: Oxford University Press. 203–220.

Cobb, William Jelani. 2007. *To the Break of Day: A Freestyle on the Hip-Hop Aesthetic.* New York: New York University Press.

Cohen, Julie. 2005. "Intellectual Property and Public Values: The Place of the User in Copyright Law." *Fordham Law Review* 74: 347–374.

Cohen, Rebecca. 1997. "Painting Race." *Austin Chronicle,* October 27.

Colebrook, Clair. 2004. *Irony.* New York: Routledge.

Conde, Mary. 1996. "Some African-American Fictional Responses to *Gone With the Wind.*" *Yearbook of English Studies* 26: 208–217.

Cone, James Hal. 1991. *Martin and Malcolm and America: A Dream or a Nightmare?* Maryknoll: Orbis.

Conroy, Pat. N.d. "Pat Conroy's Declaration." From *SunTrust Bank v. Houghton Mifflin* case file. On file with author.

Coombe, Rosemary. 1998. *The Cultural Life of Intellectual Properties: Authorship, Appropriation, and the Law.* Durham: Duke University Press.

Cooper, Martha. 2004. *Hip Hop Files: Photographs 1979–1984.* Cologne: From Here to Fame.

Copeland, Huey. 2005. "'Bye, Bye Black Girl': Lorna Simpson's Figurative Retreat." *Art Journal* (Summer): 63–77.

Cornell, Drucilla. 1993. *Transformations: Recollective Imagination and Sexual Difference.* New York: Routledge.

Corrin, Lisa. 1994. "Mining the Museum: Artists Look at Museums, Museums Look at Themselves." *Mining the Museum.* By Fred Wilson. New York: New Press. 3–20.

Crenshaw, Kimberlé. 1991. "Mapping the Margins: Intersectionality, Identity Politics, and Violence Against Women of Color." *Stanford Law Review* 43 (July): 1241–1299.

Crenshaw, Kimberlé. 2002. "Critical Race Studies: The First Decade: Critical Reflections; or, 'A Foot in the Closing Door.'" *UCLA Law Review* 49 (June): 1343–1373.

Crenshaw, Kimberlé, Neil Gotanda, Gary Peller, and Kendall Thomas. 1995. "Introduction." *Critical Race Theory: The Key Writings That Formed the Movement.* New York: New Press. xi–xxxii.

*Creswill v. Grand Lodge Knights of Pythias of Georgia.* 1912. 225 U.S. 246.

Crips, Thomas. 1983. "Winds of Change: *Gone With the Wind* and Racism as a National Issue." *Recasting* Gone With the Wind *in American Culture.* Ed. Darden Pyron. Miami: University Press of Florida. 137–152.

Crouch, Stanley. 1990. "Aunt Media." *Notes of a Hanging Judge.* New York: Oxford University Press. 202–209.

Croyden, Margaret. 1994. "Toni Morrison Tries Her Hand at Playwriting." *Conversations with Toni Morrison.* Ed. Danille Taylor-Guthrie. Jackson: University Press of Mississippi. 218–222.

Cruse, Harold. 1984. *The Crisis of the Negro Intellectual.* 1967. Reprint, New York: Quill.

Darling, Marsha. 1994. "In the Realm of Responsibility: A Conversation with Toni Morrison." *Conversations with Toni Morrison.* Ed. Danille Taylor-Guthrie. Jackson: University Press of Mississippi. 246–254.

Deleuze, Gilles. 1994. *Difference and Repetition.* Trans. Paul Patton. New York: Columbia University Press.

Delgado, Richard. 1993. "Words That Wound: A Tort Action for Racial Insults, Epithets, and Name Calling." *Words That Wound: Critical Race Theory, Assaultive Speech, and the First Amendment.* Ed. Charles Lawrence III, Mari Matsuda, Richard Delgado, and Kimberlé Crenshaw. Boulder: Westview. 89–110.

Delgado, Richard. 1995. *The Rodrigo Chronicles: Conversations about America and Race.* New York: New York University Press.

Delgado, Richard. 2003. "Crossroads and Blind Alleys: A Critical Examination of Recent Writing about Race, *Crossroads, Directions, and A New Critical Race Theory.*" *Texas Law Review* 82 (November): 121–151.

Delgado, Richard, and Jean Stefancic. 1994. *Failed Revolutions: Social Reform and the Limits of the Legal Imagination.* Boulder: Westview Press.

DeLong, James. 2002. "Defending Intellectual Property." *Copy Fights: The Future of Intellectual Property in the Information Age.* Washington, D.C.: Cato Institute. 17–36.

Demers, Joanna. 2006. *Steal This Music: How Intellectual Property Law Affects Musical Creativity.* Athens: University of Georgia Press.

Dickson-Carr, Darryl. 2001. *African American Satire: The Sacredly Profane Novel.* Columbia: University of Missouri Press.

Dinerstein, Joel. 2003. *Swinging the Machine: Modernity, Technology, and African American Cultures between the World Wars.* Amherst: University of Massachusetts Press.

Dixon, Annette, ed. 2002. *Kara Walker: Pictures from Another Time.* Ann Arbor: University of Michigan Museum of Art.

Doellinger, Chad. 2005. "Recent Developments in Trademark Law: Confusion,

Free Speech, and the Question of Use." *Marshall Review of Intellectual Property Law* 4 (Spring): 387–405.

Douglass, Frederick. 1969. *My Bondage and My Freedom.* 1855. Reprint, New York: Dover.

Douglass, Frederick. 1997a. *Narrative of the Life of Frederick Douglass: Authoritative Text, Contexts, Criticism.* Ed. William Andrews and William McFeely. New York: Norton.

Douglass, Frederick. 1997b. "What to the Slave Is the Fourth of July?" *Narrative of the Life of Frederick Douglass: Authoritative Text, Contexts, Criticism.* Ed. William Andrews and William McFeely. New York: Norton. 116–127.

Dubey, Madhu. 1999. "The Politics of Genre in *Beloved.*" *Novel* (Spring): 187–206.

Du Bois, W. E. B. 1969. *The Souls of Black Folks.* 1903. Reprint, New York: Signet.

Du Bois, W. E. B. 2000. "Criteria of Negro Art." *African American Literary Theory: A Reader.* Ed. Winston Napier. New York: New York University Press. 17–23.

Dussere, Erik. 2003. *Balancing the Books: Faulkner, Morrison, and the Economies of Slavery.* New York: Routledge.

Dyson, Michael Eric. 2000. *I May Not Get There With You: The True Martin Luther King Jr.* New York: Free Press.

Eakin, Emily. 2002. "Malcolm X Family Fights Auction of Papers." *New York Times,* March 7.

Eckstein, Lars. 2006. "A Love Supreme: Jazzthetic Strategies in Toni Morrison's *Beloved.*" *African American Review* 40.2: 271–283.

Ellis, Trey. 2003. *Platitudes.* 1988. Reprint, Boston: Northeastern University Press.

Ellis, Trey. 1989. "The New Black Aesthetic." *Callaloo* 38 (Winter): 233–243.

Ellison, Ralph. 1995. *Invisible Man.* 1952. Reprint, New York: Random House.

EPMD. 1988. "The Steve Martin." *Strictly Business.* Priority Records.

Equiano, Olaudah. 1995. *The Interesting Narrative of the Life of Olaudah Equiano, Written by Himself.* Ed. Robert J. Allison. 1789. Reprint, New York: Bedford/St. Martin's.

Everett, Percival. 2001. *Erasure.* Hanover: University Press of New England.

Farber, Daniel, and Suzanna Sherry. 1997. *The Radical Assault on Truth in American Law.* New York: Oxford University Press.

*Field v. Google.* 2006. CV-S-04-0413-RCJ-LRL (U.S.D.C. Nevada).

Fisher, Jean. 1999. "The Breath between Words." *Adrian Piper: A Retrospective.* New York: Distributed Art. 35–44.

Folami, Akilah. N.d. "The Telecommunications Act of 1996 And Its Contribution to the Overdevelopment of Gangsta Rap and the Underdevelopment of Hip Hop." On file with author.

Forness, Norman. 1980. "The Master, the Slave, and the Patent Laws: A Vignette of the 1850s." *Prologue* 12.1: 22–27.

Foucault, Michel. 1990. *The History of Sexuality: An Introduction, Volume 1.* Trans. Robert Hurley. New York: Vintage.

Foucault, Michel. 1995. *Discipline & Punish: The Birth of the Prison.* Trans. Alan Sheridan. 2nd ed. New York: Vintage.

Fouché, Rayvon. 2003. *Black Inventors in the Age of Segregation: Granville T. Woods, Lewis H. Latimer and Shelby J. Davidson.* Baltimore: John Hopkins University Press.

Fouché, Rayvon. 2006. "Say it Loud, I'm Black and I'm Proud: African Americans, American Artifactual Culture, and Black Vernacular Technological Creativity." *American Quarterly* 58.3: 639–661.

*Freestyle.* 2001. New York: Studio Museum.

Fricke, Jim. and Charlie Ahearn. 2002. *Yes Yes Y'all: The Experience Music Project Oral History of Hip Hop's First Decade.* New York: Da Capo.

Frye, Northrop. 1957. *Anatomy of Criticism: Four Essays.* New York: Atheneum.

Fussell, Betty. 1994. "All That Jazz." *Conversations with Toni Morrison.* Ed. Danille Taylor-Guthrie. Jackson: University Press of Mississippi. 280–288.

Gaines, Jane. 1991. *Contested Culture: The Image, The Voice, and the Law.* Chapel Hill: University of North Carolina Press.

Gaines, Jane. 1998. "The Absurdity of Property in the Person." *Yale Journal of Law and Humanities* 10.2: 537–548.

Garofalo, Reebee. 2002. "Crossing Over: From Black Rhythm and Blues to White Rock 'n' Roll." *Rhythm and Business: The Political Economy of Black Music.* Ed. Norman Kelley. New York: Akashic. 112–137.

Gates, Henry Louis. N.d. "Declaration of Henry Louis Gates, Jr." From *SunTrust Bank v. Houghton Mifflin* case file. On file with author.

Gates, Henry Louis. 1987. "Introduction." *The Classic Slave Narratives.* Ed. Henry Louis Gates. New York: Mentor. ix–xviii.

Gates, Henry Louis. 1990. "2 Live Crew Decoded: Rap Music Group's Use of Street Language in Context of Afro-American Cultural Heritage Analyzed." *New York Times,* June 19.

Gates, Henry Louis. 1992. *Loose Canons.* New York: Oxford University Press.

Gates, Henry Louis. 1998. *The Signifying Monkey: A Theory of African-American Literary Criticism.* New York: Oxford University Press.

George, Nelson. 1998. *Hip Hop America.* New York: Penguin.

George, Nelson. 2004. *Post-Soul Nation.* New York: Penguin

Gillespie, Tarleton. 2007. *Wired Shut: Copyright and the Shape of Digital Culture.* Cambridge: MIT Press.

Gilroy, Paul. 2000. *Against Race: Imagining Political Culture beyond the Color Line.* Cambridge: Harvard University Press.

Golden, Thelma. 2001. "Post . . ." *Freestyle.* New York: Studio Museum. 14–15.

Gonzalez, Jennifer. 2001. "Against the Grain: The Artist as Conceptual Materialist." *Fred Wilson: Objects and Installations: 1979–2000.* Baltimore: Center for Art and Visual Culture. 22–31.

Goodrich, Peter. 1998. "Translating Legendre; or, the Poetical Sermon of a Contemporary Jurist." *Law and the Postmodern Mind: Essays on Psychoanalysis and Jurisprudence.* Ed. Peter Goodrich and David G. Carlson. Ann Arbor: University of Michigan Press. 223–237.

*Grand Upright Music v. Warner Brothers.* 1991. 780 F. Supp. 182 (S.D.N.Y.).

Greene, K. J. 1999. "Copyright, Culture, and Black Music: A Legacy of Unequal Protection." *Hastings Communication and Entertainment Law Journal* 21 (Winter): 339–392.

Greene, Stephanie. 2006. "Sorting Out 'Fair Use' and 'Likelihood of Confusion' in Trademark Law." *American Business Law Journal* 43 (Spring): 43–77.

Guinier, Lani. 1994. *The Tyranny of the Majority: Fundamental Fairness in Representative Democracy.* New York: Free Press.

Guinier, Lani. 1998. *Lift Every Voice: Turning a Civil Rights Setback into a New Vision of Social Justice.* New York: Simon and Schuster.

Gutièrrez-Jones, Carl. 2001. *Critical Race Narratives: A Study of Race, Rhetoric, and Injury.* New York: New York University Press.

Halpern, Sheldon. 2005. "A High Likelihood of Confusion: Wal-Mart, Traffix, Moseley, and Dastar—The Supreme Court's New Trademark Jurisprudence." *New York University Annual Survey of American Law* 61: 237–271.

Haney Lopez, Ian. 1998. *White by Law: The Legal Construction of Race.* New York: New York University Press.

Hansberry, Lorraine. 1994. *A Raisin in the Sun.* 1959. Reprint, New York: Vintage.

*Hansberry v. Lee.* 1940. 311 U.S. 32.

Harris, Cheryl. 1993. "Whiteness as Property." *Harvard Law Review* 106 (June): 1707–1791.

Harris, Michael. 2003. *Colored Pictures: Race and Visual Representation.* Chapel Hill: University of North Carolina Press.

Harris, Middleton. 1974. *The Black Book.* New York: Random House.

Harvey, David. 1989. *The Conditions of Postmodernity.* New York: Blackwell.

Hayt-Atkins, Elizabeth. 1991. "The Indexical Present: A Conversation with Adrian Piper." *Arts Magazine* (March): 48–51.

Headley, Clevis. 2006. "Black Studies, Race, and Critical Race Theory: A Narrative Deconstruction of Law." *A Companion to African-American Studies.* Ed. Lewis Gordon and Jane Gordon. Malden: Blackwell. 330–359.

Heath, R. Scott. 2006. "True Heads: Historicizing the Hip Hop 'Nation' in Context." *Callaloo* 29.3: 846–866.

Heller, Steven. 1998. "Black on Black." *Print* 53.3: 66–70.

hooks, bell. 1995. *Art on My Mind: Visual Politics.* New York: New Press.

hooks, bell. 2003. *Teaching Community: A Pedagogy of Hope.* New York: Routledge.

Horowitz, Steven. 2005. "Rethinking Lockean Copyright and Fair Use." *Deakin Law Review* 10.1: 209–232.

Hurston, Zora Neale. 2000. "Characteristics of Negro Expression." *African American Literary Theory: A Reader.* Ed. Winston Napier. New York: New York University Press. 31–44.

Hutcheon, Linda. 1994. *Irony's Edge: The Theory and Politics of Irony.* New York: Routledge.

Jackson, John, Jr. 2008. *Racial Paranoia.* New York, Basic Books.

Jackson, Kennell. 2005. "Introduction: Traveling While Black." *Black Cultural Traffic: Crossroads in Global Performance and Popular Culture.* Ed. Harry J. Elam Jr. and Kennell Jackson. Ann Arbor: University of Michigan Press. 1–39.

Jacobs, Harriet. 1988. *Incidents in the Life of a Slave Girl.* New York: Oxford University Press.

*Jarvis v. A&M Music.* 1992. 827 F. Supp. 282 (D.C. New Jersey).

Jenkins, Henry. 1992. *Textual Poachers: Television Fans and Participatory Culture.* New York: Routledge.

Jenkins, Henry. 2006. *Convergence Culture: Where Old and New Media Collide.* New York: New York University Press.

Johnson, Alex. 1996. "Rethinking the Process of Classification and Evaluation: Destabilizing Racial Classifications Based on Insights Gleaned From Trademark Law." *California Law Review* 84 (July): 887–952.

Johnson, Kevin. 2004. "Roll Over Beethoven: A Critical Examination of Recent Writing about Race." *Texas Law Review* 82 (February): 717–734.

Jones, Edward P. 2003. *The Known World.* New York: HarperCollins.

Jones, Gayl. 1975. *Corregidora.* Boston: Beacon.

Jones, LeRoi. 1963. *Blues People: Negro Music in White America.* New York: William Morrow.

Judy, R. A. T. 2004. "On the Question of Nigga Authenticity." *That's the Joint! The Hip Hop Studies Reader.* Ed. Murray Forman and Mark Anthony Neal. New York: Routledge. 105–117.

Katyal, Sonia. 2006. "Semiotic Disobedience." *Washington University Law Review* 84.3: 489–571.

Kelley, Norman, ed. 2002. *Rhythm and Business: The Political Economy of Black Music.* New York: Akashic.

Kelley, Norman. 2003. *Phat Death.* New York: Akashic.

Kelley, Norman. 2004. *The Head Nigger in Charge Syndrome: The Dead End of Black Politics.* New York: Nation.

Kelley, Robin. 1997. *Yo' Mama's Disfunktional: Fighting the Culture Wars in Urban America.* Boston: Beacon Press.

Kelley, Robin. 1998. "Playing for Keeps: Pleasure and Profit on the Postindustrial Playground." *The House That Race Built.* Ed. Wahneema Lubiano. New York: Random House. 195–231.

Kelman, Mark. 1984. "Trashing." *Stanford Law Review* 36 (January): 293–348.

Kelman, Mark. 1987. *A Guide to Critical Legal Studies.* Cambridge: Harvard University Press.

Kennedy, Randall. 2002. *Nigger: The Strange Career of a Troublesome Word.* New York: Pantheon.

Kern-Foxworth, Marilyn. 1994. *Aunt Jemima, Uncle Ben, and Rastus: Blacks in Advertising, Yesterday, Today, and Tomorrow.* Westport: Greenwood Press.

Kern-Foxworth, Marilyn. 1997. "Painting Positive Pictures of Images That Injure: Michael Ray Charles's Dueling Dualities." *Michael Ray Charles, An American Artist's Work, 1989–1997.* Houston: University of Houston Baffler Gallery.

Kilgannon, Corey. 2006. "Epithet 'Has Many Meanings,' A Harvard Professor Testifies." *New York Times,* June 8.

King, Dexter, Jr., and Ralph Wiley. 2003. *Growing Up King: An Intimate Memoir.* New York: Warner.

King, Lovalerie. 1998. "The Disruption of Formulaic Discourse: Writing Resistance and Truth in *Beloved.*" *Critical Essays on Toni Morrison's* Beloved. Ed. Barbara Solomon. New York: G. K. Hall. 272–283.

King, Lovalerie. 2007. *Race, Theft, and Ethics: Property Matters in African American Literature.* Baton Rouge. Louisiana State University Press.

King, Martin Luther. 1969. "Letter from the Birmingham Jail." *On Civil Disobedience: American Essays, Old and New.* Ed. Robert Goldwin. Chicago: Rand McNally. 61–77.

King, Martin Luther. 2001. "I Have a Dream." *A Call to Conscience: The Landmark Speeches of Dr. Martin Luther King, Jr.* Ed. Clayborne Carson and Kris Shepard. New York: Time Warner. 81–87.

King-Hammond, Leslie. 1994. "A Conversation with Fred Wilson." *Mining the Museum.* By Fred Wilson. New York: New Press. 23–34.

Kiracofe, Roderick. 1993. *The American Quilt: A History of Cloth and Comfort, 1750–1950.* New York: Clarkson Potter.

Kitwana, Batari. 2002. *The New Hip Hop Generation: Young Blacks and the Crisis in African-American Culture.* New York: Basic Books.

Kofsky, Frank. 1998. *Black Music, White Business: Illuminating the History and Political Economy of Jazz.* New York: Pathfinder.

Krims, Adam. 2000. *Rap Music and the Poetics of Identity.* New York: Cambridge University Press.

Krumholz, Linda. 1999. "The Ghosts of Slavery: Historical Recovery in Toni Morrison's *Beloved.*" *Toni Morrison's* Beloved: *A Casebook.* Ed. William Andrews and Nellie McKay. New York: Oxford University Press. 107–126.

Lamar, Jake. 1996. *The Last Integrationist.* New York: Crown.

Landes, William, and Richard Posner. 2003. *The Economic Structures of Intellectual Property Law.* Cambridge: Harvard University Press.

Lawrence, Charles R. 1987. "The Id, the Ego, and Equal Protection: Reckoning with Unconscious Racism." *Stanford Law Review* 39 (January): 317–388.

Lee, Paul. 2002. "Why Malcolm X's Papers Shouldn't Be Auctioned." February 28. H-Afro-Am. August 9, 2004. http://h-net.msu.edu/cgi-bin/logbrowse.pl?trx= vx&list=H-Afro-Am&month=0202&week=d&msg=pdAi5ycBrOQTa3CbqHa AuA&user=&pw=.

Lessig, Lawrence. 2001. "Let the Stories Go." *New York Times,* April 30.

Lessig, Lawrence. 2002. *The Future of Ideas: The Fate of the Commons in a Connected World.* New York: Vintage.

Lessig, Lawrence. 2004. *Free Culture: How Big Media Uses Technology and the Law to Lock Down Culture and Control Creativity.* New York: Penguin.

Leval, Pierre. 1990. "Toward a Fair Use Standard." *Harvard Law Review* 103 (March): 1105–1136.

Levine, Lawrence. 1996. *The Opening of the American Mind: Canons, Culture, and History.* Boston, Beacon.

Lewis, David Levering, and Deborah Willis. 2003. *A Small Nation of People: W. E. B. Du Bois and African American Portraits of Progress.* New York: Amistad.

Liazos, Ariane, and Marshall Ganz. 2004. "Duty to the Race: Fraternal Orders in Defense of the Right to Organize." *Social Science History* 28.3: 485–534.

Liebowitz, Stan. 2002. "Copyright in the Post-Napster World: Legal or Market Solutions?" *Copy Fights: The Future of Intellectual Property in the Information Age.* Ed. Adam Thierer and Clyde Wayne Crews Jr. Washington, D.C.: Cato Institute. 197–204.

Lippard, Lucy. 1990. *Mixed Blessings: New Art in a Multicultural America.* New York: New Press.

Litman, Jessica. 2002. "Revising Copyright for the Information Age." *Copy Fights: The Future of Intellectual Property in the Information Age.* Ed. Adam Thierer and Clyde Wayne Crews Jr. Washington, D.C.: Cato Institute. 125–145.

Locke, Alain. 1997. "The New Negro." *The New Negro.* Ed. Alain Locke. 1925. Reprint, New York: Touchstone. 3–16.

Locke, John. 1980. *Second Treatise of Government.* Ed. C. B. Macpherson. Indianapolis: Hackett.

Lubar, Steven. 1991. "The Transformation of Antebellum Patent Law." *Technology and Culture* 32.4: 932–59.

Lubiano, Wahneema. 1996. "Like Being Mugged by a Metaphor." *Mapping Multiculturalism.* Ed. Avery Gordon and Christopher Newfield. Minneapolis: University of Minnesota Press. 64–75.

Madison, Michael. 2005. "Rewriting Fair Use and the Future of Copyright Reform." *Cardozo Arts & Entertainment Law Journal* 23: 391–418.

Marshall, Richard. 1993. "Repelling Ghosts." *Jean-Michel Basquiat.* Ed. Richard Marshall. New York: Whitney Museum. 9–26.

Martin, Carol. 1993. "Anna Deavere Smith: The Word Becomes You." *Drama Review* 37.4: 45–62.

Matsuda, Mari, Charles R. Lawrence III, Richard Delgado, and Kimberlé Crenshaw, eds. 1993. *Words That Wound: Critical Race Theory, Assaultive Speech, and the First Amendment.* Boulder: Westview Press.

McBride, Dwight. 1997. "Speaking the Unspeakable: On Toni Morrison, African American Intellectuals and the Uses of Essentialist Rhetoric." *Toni Morrison: Critical and Theoretical Approaches.* Ed. Nancy J. Peterson. Baltimore: Johns Hopkins University Press. 131–154.

McDonough, Walter. 2006. "Copyright Law in the Digital Age." Future of Music Coalition, November 3. http://www.futureofmusic.org/articles/waltercopyright.cfm.

McGruder, Aaron. 2003. *A Right to Be Hostile: The Boondocks Treasury.* New York: Three Rivers.

McLeod, Kembrew. 2001. *Owning Culture: Authorship, Ownership, and Intellectual Property Law.* New York: Peter Lang.

McLeod, Kembrew. 2007. *Freedom of Expression®: Overzealous Copyright Bozos and Other Enemies of Creativity.* Rev. ed. New York: Doubleday.

*MGM Studios v. Grokster.* 2005. 545 US 913.

Mercer, Kobena. 1999. "Decentering and Recentering: Adrian Piper's Spheres of Influence." *Adrian Piper: A Retrospective.* New York: Distributed Art Pub. 46–59.

Merry, Sally Engle. 1998. "Law, Culture, and Cultural Appropriation." *Yale Journal of Law and Humanities* 10.2: 575–603.

Miller, Paul. 2006. "The City in *Public* versus Private: Through a Scanner Darkly." *Total Chaos: The Art and Aesthetics of Hip Hop.* Ed. Jeff Chang. New York: Basic. 149–157.

Minda, Gary. 1995. *Postmodern Legal Movements: Law and Jurisprudence at Century's End*. New York: New York University Press.

Mitchell-Kernan, Claudia. 1999. "Signifying, Loud-Talking, and Marking." *Signifyin(g), Sanctifyin', & Slam Dunking: A Reader in African American Expressive Culture*. Ed. Gena Caponi. Amherst: University of Massachusetts Press. 309–330.

Miyakawa, Felicia M. 2005. *Five Percenter Rap: God's Hop Music, Message, and Black Muslim Mission*. Bloomington: Indiana University Press.

Modleski, Tania. 1997. "Doing Justice to the Subjects—Mimetic Art in a Multicultural Society: The Works of Anna Deavere Smith." *Female Subjects in Black and White: Race, Psychoanalysis, Feminism*. Ed. Barbara Christian, Elizabeth Abel, and Helene Moglen. Berkeley: University of California Press. 57–76.

Moffat, Viva. 2004. "Mutant Copyrights and Backdoor Patents: The Problem of Overlapping Intellectual Property Protection." *Berkeley Technology Law Journal* 19 (Fall): 1473–1532.

Moreland, Richard. 1997. " 'He Wants to Put His Story Next to Hers': Putting Twain's Story Next to Hers in Morrison's *Beloved*." *Toni Morrison: Critical and Theoretical Approaches*. Ed. Nancy J. Peterson. Baltimore: Johns Hopkins University Press. 155–180.

Morrison, Toni. N.d. "Declaration." From *SunTrust Bank v. Houghton Mifflin* case file. On file with author.

Morrison, Toni. 1987a. *Beloved*. New York: Knopf.

Morrison, Toni. 1987b. "The Site of Memory." *Inventing the Truth: The Art and Craft of Memoir*. Ed. William Zinsser. Boston: Houghton Mifflin. 103–124.

Morrison, Toni. 1992a. *Jazz*. New York: Knopf.

Morrison, Toni. 1992b. *Playing in the Dark: Whiteness and the Literary Imagination*. New York: Random House.

Morrison, Toni. 1994. *The Nobel Prize Speech*. New York: Knopf.

Morrison, Toni. 1996. "Unspeakable Things Unspoken: The Afro-American Presence in American Literature." *Criticism and the Color Line: Desegregating American Literary Studies*. Ed. Henry Wonham. New Brunswick: Rutgers University Press. 16–29.

Morrison, Toni, and Cornel West. 2004. "Blues, Love and Politics." *Nation*, May 24, 18–28.

Moses, Cat. 1999. "The Blues Aesthetic in Toni Morrison's *The Bluest Eye*." *African American Review* 33.4: 623–637.

Murray, Albert. 1973. *The Hero and the Blues*. Columbia: University of Missouri Press.

Murray, Albert. 1976. *Stomping the Blues*. New York: Da Capo Press.

Murray, Albert. 1997. *The Blue Devils of Nada*. New York: Vintage.

Murray, Derek, and Soraya Murray. 2005. "A Rising Generation and the Pleasures of Freedom." *International Review of African American Art* 20.2: 3–11.

Neal, Mark Anthony. 2002. *Soul Babies: Black Popular Culture and the Post-Soul Aesthetics*. New York: Routledge.

Neal, Mark Anthony. 2004. "Up From Hustling: Power, Plantations and the Hip-Hop Mogul." *Socialism and Democracy* 18.2: 157–181.

Neal, Mark Anthony. 2006. "Post–Civil Rights Period." *African American Music: An Introduction.* New York: Routledge. 624–642.

Netanel, Neil. 2008. *Copyright's Paradox.* New York: Oxford University Press.

New, Michael. N.d. "'Nothing but a Man': Racial Identity and Musical Production in *John Henry Days.*" On file with author.

*Newton v. Diamond.* 2003. 349 F.3d. 591 (9th Cir.).

Nielsen, Aldon. 1997. *Black Chant: Languages of African-American Postmodernism.* New York: Cambridge University Press.

Nimmer, David. 2003. "'Fairest of Them All' and Other Fairy Tales of Fair Use." *Law & Contemporary Problems* 66 (Winter–Spring): 263–287.

Norfleet, Dawn. 2006. "Hip Hop and Rap." *African American Music: An Introduction.* Ed. Mellonee Burnim and Portia Maultsby. New York: Routledge. 353–390.

N.W.A. 1988. "Fuck Tha Police." *Straight Outta Compton.* Priority.

Omi, Michael. 1996. "Racialization in the Post–Civil Rights Era." *Mapping Multiculturalism.* Ed. Avery Gordon and Christopher Newfield. Minneapolis: University of Minnesota Press. 178–186.

Outkast. 1998. "Rosa Parks." *Aquemini.* Arista.

Overton, Spencer. 2002. "Racial Disparities and the Political Function of Property." *UCLA Law Review* 49: 1553–1574.

Parks, Suzan-Lori. 2003. *Getting Mother's Body: A Novel.* New York: Random House.

*Parks v. Laface Records.* 2003. 329 F. 3d. 437 (6th Cir.).

Penalver, Eduardo, and Sonia Katyal. 2007. "Property Outlaws." *University of Pennsylvania Law Review* 155 (May): 1095–1186.

Penningroth, Dylan. 2003. *Claims of Kinfolk: African American Property and Community in the 19th Century South.* Chapel Hill: University of North Carolina Press.

Perez-Torres, Rafael. 1997. "Knitting and Knotting the Narrative Thread—*Beloved* as Postmodern Novel." *Toni Morrison: Critical and Theoretical Approaches.* Ed. Nancy J. Peterson. Baltimore: Johns Hopkins University Press. 91–109.

Perkins, William. 1996. "Youth's Global Village: An Epilogue." *Droppin' Science: Essays on Rap Music and Hip Hop Culture.* Ed. William Perkins. Philadelphia: Temple University Press. 258–273.

Perry, Imani. 2004. *Prophets of the Hood: Politics and Poetics in Hip Hop.* Durham: Duke University Press.

Peterson, James. 2006. "'Dead Prezence': Money and Mortal Themes in Hip Hop Culture." *Callaloo* 29.3: 895–909.

*Pictures, Patents, Monkeys, and More . . . On Collecting.* 2001. New York: Independent Curators International.

Pinckney, Darryl. 1992. *High Cotton.* New York: Farrar Straus Giroux.

Piper, Adrian. 1996. *Out of Order, Out of Sight, Volumes I and II.* Cambridge: MIT Press.

Posner, Richard. 2002. "The Law and Economics of Intellectual Property." *Daedalus* (Spring): 5–12.

Pough, Gwendolyn. 2004. *Check It While I Wreck It: Black Womanhood, Hip-Hop Culture, and the Public Sphere.* Boston: Northeastern University Press.

Powell, Richard. 1998. "Art History and Black Memory: Toward a 'Blues Aesthetic.'" *The Jazz Cadence of American Culture.* Ed. Robert O'Meally. New York: Columbia University Press. 182–195.

Powell, Richard. 2002. *Black Art: A Cultural History.* 2nd ed. New York: Thames & Hudson.

Public Enemy. 1990. "Burn Hollywood Burn." *Fear of a Black Planet.* Def Jam.

Radano, Ronald. 2003. *Lying Up a Nation: Race and Black Music.* Chicago: University of Chicago Press.

Radin, Margaret. 1996. *Contested Commodities.* Cambridge: Harvard University Press.

Randall, Alice. 2001. *The Wind Done Gone.* New York: Houghton Mifflin.

Randall, Alice. 2002. Interview with Ken Paulson. *Speaking Freely,* April 2. June 30, 2006. http://www.firstamendmentcenter.org/about.aspx?id=12787.

Randall, Alice. 2004. *Pushkin and the Queen of Spades.* New York: Houghton Mifflin.

Randle, Gloria. 2001. "Lady Sings the Blues: Toni Morrison and the Jazz/Blues Aesthetic." *African American Jazz and Rap: Social and Philosophical Examinations of Black Expressive Behavior.* Ed. James Conyers. Jefferson: McFarland. 131–144.

Reed, Lou. 1990. "Walk on the Wild Side." *Walk on the Wild Side: The Best of Lou Reed.* RCA.

Reid, Calvin. 1998. "Air Sambo." *Michael Ray Charles.* New York: Tony Shafrazi, 4–7.

Reinelt, Janelle. 1996. "Performing Race: Anna Deavere Smith's *Fire in the Mirror.*" *Modern Drama* 39: 609–617.

Rice, Alan. 2000. "It Don't Mean a Thing if It Ain't Got That Swing: Jazz's Many Uses for Toni Morrison." *Black Orpheus: Music in African American Fiction from the Harlem Renaissance to Toni Morrison.* Ed. Saadi Sinawe. New York: Garland. 153–180.

Richards, Phillip. 2006. *Black Heart: The Moral Life of Recent African American Letters.* New York: Peter Lang.

Riding, Alan. 2006. "Rap and Film at the Louvre? What's Up With That?" *New York Times,* November 21.

*Ringgold v. Black Entertainment Television.* 1997. 126 F.3d. 70 (2nd Cir.).

Ripani, Richard. 2006. *The New Blue Music: Changes in Rhythm and Blues, 1950–1999.* Jackson: University Press of Mississippi.

Robinson, Randall. 2000. *The Debt: What America Owes to Blacks.* New York: Dutton.

*Rogers v. Koons.* 1992. 960 F.2d 301 (2nd Cir.).

Rorty, Richard. 1989. *Contingency, Irony and Solidarity.* New York: Cambridge University Press.

Rose, Carol. 2005. "Property in all the Wrong Places" *Yale Law Review* 114 (March): 991–1019.

Rose, Mark. 1993. *Authors and Owners: The Invention of Copyright.* Cambridge: Harvard University Press.

Rose, Tricia. 1994. *Black Noise: Rap Music and Black Culture in Contemporary America.* Hanover: University Press of New England.

Rose, Tricia. 1996. "Hidden Politics: Discursive and Institutional Policing of Rap

Music." *Droppin' Science: Critical Essays on Rap Music and Hip Hop Culture*. Ed. William Eric Perkins. Philadelphia, Temple University Press. 236–257.

Ross, Thomas. 1996. *Just Stories: How Law Embodies Racism and Bias*. Boston: Beacon.

Rubenfeld, Jed. 2002. "The Freedom of Imagination: Copyright's Constitutionality." *Yale Law Review* 112 (October): 1–60.

Rushdy, Ashraf. 1999. "Daughters Signifyin' History: The Example of Toni Morrison's *Beloved*." *Toni Morrison's* Beloved: *A Casebook*. Ed. William Andrews and Nellie McKay. New York: Oxford University Press. 37–66.

Saint-Amour, Paul. 2003. *The Copywrights: Intellectual Property and the Literary Imagination*. Ithaca: Cornell University Press.

Sanjek, David. 2006. "Ridiculing the 'White Bread Original': The Politics of Parody and Preservation of Greatness in *Campbell v. Acuff-Rose*." *Cultural Studies* 20.2–3: 262–281.

Sanjek, Russell, and David Sanjek. 1996. *Pennies from Heaven: The American Popular Music Business in the Twentieth Century*. New York: Da Capo.

Scafidi, Susan. 2005. *Who Owns Culture? Appropriation and Authenticity in American Law*. New Brunswick: Rutgers University Press.

Schietinger, John. 2005. "*Bridgeport Music v. Dimension Films:* How the Sixth Circuit Missed a Beat on Digital Sampling." *DePaul Law Review* 55 (Fall): 209–248.

Schloss, Joseph. 2004. *Making Beats: The Art of Sample-Based Hip Hop*. Middletown: Wesleyan University Press.

Schmidt, Alvin, and Nicholas Babchuk. 1973. "The Unbrotherly Brotherhood: Discrimination in Fraternal Orders." *Phylon* 34.3: 275–282.

Schumacher, Thomas. 2004. "'This Is a Sampling Sport': Digital Sampling, Rap Music, and the Law in Cultural Production." *That's the Joint! The Hip Hop Studies Reader*. Ed. Murray Forman and Mark Anthony Neal. New York: Routledge. 443–458.

Schur, Richard. 2003. "*The Wind Done Gone* Controversy: American Studies, Copyright Law, and the Imaginary Domain." *American Studies* 44.1–2: 5–33.

Schur, Richard. Forthcoming. "Narrating African American Subjectivity through the Body: Critical Race Theory and Legal Discourse." *America and the Black Body: Identity Politics in Print and Visual Culture*. Ed. Carol Henderson. Madison: Farleigh Dickinson University Press.

*Seale v. Gramercy*. 1997. 964 F. Supp. 918 (E.D. Penn).

*Shelley v. Kraemer*. 1948. 334 U.S. 1.

Sims, Lowery Stokes. 1987. *Robert Colescott, a Retrospective, 1975–1986*. San Jose: San Jose Museum of Art.

Sirmans, Franklin. 2005. "In the Cipher: Basquiat and Hip Hop Culture." *Basquiat*. Ed. Marc Mayer. New York: Merrill. 91–128.

Sluby, Patricia. 2004. *The Inventive Spirit of African Americans: Patented Ingenuity*. Westport: Praeger.

Smethurst, James. 2005. *The Black Arts Movement: Literary Nationalism in the 1960s and 1970s*. Chapel Hill: University of North Carolina Press.

Smith, Anna Deavere. 1993. *Fires in the Mirror*. New York: Doubleday.

Smith, Anna Deavere. 1994. *Twilight—Los Angeles, 1992*. New York: Doubleday.

Spann, Girardeau. 1994. *Race against the Court: The Supreme Court and Minorities in Contemporary America*. New York: New York University Press.

Spearhead. 1994. "Dream Team." *Home*. Capitol.

Spears, James. 2001. "Black Folk Elements in Margaret Walker's *Jubilee*." *Fields Watered with Blood: Critical Essays on Margaret Walker*. Ed. Maryemma Graham. Athens: University of Georgia Press. 225–230.

Spivak, Gayatri. 1994. "Can the Subaltern Speak?" *The Post-Colonial Studies Reader*. Ed. Bill Ashcroft, Gareth Griffins, and Helen Tiffin. New York: Routledge. 24–28.

Stepto, Robert. 1991. *From Behind the Veil: A Study of Afro-American Narrative*. 2nd ed. Urbana: University of Illinois Press.

Stocking, George. 1985. *Objects and Others: Essays on Museums and Material Culture*. Madison: University of Wisconsin Press.

Storr, Robert. 1996. "Foreword." *Out of Order, Out of Sight, Vol 1*. Cambridge: MIT Press. xv–xxvii.

Strathern, Marilyn. 2005. "Imagined Collectivities and Multiple Authorship." *CODE: Collaborative Ownership and the Digital Economy*. Ed. Rishab Ghosh. Cambridge: MIT Press. 13–28.

Stromberg, Frederik. 2003. *Black Images in the Comics: A Visual History*. Seattle: Fantagraphics.

Suggs, Jon-Christian. 2000. *Whispered Consolations: Law and Narrative in African American Life*. Ann Arbor: University of Michigan Press.

Sunder, Madhavi. 2005. "Property in Personhood." *Rethinking Commodification: Cases and Readings in Law and Culture*. Ed. Martha Ertman and Joan Williams. New York: New York University Press. 164–176.

*SunTrust Bank v. Houghton Mifflin Company*. 2001. 268 F. 3d 1257 (11th Cir.).

Swedenburg, Ted. 2004. "Homies in the 'Hood: Rap's Commodification of Insubordination." *That's the Joint! The Hip Hop Studies Reader*. Ed. Murray Forman and Mark Anthony Neal. New York: Routledge. 579–592.

Tate, Greg. 1992. *Flyboy in the Buttermilk: Essays on Contemporary America*. New York: Simon and Schuster.

Tate, Greg, ed. 2003. *Everything but the Burden: What White People Are Taking from Black Culture*. New York: Harlem Moon.

Tate, Greg, Vijay Prashad, Mark Anthony Neal, and Brian Cross. 2006. "Got Next: A Roundtable on Identity and Aesthetics after Multiculturalism." *Total Chaos: The Art and Aesthetics of Hip Hop*. Ed. Jeff Chang. New York: Basic. 33–51.

Taylor, Helen. 2001. *Circling Dixie: Contemporary Southern Culture through a Transatlantic Lens*. New Brunswick: Rutgers University Press.

Thompson, Debby. 2003. "Is Race a Trope? Anna Deavere Smith and the Question of Racial Performativity." *African American Review* 37.1: 127–140.

Toop, David. 2000. *Rap Attack #3: African Rap to Global Hip Hop*. London: Serpent's Tail.

Trademark Dilution Revision Act of 2006. 2006. H.R. 683. January 3.

A Tribe Called Quest. 1990. "Can I Kick It?" *People's Instinctive Travels and the Paths of Rhythm*. BMG.

Troutt, David. 2005. "A Portrait of the Trademark as a Black Man: Intellectual

Property, Commodification, and Redescription." *University of California Law Review* 38 (April): 1141–1207.

*Tuff 'N' Rumble Management v. Profile Records.* 1997. 42 U.S. P.Q. (S.D.N.Y.).

Tushnet, Rebecca. 2004. "Copy This Essay: How Fair Use Doctrine Harms Free Speech and How Copying Serves It." *Yale Law Journal* 114 (December): 535–590.

*Ty v. Publications International Limited.* 2002. 292 F.3d 512 (7th Cir.).

Unger, Roberto. 1986. *The Critical Legal Studies Movement.* Cambridge: Harvard University Press.

United Nations Educational, Scientific, and Cultural Organization (UNESCO). 2005. "Convention on the Protection and Promotion of the Diversity of Cultural Expressions." Paris. October 20.

U.S. House of Representatives. 2000. "Online Music: Will Small Music Labels and Entrepreneurs Prosper in the Internet Age?" Committee on Small Businesses. May 24. November 3, 2006. http://wwwc.house.gov/smbiz/hearings/106th/2000/000524/transcript.asp.

Vaidhyanathan, Siva. 2003. *Copyrights and Copywrongs: The Rise of Intellectual Property and How It Threatens Creativity.* New York: New York University Press.

Vaidhyanathan, Siva. 2004. *The Anarchist in the Library: How the Clash between Freedom and Control Is Hacking the Real World and Crashing the World.* New York: Basic Books.

Valdes, Francisco, Jerome Culp, and Angela Harris, eds. 2002. *Crossroads, Directions, and a New Critical Race Theory.* Philadelphia: Temple University Press.

Vlach, Michael. 1978. *The Afro-American Tradition in Decorative Arts.* Cleveland: Cleveland Museum of Art.

Walker, Alice. 1982. *The Color Purple.* New York: Washington Square.

Wallace, Michele. 1994. *Invisibility Blues: From Pop to Theory.* 1990. Reprint, New York: Verso.

Wallace, Michele. 2004. *Dark Designs and Visual Culture.* Durham: Duke University Press.

Washington, Booker. 1959. *Up from Slavery.* 1900. Reprint, New York: Bantam.

Watkins, Mel. 1994. *On the Real Side: A History of African American Comedy.* Chicago: Lawrence Hill.

Watkins, S. Craig. 2004. "Black Youth and the Ironies of Capitalism." *That's the Joint! The Hip Hop Studies Reader.* Ed. Murray Forman and Mark Anthony Neal. New York: Routledge. 557–578.

Watkins, S. Craig. 2005. *Hip Hop Matters: Politics, Pop Culture, and the Struggle for the Soul of a Movement.* Boston: Beacon.

Weheliye, Alexander. 2005. *Phonographies: Grooves in Sonic Afro-Modernity.* Durham: Duke University Press.

Weisenburger, Steven. 1998. *Modern Medea: A Family Story of Slavery and Child-Murder from the Old South.* New York: Hill & Wang.

West, Cornell. 1993. "Foreword." *Fires in the Mirror.* By Anna Deavere Smith. New York: Doubleday.

West, Dorothy. 1995. "The Penny." *The Richer, The Poorer.* New York: Anchor. 77–82.

White, Hayden. 1973. *Metahistory: The Historical Imagination in Nineteenth-Century Europe*. Baltimore: Johns Hopkins University Press.

Whitehead, Colson. 1999. *The Intuitionist*. New York: Random House.

Whitehead, Colson. 2001. *John Henry Days*. New York: Random House.

Whitehead, Colson. 2006. *Apex Hides the Hurt*. New York: Random House.

Williams, Joan, and Viviana Zelizer. 2005. "To Commodify or Not to Commodify: That is *Not* the Question." *Rethinking Commodification: Cases and Readings in Law and Culture*. Ed. Martha Ertman and Joan Williams. New York: New York University Press. 362–382.

Williams, Patricia. 1991. *The Alchemy of Race and Rights*, Cambridge: Harvard University Press.

Williams, Patricia. 1998. *Seeing a Color-Blind Future: The Paradox of Race*. New York: Farrar, Strauss and Giroux.

Williams, Patricia. 2004. *Open House: Of Family, Friends, Food, Piano Lessons, and the Search for a Room of My Own*. New York: Farrar, Strauss and Giroux.

Williams, Sherley Anne. 1986. *Dessa Rose*. New York: Morrow.

Wilson, Fred. 1994. *Mining the Museum*. New York: New Press.

Wilson, Fred. 2001a. *Fred Wilson: Objects and Installations: 1979–2000*. Baltimore: Center for Art and Visual Culture.

Wilson, Fred. 2001b. "Mining the Museum in Me." *Pictures, Patents, Monkeys, and More . . . On Collecting*. New York: Independent Curators International. 53–55.

Wilson, Fred. 2003. Interview with Kathleen Goncharov. *Fred Wilson: Speak of Me as I Am*. Ed. Reiko Tomii and Kathleen M. Friello. Cambridge: MIT List Visual Arts Center.

Wilson, Fred. 2006. Interview with Richard Klein. *Fred Wilson: Black Like Me*. Ridgefield, CT: Aldrich Contemporary Art Museum. 9–20.

Wilson, Stephen. 2002. "Music Sampling Lawsuits: Does Looping Music Samples Defeat the De Minimis Defense?" *Journal of High Technology Law* 1: 179–194.

Winter, Irene J. 1996. "Exhibit/Inhibit: Archaeology, Value, History in the Work of Fred Wilson." *New Histories*. Ed. Milena Kalinovska. Boston: Institute of Contemporary Art. 182–191.

Woidat, Caroline. 1997. "Talking Back to Schoolteacher: Morrison's Confrontation with Hawthorne in *Beloved*." *Toni Morrison: Critical and Theoretical Approaches*. Ed. Nancy J. Peterson. Baltimore: Johns Hopkins University Press. 181–200.

Wood, Joe. 1992. "Malcolm X and the New Blackness." *Malcolm X: In Our Own Image*. Ed. Joe Wood. New York: St. Martin's Press. 1–17.

Woodmansee, Martha, and Peter Janzi, eds. 1994. *The Construction of Authorship: Textual Appropriation in Law and Literature*. Durham: Duke University Press.

Wright, Kristine. 2004. "Rise Up Hip Hop Nation: From Deconstructing Racial Politics to Building Positive Solutions." *Socialism and Democracy* 18.2: 9–19.

X, Malcolm. 1965a. "The Ballot or the Bullet." *Malcolm X Speaks*. Ed. George Breitman. New York: Pathfinder. 23–44.

X, Malcolm. 1965b. "Message to the Grass Roots." *Malcolm X Speaks*. Ed. George Breitman. New York: Pathfinder. 3–17.

Yu, Peter. 2007. "Ten Common Questions about Intellectual Property and Human Rights." http://ssrn.com/abstract=979193, 2007. Accessed April 7, 2007.

# Index